THE UNFOLDING DRAMA
OF REDEMPTION

VOLUME III

The Unfolding Drama of Redemption

THE BIBLE AS A WHOLE

VOLUME III

ACT II AND THE EPILOGUE OF THE DRAMA

EMBRACING THE EPISTLES AND
THE BOOK OF REVELATION

ALSO CONTAINS COMPLETE INDICES TO VOLUMES I, II and III

W. GRAHAM SCROGGIE, D.D.(Edin.)

LONDON
PICKERING & INGLIS LTD.
1970

PICKERING & INGLIS LTD.
29 LUDGATE HILL, LONDON, E.C.4
26 BOTHWELL STREET, GLASGOW, C.2

Printed in Great Britain

Other Volumes in the Series

FOREWORD

'He being dead yet speaketh.'

With the issue, after much delay, of this final volume, it is necessary to explain that editing progress has been slow and arduous for many reasons. Following the printing of Volume II (four years after Volume I) my husband's relapse and continuing illness had prevented his ordered gathering together of the material prepared for the third volume. This, though written in full and largely in rough proof form partly consisted of typed and hand-written sheets which had been put aside while working on the earlier volumes.

Six months later, however, doctors prescribed what proved to be a grievous overdose. His mind became clouded and his work closed (despite signs of hope for his recovery) a year before his Home-call. Hence it fell to me, aided by the prayers of many, to try to assess what material was missing, to sift through the mass of his papers, to determine which of the many manuscripts were the portions destined for this book; and also to tackle the proof he had been correcting a year beforehand. Concentration was difficult, as the long strain of such nursing brought its natural and prolonged reaction.

Meanwhile I had gladly accepted a most kind offer from the Rev. H. Brash Bonsall, Founder and Principal of the Birmingham Bible Institute, to help in the onerous task of checking the material and reading the proofs; and also to index the three volumes as a last tribute to my husband, and 'for the joy of setting this final seal upon his Bible studies'. He has spared no effort in checking and collating, and has made his indices as helpful as possible to both scholar and preacher. The latter will appreciate the index of Scripture passages referring him to the author's comment on any given text. He hopes that by this means the three volumes will serve not only as an introduction to Scripture, but in a limited way as a commentary upon it.

For Mr. Brash Bonsall's masterly oversight of the whole enter-prise, despite the extreme pressure of engagements at Birmingham and elsewhere, I am supremely grateful and readers will be forever indebted. Warm thanks go also to the other kind friends who have helped us in various ways.

I am confident that this final volume, the climax of my beloved husband's ministry, is, in God's overruling mercy, 'according to the pattern shewed', and as he himself had planned (had he lived) to present it.

May our Lord Jesus Christ, Whom he loved and served so faithfully, use his unfolding of the drama of Redemption to make the Gospel Story dearer and clearer than ever before.

JOAN M. SCROGGIE

ANALYSIS OF CONTENTS

CONTENTS

x

CONTENTS

CONTENTS

EPILOGUE

THE REVELATION

CHARTS

MAPS

ACT II

SCENE 2

THE DOCTRINAL EXPRESSION OF CHRISTIANITY

THE EPISTLES

ACT II

In ACT II of the *Drama of Redemption* there are two Scenes:

1. *The Introduction of Christianity into the World by Jesus the Messiah.*
2. *The Progress of Christianity in the World to the End of the First Century A.D.*

The First Scene which has been dealt with in Volume II, page 115 embraces the period B.C.5-A.D. 30, and the Second Scene, the period A.D. 30-95, so that ACT II covers the first century of the Christian era.

The second of the two Scenes of ACT II is presented in two parts. The first tells of the *Historical Expansion of Christianity*, and the second tells of its *Doctrinal Expression*. The record of the former is the Book of the *Acts*, and of the latter, the New Testament *Epistles* (see *The Drama*, Vol. 2, pp. 167, 169). These records are not consecutive, but partly contemporaneous, that is, the *Acts* does not record the whole history of the Christian Church from Pentecost to the end of the century, but only 33 years of it, and within that generation eleven of the twenty-one Epistles were written, and the other ten belong to the period beyond the Acts. (See *The Drama*, Vol. 2, p. 87).

We have already considered the *Historical Expansion of Christianity* as far as it is recorded in the Acts, and now we shall contemplate the *Doctrinal Expression* of it which is richly presented in twenty-one Epistles.

2

SCENE 2

THE DOCTRINAL EXPRESSION OF CHRISTIANITY

LETTERS

The great truths of Christianity are not presented in the form of treatises, or essays, but of letters, which are the most personal form of literature. The title of innumerable books—The Life and Letters of—shows how closely related letters are to life, for in them personality is revealed as it could not be in literary disquisitions and compendiums. We are all more interested in people than in events, and we prefer the concrete to the abstract, and so, in God's good providence, the sublimest truths are presented in this most homely form. Of the twenty-seven Writings of the New Testament twenty-one are Letters, three-quarters of the whole.

'In this respect', says Farrar, 'the records of Christianity are absolutely unique in the religious history of the world. Of all the sacred books which the world has seen there is not one which is composed mainly, or at all, of letters, with the single exception of the New Testament. The Bibles of the world—the *Vedas*, the *Zend Avesta*, the *Tripitaka*, the *Koran*, and the writings of Confucius—are poems, or rhythmic addresses, or legendary histories, or philosophic discourses. In this, as in all other respects, the ways of God's providence differ from man's expectations. We may thank God that we derive some of the deepest truths of our belief from documents so simple, so individual, so full of human interest and love—written, most of them, in a style the most personal that ever existed' (*Messages of the Books*, pp. 143-4).

LETTER-WRITING

Letter-writing is of great antiquity. Excavations have brought to light this form of literature as early as 2275 B.C. The art is referred to very frequently in the Old Testament, and a postal service is indicated in Esther iii. 13, 15; viii. 10, 14; Job ix. 25; and elsewhere.

The Old Testament Apocrypha also contains specimens of personal and official letters; and in the Acts fine examples of this form of communication are in xv. 23-29; xxiii. 25-30; and elsewhere in this book reference is made to letter-writing (ix. 2; xviii. 27; xxii. 5; xxviii. 21).

Paul refers several times to letters having been written (1 Cor. vii. 1; xvi. 3; 2 Cor. iii. 1). Also in the Book of the Revelation are seven Letters addressed to seven churches in Asia Minor (ii. 1-iii. 22).

Much of sub-apostolic literature was in letter-form and increasingly to our day it has become one of the largest and most valuable forms of literature. It is said that, in preparation for writing the biography of William Ewart Gladstone, John Morley read 50,000 of the statesman's letters.

It is not wholly surprising, therefore, that Epistles, or Letters, have a prominent place in the revelation of the New Testament. Deissmann in his *Light from the Ancient East* has drawn a sharp distinction between a letter and an epistle, but he makes the distinction too formal and rigid, says Ramsay. There is, however, a difference between the informal letter and the literary epistle, and, in any case, Paul's letters are unique in that they are distinctively *religious*. 'Paul was apparently the first to recognize the full possibilities that lay in a letter as a means of conveying religious instruction' (G. Milligan). What we commonly understand by a letter is something personal, spontaneous and confidential, and not intended for publication, but an epistle is more general in aim. Paul's writings cannot belong to either of these categories, for his letters interpenetrate his epistles, and his epistles, his letters. For example, in *Philippians*, personal and intimate, is a great Christological passage (ii. 5-11), and in *Romans*, so theological, are personal and intimate passages (xv-xvi).

Strictly speaking, JAMES is not a letter, but was intended to be copied and widely distributed (i. 1); and its contents are meditations on various subjects. Also 1-2 PETER are not letters, being addressed to people widely scattered (1. i. 1; 2. i. 1). The same may be said of JUDE. 2 and 3 JOHN are letters, but this can scarcely be said of 1 JOHN. Although GALATIANS is addressed to 'the churches in Galatia', the contents make it clear that this is a letter, and not an epistle. Of Paul's writings ROMANS is least like a letter, yet it is addressed to a single Church (i. 7). Notwithstanding ch. xiii. 22-24, HEBREWS is not a letter, but a discourse designed to show how the types of the Old Testament are fulfilled.

Innumerable letters are but of antiquarian interest, but those of the New Testament are for ever 'living and powerful.'

NEW TESTAMENT LITERATURE

It will be well at this point to see the chronological relation to one another of the twenty-seven Writings of the New Testament. The dates are approximately correct. (*The Drama*, Vol. 2, Chart 120, p. 87).

CHART 139

CHRONOLOGY OF NEW TESTAMENT LITERATURE				
Decade	Writing	Date	Place	Period
A.D. 40–50	JAMES	A.D. 44-49	Jerusalem	I N I T I A L
50–60	MARK	50	Rome (?)	
	1 THESSALONIANS	52	Corinth	
	2 THESSALONIANS	53	Corinth	
	1 CORINTHIANS	57	Ephesus	
	2 CORINTHIANS	57	Macedonia	
	GALATIANS	57	Corinth	
	ROMANS	58	Corinth	
	MATTHEW	52-56	Judaea	
	LUKE	59-62	Caesarea	
60–70	EPHESIANS	62-63	Rome	C E N T R A L
	COLOSSIANS	62-63	Rome	
	PHILEMON	62-63	Rome	
	PHILIPPIANS	62-63	Rome	
	ACTS	62-63	Rome	
	1 PETER	64-67	'Babylon'	
	JUDE	65-68	Jerusalem (?)	
	1 TIMOTHY	65-67	Macedonia	
	TITUS	66-67	Ephesus	
	2 TIMOTHY	67-68	Rome	
	2 PETER	67-68	(?)	
	HEBREWS	67-68(?)	(?)	
70–80	—	—	—	
80–90	—	—	—	F I N A L
90–100	JOHN'S GOSPEL	90-95	Ephesus	
	JOHN'S 1st EPISTLE	90-95	Ephesus	
	JOHN'S 2nd EPISTLE	90-95	Ephesus	
	JOHN'S 3rd EPISTLE	90-95	Ephesus	
	THE REVELATION	95-96	Patmos	

This chart shows that apostolic history is divisible into three main periods, the first ending in A.D. 60; the second, in A.D. 68; and the third in or about A.D. 95.

From this chart we see that, in all likelihood, the Epistle of James was the earliest New Testament Writing, and that Mark's Gospel was the first of the Four.

During A.D. 58-60 Luke was with Paul in Caesarea, and it is most probable that he wrote his Gospel then and there. At the same time he may have written a large part of the Acts, and have completed it in Rome in A.D. 63; for while in Caesarea Luke had ample opportunity for collecting valuable information concerning the early history of the Church from many who were in the foreground of the story. Probably Luke made contact with Paul during the second missionary journey (chapter xvi) but he had thoroughly reliable sources of information of the period before that, so that chapters i-xv are as historically reliable as the remainder of the Book. (*The Drama*, Vol. 2, p. 172.)

LOST AND FORGED LETTERS

Before looking at the twenty-one Letters of the New Testament a word must be said about apostolic letters which have not survived, and also about early letter forgeries to which Paul refers.

LOST LETTERS

That Paul must have written many letters which have not been preserved may be safely assumed. Farrar, after summarizing Paul's Epistles, has well said: 'He must doubtless have written others besides these, but intense as would have been for us the theologic and psychologic interest of even the most trivial of his writings, we may assume, with absolute certainty, that those which we still possess have been preserved in accordance with God's special providence, and were by far the most precious and important of all that he wrote'.

The idea that apostolical letters have been lost is not gratuitous, for the fact is witnessed to in the New Testament. Paul says that he autographed letters which he wrote (2 Thess. iii. 17; 1 Cor. xvi. 21; Col. iv. 18; cf. Gal. vi. 11, R.V.), and probably the writing of other letters is implied.

To the same effect are other references. In 2 Cor. x. 9, 10, Paul speaks of letters which he wrote to Corinth, and the Corinthians also speak of such; and in Ephes. iii. 3, he says: 'As I have written briefly'.

But the fact of a lost letter is plainly stated in 1 Cor. v. 9, 11, 'I wrote to you in my letter'. This letter has not survived. Again, writing to the Colossians, Paul says: 'See that you read also the letter from Laodicea' (iv. 16). This conceivably may refer to the letter known as the Epistle to the Ephesians, but if this is not so, it is a lost letter.

Such loss need not be wondered at, seeing that so much of what Christ said and did is unrecorded (John xxi. 25).

FORGED LETTERS

That the forgery of letters was early practised is plainly indicated in 2 Thess. ii. 2, where Paul refers to *letters purporting to be from him* on the subject of the LORD's return. Because of such forgery the salutation in Paul's letters was written by his own hand, although the letters themselves were dictated (Rom. xvi. 22). Nor are we without other instances of forgeries. Of such we may mention a letter which, it was claimed, our LORD sent to Abgarus, king of Edessa, saying that He could not visit his country to heal him.

The *Clementine Homilies* is a work attributed to Clement of Rome, but it is fiction; and in it is a letter which Peter is supposed to have written to James.

There is also a spurious *Epistle from Laodicea* which seeded from the reference in Col. iv. 16.

Also it is claimed that Paul wrote six letters to Seneca, and Seneca, eight letters to Paul. Of these Bishop Lightfoot says: 'This correspondence was probably forged in the 4th century, either to recommend Seneca to Christian readers, or to recommend Christianity to students of Seneca'.

When we think of letters lost and forged belonging to the apostolic age how great should be our gratitude that we have twenty-one letters written in the second half of the first century which have the seal of divinity upon them.

THE WRITERS OF THE EPISTLES

There are five and probably six writers of New Testament Epistles—*James, Jude, Peter, Paul, John*, and the author of 'Hebrews'; and these writers present Christian truth in quite distinctive ways. Paul is theological; Peter is practical; James and Jude are ethical; and John is mystical. Paul is the scholar; Peter is the comforter; James and Jude are the challengers; and John is the dreamer. These will appeal to us at different times, according to our circumstances, but rarely, one would think, do they all appeal to all Christians all the time.

There is one epistle from *James*, one from *Jude*, two from *Peter*, three from *John*, thirteen from *Paul*, and one anonymous. Two of these writers were Jesus' brothers—*James* and *Jude*; two were Jesus' Apostles—*Peter* and *John*; *Paul* has a place entirely his own; and one is unknown—the author of Hebrews.

THE PAULINE AND CATHOLIC EPISTLES

That the twenty-one Epistles of the New Testament lend themselves to classification must be obvious to the most casual reader. They fall into two quite distinct groups, the *Pauline Epistles*, and the *Catholic Epistles*, and these again are sub-divisible.

The *Pauline Epistles* are, of course, Paul's, of which there are thirteen, and to which, for convenience, we add 'Hebrews'. The *Catholic Epistles* are seven in number, and are by four authors: *James*, *Jude*, *Peter*, and *John*. Eusebius, who was the first to use the word 'Catholic' with reference to these seven Epistles, appears to have meant that they were in common use in the Church. They are General Epistles in a sense in which Paul's are not. We see then that two-thirds of the Epistles are Pauline, and one-third is Catholic. The relation of these two groups to one another in time is both of interest and importance, as the following chart shows.

CHART 140

THE CATHOLIC EPISTLES IN RELATION TO PAUL'S WRITINGS					
PERIODS			DECADES		
Before	During	After	5th	7th	10th
JAMES	1–2 PETER JUDE	JOHN	JAMES	1 PETER JUDE	JOHN
A.D. 44–49	A.D. 64–68	A.D. 90–95		2 PETER	

EMPHASES OF THE EPISTOLARY WRITERS

The emphasis of *James* and *Jude* is *ethical*; of *Peter*, it is *experimental*; of *Paul*, it is *doctrinal*; of *John*, it is *mystical*; and of the author of *Hebrews*, it is *antitypical*. These characteristics are not exclusive, but they are distinctive.

James and *Jude* emphasize *law* and *works*; *Peter* emphasizes *hope*; *Paul* emphasizes *faith*; *John* emphasizes *love*; and the author of *Hebrews* emphasizes *finality*.

CHART 141

EMPHASES OF THE EPISTOLARY WRITERS					
JAMES	JUDE	PETER	PAUL	JOHN	HEBREWS
ETHICAL		EXPERI-MENTAL	DOCTRINAL	MYSTICAL	ANTI-TYPICAL
LAW and WORKS		HOPE	FAITH	LOVE	FINALITY

THE EPISTLES AND THE OLD TESTAMENT

These Epistles are related also to the Old Testament in different ways. To *James* and *Jude* Christianity is the fulfilment of the *Law*; to *Peter* it is the fulfilment of the *Theocracy*; to *Paul* it is the fulfilment of the *Covenant* and *Sacraments*; to *John* it is the fulfilment of Old Testament *Symbolism*; and in Hebrews Christianity is the fulfilment of all the *Types* of the Old Testament.

CHART 142

THE EPISTLES AND THE OLD TESTAMENT					
JAMES	JUDE	PETER	PAUL	JOHN	HEBREWS
CHRISTIANITY AND THE FULFILMENT OF THE—					
LAW		THEOCRACY	COVENANT and SACRAMENTS	SYMBOLISM	TYPES

RELATION OF THE EPISTLES TO THE GOSPELS

The Epistles of *James* and *Jude* naturally relate themselves to *Matthew's* Gospel; *Peter's* Epistles, to *Mark's* Gospel; *Paul's* Epistles, to *Luke's* Gospel; *John's* Epistles, to his own Gospel; and *Hebrews* to them all.

CHART 143

RELATION OF THE EPISTLES TO THE GOSPELS					
JAMES	JUDE	PETER	PAUL	JOHN	HEBREWS
MATTHEW		MARK	LUKE	JOHN	ALL

CHART 144

RELATION OF THE EPISTLES TO THE ACTS			
Within the Period of the Acts		Beyond the Period of the Acts	
A.D. 44-63		A.D. 63-95	
44-49	JAMES	64-67	1 PETER
52-53	1-2 THESSALONIANS	67-68	JUDE
57	1-2 CORINTHIANS	65-67	1 TIMOTHY
57	GALATIANS	67	TITUS
58	ROMANS	67-68	2 TIMOTHY
62-63	EPHESIANS	64-67	HEBREWS
„	COLOSSIANS	66-68	2 PETER
„	PHILEMON	90-95	1-2-3 JOHN
„	PHILIPPIANS		

THE CATHOLIC EPISTLES AND THE FALL OF JERUSALEM

The Catholic Epistles should also be viewed in relation to the greatest catastrophe that ever befell the Jewish People—the Fall of Jerusalem in A.D. 70.

CHART 145

THE CATHOLIC EPISTLES AND THE FALL OF JERUSALEM IN A.D. 70					
BEFORE			AFTER		
BOOK	DATE	Place of Writing	BOOK	DATE	Place of Writing
JAMES	44–49	Jerusalem	1 JOHN	95–96	Ephesus
1 PETER	64–67	Babylon(?)			
JUDE	65–68	Jerusalem	2 JOHN	95–96	Ephesus
2 PETER	67–68	Rome(?)	3 JOHN	95–96	Ephesus

RELATION OF THE EPISTOLARY WRITERS TO CENTRES OF INFLUENCE

It is worth while noticing that the epistolary writers are prominently related to certain centres of great influence in the world of their day; and perhaps it is not an exaggeration to say that some of these centres derived their fame, from a Biblical point of view, from the connection of these men with them.

James, *Jude*, and *Peter* belonged specially to *Jerusalem*; *Paul* to *Antioch*, *Ephesus*, and *Rome*; *John* to *Ephesus*; and if, as Luther believed, *Apollos* wrote Hebrews, *Alexandria* and *Corinth* owed much to his connection with them.

CHART 146

RELATION OF THE EPISTOLARY WRITERS TO CENTRES OF INFLUENCE					
JAMES	JUDE	PETER	PAUL	JOHN	APOLLOS ?
JERUSALEM			ANTIOCH EPHESUS ROME	EPHESUS	ALEXANDRIA CORINTH

Peter's Epistles represent the middle position between *James* and *Jude* on the one hand, and *Paul* on the other hand. No one of these writers alone represents Christianity—not even Paul— but together they describe the full circle of Christian truth. Their presentations are not contradictory but complementary.

THE DOCTRINAL EXPRESSION
OF CHRISTIANITY

THE EPISTLES

PAULINE

GENERAL

PAULINE EPISTLES

THE PAULINE EPISTLES

The thirteen Epistles which Paul wrote can be classified in various ways, and each way is of some value.

THE ORDER OF PAUL'S EPISTLES

This relates to the time of writing, which was as follows:—

A.D. 52, 1 Thessalonians. A.D. 53, 2 Thessalonians.
A.D. 57, 1-2 Corinthians; Galatians. A.D. 58, Romans.
A.D. 62-63, Ephesians, Colossians, Philemon, Philippians.
A.D. 66-67, 1 Timothy, Titus. A.D. 67-68, 2 Timothy.

If these letters are carefully considered it will be seen that the first two and the last three greatly differ from the other eight. It may be said that the two and the three are related to the eight as introduction and conclusion, as prologue and epilogue, as preface and postscript; the substance of the Pauline teaching being in the central eight Epistles; and these eight, it should be observed, divide into two groups, the first of which is characterized by controversy, and the second by contemplation.

CHART 147

ORDER OF PAUL'S EPISTLES			
Prological	*Controversial*	*Contemplative*	*Epilogical*
1 Thessalonians 2 Thessalonians	1 Corinthians 2 Corinthians Galatians Romans	Ephesians Colossians (Philemon) Philippians	1 Timothy Titus 2 Timothy
A.D. 52-53	A.D. 57-58	A.D. 62-63	A.D. 65-67
The Coming	The Cross	The Christ	The Congregation

This order is impressive and important. The Prologue points onward to the end of the Christian age; and the Epilogue points outward to an undefined period of the Christian Church, which began in Paul's day. These views are not contradictory, but the end is presented before that of which it is the end is set forth.

Between these views are the controversial and contemplative Epistles, and in this order. The calm follows the storm. Before the superstructure is built the foundation is laid. What has to be fought for is shown before enjoyment of the victory is described.

For about fifteen years Paul was writing letters, of which, providentially, these thirteen have been preserved.

(See on Lost Letters, pp. 9, 10.)

THE DESTINATIONS OF PAUL'S EPISTLES

It is important to distinguish between the Letters which the Apostle sent to Churches, and those which he sent to individuals. Of the former there are nine, and of the latter, four.

Of the nine letters sent to churches, seven went to local, and two to scattered churches. The local churches were at Thessalonica, Corinth, Rome, Colossae, and Philippi; and the scattered churches were in Galatia and West Asia Minor—Galatians and Ephesians.

Of the letters to individuals, Paul wrote four to three persons—one to Philemon, one to Titus, and two to Timothy.

It is noteworthy that there is no indication that the Apostle ever wrote to any Church in Palestine and Syria, or to Beroea, or Athens.

These particulars may be summarized as follows:—

CHART 148

DESTINATIONS OF PAUL'S EPISTLES		
To CHURCHES		To INDIVIDUALS
SINGLE (7)	GROUPS (2)	(3)
1-2 Thessalonians 1-2 Corinthians Romans Colossians Philippians	Galatians Ephesians	Philemon Titus Timothy (2)
To ASIA (3)		To EUROPE (6)
Galatians Colossians Ephesians		1-2 Thessalonians 1-2 Corinthians Romans Philippians

THE DESTINATIONS OF PAUL'S EPISTLES

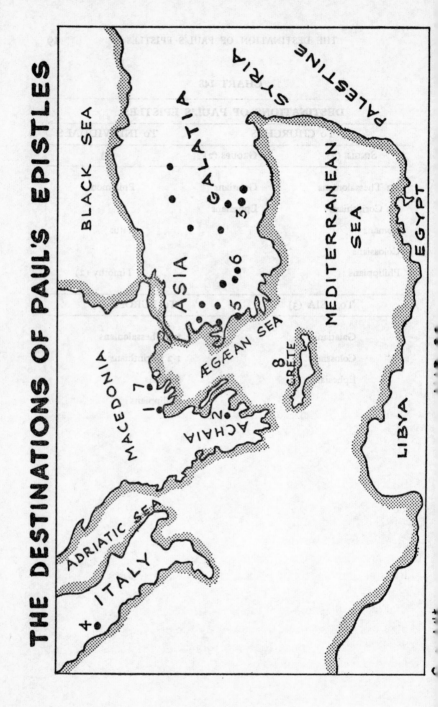

KEY TO MAP

Paul wrote thirteen Epistles, and they went to eight destinations, which are numbered on the map.

Two went to No. 1; two to No. 2; one to No. 3; one to No. 4; three to No. 5; two to No. 6; and one each to Nos. 7 and 8. Two of these Epistles, 5 and 3, went to groups of churches.

1. Two Epistles to Thessalonica.

2. Two extant Epistles to Corinth. Others are lost.

3. An Epistle to 'the churches of Galatia' (Gal. i. 1. 1 Cor. xvi. 1). What this expression means is a matter of controversy. We should try to understand what is meant by 'Galatia'.

(a) Galatia proper, the Northern territory inhabited by the Gauls, had three chief cities—Pessinus, Ancyra, and Tavium (W. to E.).

(b) The Roman Province of Galatia embraced also part of Phrygia, Pisidia, Isauria, and part of Lycaonia, and in this Southern Galatia were the churches which Paul planted on his first missionary journey.

Lightfoot, and many others, take the view that 'the churches of Galatia' were in the Northern Province. Ramsay, and many others, hold that the reference is to the Southern Province, to the churches of the first missionary journey.

If the latter view is correct the Galatian Letter was sent to Antioch in Pisidia, Iconium, Lystra, and Derbe.

4. The letter to the Romans went to the Christians in the capital of the Empire.

5. The Epistle to the Ephesians was an encyclical letter, and most probably was circulated to the churches in Pergamum, Thyatira, Smyrna, Sardis, Philadelphia, Laodicea, and, perhaps, Colossae.

But the two letters to Timothy also went to Ephesus where Timothy was at the time (1 Tim. i. 3; 2 Tim. iv. 19).

6. Two letters went to Colossae; one to the church there, and one was private—to Philemon.

7. The letter to Philippi. It would seem, however, that there were other letters to this city, which have been lost.

8. Titus was in Crete when Paul wrote to him (i. 5), so the letter must have been taken there by someone.

As already stated, so far as we know, Paul wrote no letter to Palestine, to Syria, to Athens, or to Beroea.

The carrying of these Letters must have been a matter of great concern to Paul, but he was not lacking in postmen. Timothy, Titus, Luke, Silvanus, Tychicus, Trophimus, Clement, Artemas, Erastus, Epaphroditus, Crescens, Gaius, Aristarchus, Secundus, Sopater, and others were continually passing to and fro between the Apostle and his Churches, but we do not know how often or in what directions he employed them to convey messages.

CLASSIFICATION OF PAUL'S EPISTLES

The Apostle's Letters fall naturally into four groups which are separated from one another by about four years.

GROUP 1, 1-2 Thessalonians.
GROUP 2, 1-2 Corinthians, Galatians and Romans.
GROUP 3, Ephesians, Colossians, Philemon and Philippians.
GROUP 4, 1-2 Timothy, and Titus.

GROUP 1 is *Prophetical*, dealing with Christian Hope: Christ and the Coming, and the Perfecting of Salvation.

GROUP 2 is *Polemical*, dealing with Christian Faith: Christ and the Cross, and the Plan of Salvation.

GROUP 3 is *Philosophical*, dealing with Christian Love: Christ and the Church, and the Privileges of Salvation.

GROUP 4 is *Pastoral*, dealing with Christian Order: Christ and the Congregation, and the Purpose of Salvation.

GROUP 1 conveys *Consolation* to Christians facing death.
GROUP 2 reveals the *Conflict* which rages round the Cross.
GROUP 3 discloses the *Conquest* which life in Christ assures.
GROUP 4 calls for *Consistency* in creed and conduct.

GROUP 1 is *Eschatological*, speaking of the Last Things.
GROUP 2 is *Soteriological*, speaking of Salvation.
GROUP 3 is *Christological*, speaking of Christ Himself.
GROUP 4 is *Ecclesiological*, speaking of Church Organization.

The following chart summarizes these aspects of Paul's four groups of Letters.

CHART 149

CLASSIFICATION OF PAUL'S EPISTLES			
Group 1 1 THESSALONIANS 2 THESSALONIANS	Group 2 1 CORINTHIANS 2 CORINTHIANS GALATIANS ROMANS	Group 3 EPHESIANS COLOSSIANS PHILEMON PHILIPPIANS	Group 4 1 TIMOTHY TITUS 2 TIMOTHY
A.D. 52–53	A.D. 57–58	A.D. 62–63	A.D. 65–68
Prophetical	Polemical	Philosophical	Pastoral
Christian Hope	Christian Faith	Christian Love	Christian Order
CHRIST and the COMING	CHRIST and the CROSS	CHRIST and the CHURCH	CHRIST and the CONGREGATION
Perfecting of Salvation	Plan of Salvation	Privileges of Salvation	Purpose of Salvation
Consolation	Conflict	Conquest	Consistency
Eschatological	Soteriological	Christological	Ecclesiological

It must be pointed out that in Group 3 two of the four Epistles are *personal*—Philemon and Philippians—and the descriptions do not characterize these, except *Christian Love*. By *Philosophical* in this Group is meant *ultimate reality*.

PAUL'S EPISTLES AND HIS MOVEMENTS

During the first fifteen years of Paul's ministry, A.D. 37-52, he wrote nothing which has been preserved; and during the second fifteen years he wrote what we have of his Letters.

None of these was written on his first missionary journey, A.D. 47-50; two of them were written on the second journey—1-2 Thessalonians, A.D. 51-54; four of them were written on the third journey—1-2 Corinthians, Galatians, and Romans, A.D. 54-58; four of them were written during the first Roman imprisonment—Ephesians, Colossians, Philemon, and Philippians, A.D. 61-63; two of them were written during his fourth journey, after release from imprisonment—1 Timothy, and Titus, A.D. 65-67; and one of them was written during his second Roman imprisonment—2 Timothy, A.D. 67-68.

CHART 150

PAUL'S EPISTLES AND HIS MOVEMENTS					
2nd Missionary Journey	3rd Missionary Journey	Captivity in Caesarea, and Voyage to Rome	1st Imprisonment in Rome	4th Missionary Journey	2nd Imprisonment in Rome
1 THESSA- LONIANS 2 THESSA- LONIANS	1 CORIN- THIANS 2 CORIN- THIANS GALATIANS ROMANS		EPHESIANS COLOSSIANS PHILEMON PHILIPPIANS	1 TIMOTHY TITUS	2 TIMOTHY
A.D. 51–54	A.D. 54–58	A.D. 58–61	A.D. 61-63	A.D. 63–67	A.D. 67-68
1	2		3	4	

It should be observed that 1-2 Thessalonians are *anticipative*; they look towards heaven; that 1-2 Timothy and Titus are *administrative*; they move on earth; and that these are the first and fourth groups.

A contrast is presented also in groups 2 and 3, in that group 2 is *controversial*, and group 3 is *contemplative*. (Chart 147).

Group 2 presents truths, not contradictory, but complementary. Epistles 1-2 Corinthians, Galatians, and Romans are both theological and experimental; they are objective and subjective; they teach that Christ died for us, and that we must die with Christ; they show that a great work has been done for us, and that a great work must be done in us; they reveal the ground of Christian hope, and the power of Christian life; they answer both Judaism and Hellenism—the false ground of hope of the one, and the false theory of life of the other (cf. Lightfoot). Chart 151 sets out these particulars.

CHART 151

COMPLEMENTARY CONTRASTS IN PAUL'S EPISTLES

	GROUP 1	GROUP 2	GROUP 3	GROUP 4
	Anticipative	*Controversial*	*Contemplative*	*Administrative*
	Looking towards Heaven	1 CORINTHIANS 2 CORINTHIANS GALATIANS ROMANS	EPHESIANS COLOSSIANS PHILEMON PHILIPPIANS	Moving on Earth
	1–2 THESSALONIANS			1–2 TIMOTHY. TITUS
		GROUP 2	GROUP 3	
	Theological	Experimental	Christ and The Church	Paul and his Friends
	Objective	Subjective	Christ The Head COLOSSIANS	Christian Love PHILEMON
	Christ died for us	We must die with Christ		
	Ground of Christian Hope	Power of Christian Life	The Church the Body EPHESIANS	Christian Joy PHILIPPIANS
	Judaism answered	Hellenism answered		
	THE CONFLICT		THE CONQUEST	

In the first group we see Christ Crucified; in the second, Christ Risen; and in the third, Christ Coming Again.

It is not fanciful to see in the Pauline groups of Epistles four aspects of Christ in relation to His people.

CHART 152

CHRIST IN RELATION TO HIS PEOPLE IN PAUL'S EPISTLES			
Group 1	**Group 2**	**Group 3**	**Group 4**
THE JUDGE	THE REDEEMER	THE LORD	THE AUTHORITY
Future	Past	Present	

These aspects are not exclusive, but they are distinctive.

THE TWO ORDERS OF PAUL'S EPISTLES

It should be observed that of the nine Church Epistles the order in our Bible is not chronological. Romans was not the first Epistle to be written, but the sixth; and 1-2 Thessalonians were not the last to be written, but the first. The difference is as follows:

ORDER OF READING	ORDER OF WRITING
Romans	1 Thessalonians
1 Corinthians	2 Thessalonians
2 Corinthians	1 Corinthians
Galatians	2 Corinthians
Ephesians	Galatians
Philippians	Romans
Colossians	Ephesians
1 Thessalonians	Colossians
2 Thessalonians	Philippians

The actual order of the Prison Epistles is not certain, but the matter is of little consequence as they were all written about the same time.

These Church Epistles treat of three great themes—*Justification, Sanctification,* and *Glorification.* In the order of writing

Glorification comes first—1-2 Thessalonians; *Justification* comes second—1-2 Corinthians, Galatians, and Romans; and *Sanctification* comes last—Ephesians, Colossians and Philippians. But in the Bible order *Justification* comes first—Romans, 1-2 Corinthians, and Galatians; *Sanctification* comes second—Ephesians, Philippians, and Colossians; and *Glorification* comes last—1-2 Thessalonians.

THE PAULINE EPISTLES

GROUP 1
1-2 THESSALONIANS

GROUP 2
1-2 CORINTHIANS GALATIANS ROMANS

GROUP 3
EPHESIANS COLOSSIANS PHILEMON
PHILIPPIANS

GROUP 4
1 TIMOTHY TITUS 2 TIMOTHY

THE PAULINE EPISTLES

In the order of reading *Romans* is put first, though it was the sixth Epistle to be written, because, in experience, it speaks of the first things—condemnation and justification (chapters i-v); and then it goes on to treat of sanctification and glorification (chapters vi-viii). No other Epistle does this.

Also, in the order of reading 1-2 *Thessalonians* the first Epistles to be written are put last because they deal with the Second Advent by which Church history is concluded.

PAIRS OF EPISTLES

It is not without interest that Paul's Epistles go in pairs, and each pair emphasizes an important subject.

CHART 153

1.	1 THESSALONIANS 2 THESSALONIANS	HOPE
2.	1 CORINTHIANS 2 CORINTHIANS	CONDUCT
3.	GALATIANS ROMANS	TRUTH
4.	EPHESIANS COLOSSIANS	LIFE
5.	PHILEMON PHILIPPIANS	UNITY
6.	TIMOTHY (2) TITUS	SERVICE

'IN CHRIST' IN PAUL'S EPISTLES*

The catacombs show that the early Christians had passwords which were understood among them, brief but pregnant, and of these none was more significant than *En Christō*, 'In Christ'.

*From the author's *Know Your Bible*, Vol. II, pp. 176, 178.

31

An examination of Paul's Epistles will show that this word is the key to each of them, and this is not to be wondered at as the object of these Epistles is to show the quality of the life which Christians should live. Following the canonical order we see that:

In Romans we are *Justified* 'in Christ' (iii. 24). Though Romans was the sixth Letter to be written it is placed first, because it treats of the first great thing in the new life—Justification.

In 1 Corinthians we are *Sanctified* 'in Christ' (i. 2). Paul rebukes the ethical and theological errors of the Church by showing them that what is judicially true of Christians should also be practically true.

In 2 Corinthians we are *Vindicated* 'in Christ' (xii. 19). There do arise times when 'in Christ' it is our duty to defend ourselves.

In Galatians we are *Liberated* 'in Christ' (ii. 4). This Epistle is the great Charter of our emancipation from the Law, wherein it is shown that we are dead to the Law, to self, and to the world 'in Christ' (ii. 19, 20; v. 24; vi. 14).

In Ephesians we are *Exalted* 'in Christ' (i. 3; ii. 6); by His death, burial, resurrection, and ascension, the believer is dead, buried, raised, and seated in heavenly places.

In Philippians we are *Exultant* 'in Christ' (i. 26). This is the Epistle of Christian joy, and it is shown that joy is normal Christian experience 'in Christ'.

In Colossians we are *Complete* 'in Christ' (ii. 9, 10). All of God is in Christ, and all of Christ is for us, so that, being already complete in Him, we may become complete by the gracious operations of the Holy Spirit.

In Philemon we are made *Gracious* 'in Christ' (15, 16). The spirit of forgiveness and forgetfulness of wrong done to us takes possession of us, because 'in Christ' wrongs are righted, and crookednesses are evened out.

In 1 Thessalonians we are *Hope-full* 'in Christ' (i. 3). The Flaming of His Advent Feet is all across the pages of this Epistle. He is our prospect. There will be one generation of Christians that will not die, for Christ will come for them.

In 2 Thessalonians we are *Glorified* 'in Christ' (i. 12; ii. 14). The 'day of Christ' is to precede the 'day of the Lord', and the gathering of the saints unto Him is to be accomplished before Antichrist is revealed. Though first to be written these two Epistles are put last of the Church Epistles, because they treat of the final experience, the glorification of the saints.

In 1 Timothy we are made *Faithful* 'in Christ' (i. 18, 19); faithful to the doctrine, to the worship, and to the oversight of the Church; faithful in personal walk and work.

In Titus we are made *Exemplary* 'in Christ' (ii. 7, 8); in all things showing ourselves a pattern of good works.

In 2 Timothy we are *Triumphant* 'in Christ' (iv. 6-8), and though persecuted we are at last brought forth in triumph, the good fight fought, the race run, and the faith kept.

THE PAULINE EPISTLES

GROUP 1

1-2 THESSALONIANS

A.D. 52-53

The Advent Epistles

CHRIST AND THE COMING

The Judge

———————————

1-2 THESSALONIANS

Viewing as a whole these two first Epistles of Paul there are, we observe, six factors which, taken together, make them what they are.

1. THE HISTORICAL FACTOR

This relates to the Church at Thessalonica, reference to which has already been made; but we should note that:

(a) The Church was only recently originated.

The reference in Acts xvii. 2 need not mean that Paul was in this city for three weeks only. Philippi was 100 miles distant, yet more than once the Church there sent money to Paul (Phil. iv. 15, 16); and this notwithstanding, the Apostle laboured 'night and day' at tent-making to meet his need, and that, perhaps, of Silas and Timothy also. But at most the Church could not have been in existence for more than a few months, which makes 1 Thess. i. 7, 8 the more remarkable.

(b) The Church consisted mainly of Gentiles (1 Thess. i. 9; ii. 14; Acts xvii. 4).

(c) There were in the Church some leaders, who are said to have been 'over (the members) in the Lord' (v. 12, 13). This does not mean that they were ordained bishops or elders, for they were too young in the faith, and, probably, too old in years to be that; but they would be a governing committee for purposes of administration; not ordained, but acknowledged.

(d) These young Christians were suffering much persecution (I. i. 6; ii. 14, 15; iii. 3, 4. II. i. 4-7; Acts xvii. 5-9), at the instigation of the Jews, who had slain Jesus, persecuted His prophets, and expelled His apostles. Paul had told the Thessalonian believers that they would thus suffer, so they were not unprepared.

2. THE PERSONAL FACTOR

This relates to what these Epistles reveal of Paul.

(a) He defends his conduct, while at Thessalonica, against the charge of avarice and ambition; and affirms that his motive in ministry was not selfishness but love (I. ii. I-12). This love expressed itself as in the tenderness of a mother (ii. 7), and the wisdom of a father (ii. 11).

(b) Paul's love for these converts and his longing to be with them, show how dear they were to him (ii. 17-iii. 5, R.V.).

It is doubtful if the Apostle loved any of his many converts as much as he did these, and a very practical exhibition of it is seen in his willingness rather to be left alone in Athens than that they should be without the presence and help of Timothy. This whole section is intensely personal and passionate, and has no parallel except in Philippians and Philemon.

3. THE DEVOTIONAL FACTOR

The Apostle's heart is revealed in his prayers for his converts in Thessalonica (I. i. 2; ii. 13; iii. 9-13; v. 17, 18, 23. II. i. 3, 11, 12; ii. 13, 16, 17; iii. 5, 16). These consist in thanksgiving and intercession, and reveal, as all Paul's prayers do, the spirituality of this ministry of his.

It should not be overlooked that before making request for these Christians he gives thanks to God for what they are and have done (I. i. 2; ii. 13; iii. 9. II. i. 3; ii. 13). It is always easier to criticise than to commend, but it is not so Christian. We should endeavour to see goodness wherever it exists, though it is often threatened by what is bad (iii. 10).

4. THE ETHICAL FACTOR

Timothy who brought to Paul news that gladdened his heart brought also bad news (I. iv. 1-8). Immorality characterized the Gentile world, and the Thessalonian converts had not completely divested themselves of it when they became Christians. Paul had spoken to them about this when he was with them (iv. 2), but the evil still remained; and here the Apostle tells them that the will of God is the norm for the Christian conscience. Paul uses the word sanctification three times (*hagiasmos*, iv. 3, 4, 7), which means holiness or wholeness, and only by the pursuit of this can we 'please God' (iv. 1). It is astonishing how what is good and what is bad can coexist in the same person, and people!

5. THE DOCTRINAL FACTOR

When Paul wrote these two Epistles he had been preaching for fifteen years, and it was impossible for him to think except theologically. The expression of his theological thinking was determined to a large extent by the people to whom he wrote, and to the circumstances, but it may be affirmed with confidence that in later years he did not contradict what he had said in earlier years. Naturally the emphasis changed, but the teaching remained the same.

It is not an exaggeration to say that the substance of Paul's theology is in his first two Epistles; that here we find explicitly or implicitly all that he taught in his later Epistles. This fact has received less attention than it should have done. A considerable book could be written on this subject, but here we can only indicate how theological thèse two Epistles are.

(a) *The Trinity*, the foundation of the Christian religion, is here (I. i. 3-5; iv. 6-8; v. 18, 19. II. ii. 13).

(b) *God* is mentioned 55 times.

(c) *The Second Person of the Trinity* is spoken of as: 'Jesus'; 'Lord'; 'Lord Jesus'; 'Lord Jesus Christ'; 'Christ'; 'Christ Jesus'; and 'Son'; designations which occur not fewer than 55 times; and which clearly show that Christ was both human and Divine. In several places He is spoken of with the Father under one preposition, in which passages they are co-ordinated (*en*, I. i. 1; II. i. 1. *apo*, II. i. 2. *kata*, II. i. 12).

(d) *The Death of Christ*. This is affirmed to be not only a historical fact but atoning in power and effect (I. i. 10; ii. 15; v. 9, 10).

(e) *The Resurrection of Christ* (I. i. 10; iv. 14).

(f) *Satan*. A person, with great power (I. ii. 18; iii. 5. II. ii. 9).

(g) *Sin* (I. i. 9; ii. 15; iv. 5; v. 22. II. i. 8).

(h) *The Gospel* (I. i. 5; ii. 2, 4, 8, 9; iii. 2, 6. II. i. 8; ii. 14).

(i) *The Truth* (II. ii. 10, 12, 13).

(j) *Faith* (I. i. 3, 8; iii. 2, 5, 6, 7, 10; v. 8. II. i. 3, 4, 11; iii. 2). To this must be added eight references to *believing*.

(k) *Sanctification* (I. ii. 12; iii. 13; iv. 3, 7. II. ii. 13).

(l) The *Eschatology* of these Epistles is pronounced, and it relates to *death*; *the day of the Lord*; *the Lord's return*; the *wrath* of God; the *punishment* of sinners; the *Kingdom of God*; and the *Antichrist* (I. i. 10; ii. 19; iii. 13; iv. 13-18; v. 2-4, 23. II. i. 7-10; ii. 1-12; iii. 5).

From all these references it is clear how doctrinally full these Epistles are, and how much Paul had taught these Thessalonians in so short a time.

6. THE PRACTICAL FACTOR

Doctrine which has no relation to duty is of no use. Paul is emphatic about this in these Epistles, and he had been emphatic about it when he was at Thessalonica (iv. 11). He speaks of some members of the Church who were walking *disorderly* (in 1-2 Thess. only), a word which means those who leave their place in the ranks; those who refuse to submit to discipline. They make a *noise*, and Paul bids them 'study to be quiet'. They are guilty of *gossip*, and Paul exhorts them to 'mind their own business'. They are *indolent*, and Paul commands them to 'earn their own living' (1 Thess. iv. 11. 2 Thess. iii. 6-15).

People in the churches who are guilty of these three forms of disorder should be dealt with by the Church, and in the way that Paul indicates (2 Thess. iii. 6, 14, 15).

The piety that is not practical is pernicious.

Thessalonica was a large and important Macedonian city. It was named after the wife of Cassander, the sister of Alexander the Great, about 315 B.C.

It was a flourishing commercial city situated on the sea at the head of the Gulf of Salonica. By the Egnatian Way it connected West and East.

It was the second city in Europe which Paul visited on his second missionary journey, and where he spent three weeks (Acts xvii. 1-9). The Philippians twice sent the Apostle financial help to this city (Phil. iv. 16).

THESSALONICA

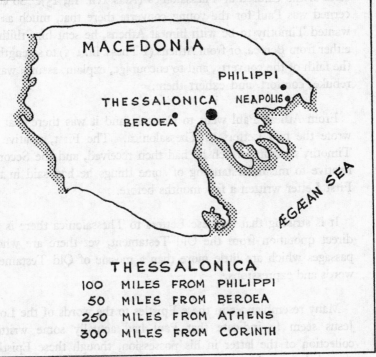

MACEDONIA

PHILIPPI

THESSALONICA   NEAPOLIS

BEROEA

ÆGÆAN SEA

THESSALONICA

100 MILES FROM PHILIPPI
 50 MILES FROM BEROEA
250 MILES FROM ATHENS
300 MILES FROM CORINTH

Copyright   MAP 30   W.G.S.

To-day it is a thriving city, and is called *Salonica*. It had a population in 1947 of 236,500, and many synagogues.

In April, 1941, the Germans took it, but it now again belongs to Greece.

So far as we know these are the first Letters which Paul wrote to a Church, and he wrote them about fifteen years after his conversion, when he was on his second missionary journey, A.D. 52, 53 (Acts xv. 36-xviii. 22), and he wrote them from Corinth (Acts xviii. 11).

Paul had visited Thessalonica, and for some weeks had proclaimed his Messianic message to the Jews, not without success, but jealous Jews had created an uproar, and the Christians, anxious for Paul's safety, sent him away by night.

Leaving Timothy at Beroea, Paul went to Athens and sent
word to Timothy and Silas to meet him there and report on the
state of the Church at Thessalonica (Acts xvii. 14, 15). So concerned was Paul for the young converts there that, much as he
wanted Timothy to be with him at Athens, he sent him thither,
either from Beroea, or from Athens (1 Thess. iii. 1-5) to strengthen
the faith of the converts, and to encourage, explain, assure, warn,
rebuke, comfort, and exhort them.

From Athens Paul went to Corinth, and it was there that he
wrote the two Letters to Thessalonica. The First, relative to
Timothy's report, which he had then received, and the Second,
relative to misunderstanding of some things he had said in the
First Letter written a few months before.

It is striking that in these Letters to Thessalonica there is no
direct quotation from the Old Testament, yet there are whole
passages which are little more than a mosaic of Old Testament
words and expressions.

Many resemblances in these Epistles to the words of the Lord
Jesus seem to indicate that Paul had actually some written
collection of the latter in his possession, though these Epistles
preceded the writing of any of the Gospels. There is no more
instructive commentary on 2 Thess. ii than Matt. xxiv.

Some of Paul's converts at Thessalonica became his intimate
friends. One of these was JASON, who was his host (Acts xvii. 7),
and who, if he be the Jason of Rom. xvi. 21, must subsequently
have travelled with the Apostle.

ARISTARCHUS was another of these friends, who, probably,
was a Gentile. He travelled with Paul on his last journey to
Jerusalem, bearing offerings for the poor saints there (Acts xx. 4).
He was with the Apostle also on the voyage to Rome, and shared
that terrible journey (Acts xxvii. 2). Also, he shared Paul's
captivity in Rome (Col. iv. 10; Phile. 24). What this friendship
meant to the great missionary it is impossible to say, but it
greatly lightened his burden.

SECUNDUS, also, was identified with Paul in service (Acts xx. 4). GAIUS figured in the Ephesian riot, and he too was a travelling companion of the Apostle (Acts xix. 29). Others of this name appear in the epistles (Rom. xvi. 23; 1 Cor. i. 14; 3 John 1).

Another associate of Paul was DEMAS, presumably a Thessalonian (2 Tim. iv. 10). The Apostle called him a 'fellow-labourer' (Phile. 24), and in the Letter to Colossae (iv, 14), he sent greetings. But he was unfaithful and forsook Paul, and a reason is given in 2 Tim. iv. 10.

The two Letters to Thessalonica are pre-eminently the Epistles of the LORD's Return. Three words are used in referring to this, and it is important to understand their different shades of meaning.

1. PAROUSIA (Παρουσία)

This word generally means *presence* in the sense of an arrival, an advent. With this significance it is found in the papyri. A certain Dionysia, who is engaged in a lawsuit, petitions for leave to return home as the care of her property demands her *presence* (P. Oxy. No. 237, A.D. 186).

The word occurs in the New Testament twenty-four times. Of these it is used six times of certain individuals (e.g. 2 Cor. x. 10; Phil. i. 26), and eighteen times of the Lord's Return. Of these eighteen, four are in 1 Thess., and two in 2 Thess. (I. ii. 19; iii. 13; iv. 15; v. 23. II. ii. 1, 8). The word is never used in the New Testament of the LORD's First Advent.

2. EPIPHANEIA ('Επιφάνεια)

This word means *a shining forth, manifestation, appearance*, and in an inscription is used of the accession of a Roman Emperor—Caligula—(*Inscriptions of Cos*, 391).

In the New Testament, the word occurs six times. It is used only by Paul, and with the exception of 2 Thess ii. 8, only in the Pastoral Epistles (I. vi. 14; II. i. 10; iv. 1, 8; Tit. ii. 13). The verb occurs in Luke i. 79; Acts xxvii. 20; Tit. ii. 11; iii. 4. It should be observed that in 2 Tim. i. 10 the word is used of Christ's First Advent.

3. APOKALUPSIS (Ἀποκάλυψις)

The verb means *to reveal*, and the substantive is an unveiling of what already exists, though hitherto it has been hidden, or only imperfectly known. It occurs seventeen times in the New Testament, of which twelve are in Paul's Epistles. The noun is used in 2 Thess. i. 7; and the verb in 2 Thess. ii. 3, 6, 8, but not of *divine* revelation.

The last book of the Bible is 'a revelation of Jesus Christ' (i. 1).

These three words illuminate New Testament eschatology. Of the first (*parousia*) Deissmann says: 'From the Ptolemaic period down into the 2nd cent. A.D. we are able to trace the word in the East as a technical expression for the arrival or the visit of the king or the emperor. In Greece a new era was reckoned from the parousia of the Emperor Hadrian, (and) all over the world advent-coins were struck after a parousia of the emperor, and we are even able to quote examples of advent-sacrifices.' (*Light from the Ancient East*).

Referring to the second and third words Trench (in his *Synonyms*) says: 'If we bring these two into comparison, ἀποκάλυψις is the more comprehensive, and, grand as is the other, the grander word. It sets forth nothing less than that progressive and immediate unveiling of (Christ) to His Church on the part of the otherwise unknown and unknowable God which has run through all ages; the body to which this revelation is vouchsafed being thereby designated or indeed constituted as His Church, the object of His more immediate care, and the ordained diffuser of this knowledge of Him to the rest of mankind.

'There is no ἀποκάλυψις save to the Church. We may say of the ἐπιφάνειαι, that they are contained in the ἀποκάλυψις, being separate points or moments therein. If God is to be immediately known to men, He must in some shape or other appear to them, to those among them whom He has chosen for this honour.

'Epiphanies must be Theophanies as well; and as such the Church has claimed not merely such communications made to

men as are recorded at Gen. xviii. 1ff; xxviii. 13ff; but all in which
the angel of the LORD or of the Covenant appears; such as Gen.
xvi. 7ff; Josh. v. 13-15; Judg. ii. 1ff; vi. 11ff; xiii. 3ff. All these it
has regarded as preludings, on the part of the Son, of His incarnation; itself the most glorious Epiphany that as yet has been,
even as His second coming is an Epiphany more glorious still
which is yet in the future.'

These references in Thessalonians, and indeed throughout
the New Testament to Christ's Second Advent, cannot be explained, or got rid of, by saying that He is always coming. In a
sense He is always coming, but no Second Advent passage refers
to this, but to a coming, yet future, as personal and visible as was
His first advent. Let it be said, however, that when a Movement
is made of any doctrine, error is more than likely to attach to it.

I THESSALONIANS

What Timothy's report was is reflected in the First Epistle which Paul sent to this Church (1 Thess. iii. 6, 7). He had brought good news of the faith, love, and patience of the Thessalonians (iii. 6); but also there was news which was not good. Some had questioned Paul's character and motives (ii. 3-12); heathen impurities still lingered among them (iv. 3-8); and there was much need for practical Christianity (v. 12-22).

To deal with these and other matters the Apostle wrote his First Letter to the Church. It is in striking contrast to his other Church Letters in that it is very personal and informal, and only broadly lends itself to analysis. We may, however, discern the following outline:

Between an Introduction, i. 1, and a Conclusion, v. 25-28, there are three parts. First, a *Word of Exultation* (i. 2-10); secondly, a *Word of Explanation* (ii-iii); and finally, a *Word of Exhortation* (iv. 1-v. 24).

Paul thanks God for the spiritual progress of the Church (i. 2-10). He reminds the members of how he had preached to them (ii. 1-12). It gladdens him to remember how they had received his message, and in doing so received strength to endure persecution (ii. 13-16). He tells them that he had endeavoured to revisit them, but Satan had prevented him (ii. 17-20). So, as he could not come to them, he had sent Timothy (iii. 1-5), and the report which he had brought back greatly comforted the Apostle (iii. 6-10), who offers a prayer on their behalf (iii. 11-13).

CHART 154

	I THESSALONIANS			
	I	II	III	
Introduction i.1	i. 2-10	ii–iii	iv–v. 24	Conclusion v. 25-28
	EXULTATION	EXPLANATION	EXHORTATION	
	1. The Faith that Received	1. Slander and Suffering	1. Christian Conduct	
	2. The Love that Served	2. Tidings and Thanksgiving	2. Christian Comfort	
	3. The Hope that Waited	3. Prayer and Purpose	3. Christian Concord	

Chapters iv-v are more didactic than i-iii. Paul exhorts his converts to practical sanctification, warning them against immorality (iv. 1-8). He enjoins upon them love and industry (iv. 9-12), and imparts to them a comforting revelation concerning those of their number who had died, and concerning the LORD's Return (iv. 13-18).

In view of the suddenness of the Day of the Lord Paul exhorts the believers to watchfulness and mutual encouragement (v. 1-11); and the Epistle ends with a series of admonitions (v. 12-24).

There are references to Christ's Second Coming in i. 10; ii. 12, 19; iii. 13; iv. 14-17; v. 1-4, 9, 23; and Paul's teaching on this subject relates to *conversion* (i. 9, 10); *evangelism* (ii. 19, 20); *unselfishness* (iii. 11-13); *bereavement* (iv. 13-18); and *holiness* (v. 23, 24). The most important passages are in iv. 13-18, and v. 1-11, which are of outstanding doctrinal importance. The subject of each of them is the LORD's Return, but, it would seem, they deal with different aspects of it.

I THESSALONIANS iv. 13-18.

'We do not want you to be under any misapprehension, brothers, about those who are falling asleep. You must not grieve for them, as others do who have no hope. For if we believe that Jesus died and rose again, then by means of Jesus God will bring back with Him those who have fallen asleep.

For we can assure you, on the Lord's own authority, that those of us who will still be living when the Lord comes will have no advantage over those who have fallen asleep, for the Lord Himself, at the summons, when the archangel calls and God's trumpet sounds, will come down from heaven, and first those who die in union with Christ will rise; then those of us who are still living will be caught up with them on clouds into the air to meet the Lord, and so we shall be with the Lord forever.

Therefore, encourage one another with this truth.'

(Goodspeed).

13. Some members of the Church had died since Paul was there, and the brethren did not know how to relate the matter to the teaching which the Apostle had given them on the LORD's Return.

'*Them that are falling asleep.*' The Apostle does not say that the bereaved *should not grieve*, but that their grief should not be like that of the unregenerate who have no prospect of a blessed resurrection.

14. That Jesus *'died and rose again'* is historical fact, and is the foundation of the Christian Gospel. For us everything depends on whether or not we *'believe'* it. *'Are fallen asleep'* (1 aor. part. pass.) means *'were put to sleep'*, not *'in'* but *'through'* (*dia*) Jesus. Here *'through'* must mean either that *Jesus put them to sleep*; or that *because of Jesus* they were persecuted and died.

When Christ returns those who were put to sleep through Him will come back with Him.

> 'As surely as our belief is rooted in the death and resurrection of Jesus, even so we are confident that God will bring along with the returning Jesus those who have fallen on sleep through Him.'
>
> (G. Milligan).

'Sleep' is used metaphorically and refers to the body, but only of the bodies of Christians. 'Cemetery' means 'the sleeping place'. The word means a dormitory. The Persians call their cemeteries 'The Cities of the Silent'.

The view that the *Soul* is the person and that it becomes unconscious at death, and remains so until the resurrection at Christ's coming, is not the teaching of the Bible. When Paul said, 'Absent from the body, present with the Lord', he certainly did not mean that between these two events he would be unconscious for nineteen hundred years.

15. Apparently Paul had received a direct revelation from the LORD on the subject about which he is writing (cf. Acts xviii. 9).

'Prevent' does not mean *hinder*, but *precede* or *anticipate*, by which is meant that when Christ comes those living will have no advantage over those who have slept (cf. Pss. xviii. 5; cxix. 148). The negative is double, for emphasis (*ou mē*).

16. *'Shout'*, summons, a word of command, given, perhaps, to the heavenly hosts as it is the voice of an archangel.

> 'With a word of command in an archangel's voice, even with the voice of the trump of God.'

The first act in the drama of the Parousia will be the resurrection of Christians who have died. There will be millions of them. What is meant by this *rising*? What about those whose bodies were blasted by bombs, those who were drowned and eaten by fish, those who were cremated?

16, 17. This is the first detailed account of what will happen when Christ comes, but it is not a full account. Nothing is said of a change of body, but about five years later further details are given (1 Cor. xv. 51-54).

The idea of two stages, with years between, was advocated by scholars such as J. N. Darby, and C. I. Scofield and is still held in evangelical circles. According to this view the Second Advent is in two stages, first to the air for the Church, and then, to the earth for the establishment of the Kingdom. The first part of the journey is 'for' the saints, and the second is 'with' them.

Other Scholars hold the view that believers meet the Lord on His way from heaven to earth and accompany Him to it, thus indicating that there is only one Second Coming, which is from heaven to earth, an event at the end of the Great Tribulation and not before it. Matt. xxiv. 29-31 is cited in support of this view, as is the Greek word *apantēsis*, 'meeting' translated 'to meet (the Lord)' in 1 Thess. 4. 17. This word occurs only three times in the New Testament, and means in each instance *a meeting to accompany*. Matt. xxv. 6, 'The bridegroom cometh, *go ye out to meet him*'. The wise virgins did this, not to remain with him where they met him, nor to return with him from whence he had come, but to *continue with him* to the marriage. Acts xxviii. 15, 16. 'When the brethren heard of us, *they came to meet us*—and we came to Rome'.

17. Some expositors affirm that by '*those of us who will still be living*' Paul expected to be alive when Christ returned. Could he have said he knew he would not live till Christ returned? He did not know, as we still do not know, when the Advent will

take place, but every Christian should live in the expectation of it. Christians are always either 'living' or 'sleeping', and one day, no one knows when, He will come to and for both.

18. '*Comfort one another with these words.*' W. E. Vine quotes a papyrus letter of the second century A.D., written by a woman to her bereaved friends. It runs: 'Irene to Taonnophris and Philon, greeting! I was as much grieved and shed as many tears over Eumoiros as I shed for Didymas. I did everything that was fitting and so did my whole family . . . But still there is nothing one can do in the face of such trouble. So *I leave you to comfort yourselves*. Farewell.'

What a difference the Christian gospel makes!

1 Thessalonians v. 1-11

'But as to times and dates, brothers, you do not need to have anyone write to you, for you yourselves know perfectly well that the Day of the Lord is to come like a thief in the night.

'When people say, "What peace and security!" then sudden destruction will be upon them, like birth-pains upon a woman about to give birth to a child, and there will be no escape.

'But you are not in darkness, brothers, so that that Day should surprise you like thieves. You all belong to the light and the day. We have nothing to do with night or with darkness. So we must not sleep like other men, but we must be vigilant and composed. For those who sleep, sleep at night, and those who get drunk do so at night, but we who belong to the day must be composed, wearing faith and love for a coat of mail, and helmeted with the hope of salvation. For God has not destined us for his wrath, but to gain salvation through our Lord Jesus Christ, who died for us so that whether we are still alive or fall asleep we may live with him. Therefore encourage one another and strengthen one another, just as you are doing.'

(Goodspeed).

Even by a casual reading of chapter iv. 13-18, and of v. 1-11 one must recognize two distinct presentations of the subject of the LORD's Return. Both passages speak of 'sleep', but the word used in chapter v is not the one used in chapter iv.

In ch. iv. 14 *koimaō* speaks of the death of the bodies of believers, though elsewhere sometimes of natural sleep (Matt. xxviii. 13; Luke xxii. 45); but in ch. v. 6, 7, 10 the word is *katheudō*, which is used only once of death in the New Testament (Matt. ix. 24).

The expression '*Day of the* LORD' may raise a difficulty here, for it seems not to have the same significance as 'the Day of Christ' in Phil. i. 10; ii. 16, and similar expressions (Phil. i. 6; 1 Cor. i. 8; v. 5). In the New Testament it occurs only here and in II. ii. 2; Acts ii. 20; 2 Pet. iii. 10; cf. Rev. i. 10; vi. 17 but in the Old Testament it occurs upwards of forty times, beginning with Amos v. 18; Isa. ii. 12, and it connotes *judgment* (cf. Zeph. 1. 7-15, etc.). The 'Day of Christ' in II. ii. 2, is changed in the Revised Version to the 'Day of the LORD', and the reference is in a judgment setting.

It thus appears that the '*Day of Christ*' refers to the *Parousia*, and the '*Day of the* LORD' to the *Epiphaneia* (2 Thess. ii. 8); and that verses 1-3 of ch. v refer to the LORD'S Return in relation to the world.

2 THESSALONIANS

This Epistle was written shortly after the First in consequence of additional information which Paul had received concerning conditions at Thessalonica. The Church had received a forged letter, purporting to have been written by him (ii. 2).

Some things he had said in his first letter had been misunderstood (ii. 2); and some of the converts were walking disorderly (iii. 6, 11). This Epistle was written to give further information on the LORD'S Return; to correct misapprehensions, to exhort steadfastness, and to enjoin industry.

Its general outline is as follows:—

CHART 155

2 THESSALONIANS			
I	II	III	IV
INTRODUCTION	ENCOURAGEMENT	EXHORTATION	CONCLUSION
i. 1-4	i. 5-ii. 12	ii. 13-iii. 15	iii. 16-18
1. Salutation (1)	1. Inspiration for the Oppressed (i. 5-12)	1. To the Devout (ii. 13-iii. 5)	1. Supplication (16)
2. Benediction (2)			2. Authentication (17)
3. Thanksgiving (3, 4)	2. Instruction for the Perplexed (ii. 1-12)	2. To the Disorderly (iii. 6-15)	3. Benediction (18)

This is the shortest of Paul's epistles to any Church, but prophetically and practically it is of great importance.

There are two practical sections, one at the beginning, and one at the end of the Epistle. The former is a word of thanksgiving and encouragement (i. 3-12). The Apostle was always generous in his recognition of what was good in others.

In the latter also is a word of thanksgiving and encouragement (ii. 13-iii. 5), but there is also a word of warning to and concerning those whose conduct was disorderly, due, it would seem, to some wrong ideas about the Second Advent (iii. 6-15).

Between these two practical sections is the famous prophetical one on the *Day of the LORD* and the *Man of Sin* (ii. 1-12).

2 Thessalonians ii. 1-12

'With regard to the arrival of our Lord Jesus Christ and our muster before Him, I beg you, brothers, not to let your minds get quickly unsettled or excited by any spirit of prophecy, or any declaration, or any letter purporting to come from me, to the effect that the Day of the Lord is already here.

'Let nobody delude you into this belief, whatever he may say. It will not come till the Rebellion takes place first of all, with the revealing of the Lawless One, the doomed One, the adversary who vaunts himself above and against every so-called god or object of worship, actually seating himself in the temple of God with the proclamation that he himself is God. Do not you remember how I used to tell you this when I was with you?

'Well, you can recall now what it is that restrains him from being revealed before His appointed time.

'For the secret force of lawlessness is at work already; only, it cannot be revealed till he who at present restrains it is removed. Then shall the Lawless One be revealed, whom the Lord Jesus will destroy with the breath of His lips, and quell by His appearing and arrival—that One whose arrival is due to Satan's activity, with the full power, the miracles and portents, of falsehood, and with the full deceitfulness of evil for those who are doomed to perish, since they refuse to love the Truth that would save them.

'Therefore God visits them with an active delusion, till they put faith in falsehood, so that all may be doomed who refuse faith in the Truth, but delight in evil.'   (Moffatt).

Confessedly this is a difficult passage. What is meant by— The day of the LORD? The apostasy? The man of sin? The son of perdition? The temple of God? That which restraineth?

The mystery of lawlessness? One that restraineth? Taken out of the way? The LORD shall slay? The working of Satan? Power and signs and wonders of falsehood?

If these twelve questions can be answered, we'll know what the passage means. One of the most satisfactory experiences any Bible student can have is to find out how colossal is his ignorance. There have been the most fantastic interpretations of this passage. Mohammed, Caligula, Titus, Simon Magus, the High Priest Ananias, Napoleon, and Luther have even been called the Antichrist; the restrainer has been regarded as Nero or Claudius; and the Second Advent has been regarded as having taken place when Jerusalem was destroyed in A.D. 70. All this would be news to Paul!

What we want to know is—Is the Man of Sin the Antichrist? Is the Antichrist a person, a tendency, or a principle? Is the Antichrist of Paul identical with the Antichrist of John? Has this prophecy been fulfilled, or is it yet to be fulfilled?

THE MAN OF SIN

Gloag says there are four views of this expression: that of the *Rationalists*, who do not regard this as a prophecy; that of the *Praeterists*, who consider that the prophecy is already fulfilled; that of the *Progressionists*, who regard it as now being fulfilled by the Roman Catholic Church; and that of the *Futurists*, who regard the fulfilment as still to come.

The reference to the *Man of Sin* is related to the book of Daniel (vii. 23-26; xi. 36-39). Antiochus Epiphanes (B.C. 200-164) undoubtedly was a type of the final Antichrist.

The three sources of information on this subject are: the book of Daniel; this Thessalonian passage; and the book of the Revelation. There are a few scattered references elsewhere (e.g. John v. 43).

When so many have failed to answer these questions we cannot hope to succeed, but we are not altogether without a clue. We should carefully ponder verses 5-6, especially verse 6.

'At present there is a power (you know what I mean) which holds him in check, so that he may not shew himself before the time appointed to him.' (R. Knox).

'Have you no memory of what I said when I was with you, giving you word of these things?

'And now it is clear to you what is keeping back his revelation till the time come for him to be seen.' (Basic English).

'You know what is restraining him now so that he may be revealed in his time.' (R.S.V.).

'You cannot have forgotten that while I was still with you, I was in the habit of telling you these things. And since then you have had experience for yourselves of the working of that power by which the full revelation of the lawless one is kept in check until his appointed time shall have arrived.' (G. Milligan).

These verses make two things perfectly clear, namely (a) that Paul gave the Thessalonians instruction on the subject of this passage, and (b) that they knew quite well what we are endeavouring to know—what the restraining power was.

Why does Paul not plainly say what or who the restrainer was? Apparently because to have said so would have endangered the Christian community had the letter fallen into the hands of an enemy, who would note that the *restrainer* is to be *removed* (cf. Acts xvii. 6-8).

The Church Fathers believed that the *Roman Empire* was the *restraining power*, and that its Caesar, at any given time, was the *restrainer*.

The passage says that when the restraining power is removed the Antichrist would be revealed, and that Christ would come and destroy him; but when the *Roman Empire* went to pieces in the fourth century neither of these things happened.

The Fathers were right so far as they could see, but we, in our time, can see that more than the Roman Empire is meant, as Antichrist has not been revealed, and Christ has not come. This something more would therefore seem to be constituted government throughout 'the times of the Gentiles' (Luke xxi. 24). When these 'times' have been fulfilled, that is, at the end of this

Christian age, conditions will arise which will give the Antichrist his chance, and which will precipitate the Lord's Return to this world, which is called the *Day of the* LORD.

THE ANTICHRIST

Whether by this word is meant a *person* or a *power* will always be a matter of controversy. Perhaps the truth is that Antichrist is *a person representing a power*. The early Church was unanimous in the belief that a person is meant, and it seems that this was the view of the Apostles. Both Paul and John regard him to be a rival Christ; both declare that his coming is preceded by an apostasy of nominal Christians; both connect his manifestation with Christ's Second Advent; both describe him as a liar and deceiver; both speak of him as an ally of Satan; and both place his coming in the future while affirming that his spirit is at work already in the world.

The record of Hitler is too recent to allow of the idea that no individual could ever exercise the power attributed to the Antichrist.

In the eleventh century the view was widely held that Antichrist was the Papacy, and from the time of the Reformation this view assumed the position of a dogma in the Protestant Churches; and the Pope was regarded as the embodiment of the whole antichristian system.

We believe that this view is not tenable, bad as the Roman Catholic system is, for the Pope has never claimed to be a rival Christ, but, on the contrary, Roman theology teaches a true doctrine of Christ's Person.

The Antichrist may be a Jew (Dan. xi. 37).

There is no ground for the view that 'the temple of God' (4) is the Christian Church.

'THE SON OF PERDITION'

These words are used again only of Judas (John xvii. 12). Was Judas a man, or an incarnate demon? (John vi. 70; Acts i. 25). Will the Antichrist be a man, or an incarnate demon?

INDOLENT CHURCH MEMBERS

Paul's warning to those who were disorderly in their behaviour, on the ground that the Advent of Christ was near at hand, is full of pathos and practical sense.

Before the Apostle left Thessalonica there were some who were acting in this foolish manner for he says:

> 'When I was with you, I gave you this rule:
> 'If anyone refuses to work,
> Give him nothing to eat!'   (10).

That is fundamental. A man's stomach settles a lot of problems. The idler does not, or should not, suffer from indigestion. The hands of these people were inactive but their tongues were not (11). They were busy only by being busybodies. Indolence and indiscretion are first cousins. To these stupid Church members Paul says:

> 'Keep quiet and do your work,
> and earn your own living.'   (12).

These idlers were not to be taken off the Church roll, nor to be regarded as enemies, but they were to be left to themselves until they felt ashamed of themselves and put their hands to some job (14).

Christian belief should never lead to ethical disorder. If we believe that Christ may come soon, it should not only delight us, but make us the more diligent.

A lady once asked John Wesley: 'Suppose you knew that you were to die at twelve o'clock tomorrow night, how would you spend the intervening time?'

'How, madam?,' he replied. 'Why, just as I intend to spend it now. I should preach this night at Gloucester, and again at five tomorrow morning. After that I should ride to Tewkesbury, preach in the afternoon, and meet the Societies in the evening. I should then repair to friend Martin's house, who expects to entertain me, converse and pray with the family as usual, retire to my room at ten o'clock, commend myself to my heavenly Father, lie down to rest, and wake up in glory'.

A story is told of the old American Puritans, that at one of the gatherings of their statesmen the daylight was suddenly obscured by some deep and unusual darkness; and at last the assembly became so alarmed, that one of them got up and moved that the meeting should at once be adjourned, because it seemed as if this would be the Judgment Day. Whereupon another, and a wiser senator, got up and said, 'If this be indeed the Judgment Day, it cannot find us better employed in any respect than in quietly doing our duty. I move simply that candles be lighted'.

Paul, who had been speaking so much about the LORD's Return, was very busy all the time he was at Thessalonica. He says:

> 'I did not eat anybody's bread without paying for it, but with toil and labour I worked night and day, in order not to be a burden to any of you.' (8).

He did this to set them a good example, and to give them no occasion to say that they paid him (9).

Relative, then, to the Second Advent, the subjects of this Epistle are: *The Coming and Persecution* (i. 5-12); *The Coming and Apostasy* (ii. 1-12); and *The Coming and Conduct* (iii. 6-15).

When Paul wrote these two letters to Thessalonica, the Church there was about a year old only, and this fact makes us more surprised at its spiritual progress than at its ethical shortcomings.

From A.D. 52-53 the Thessalonian Church disappears from Apostolic history. A reference to it in the middle of the second century shows it to be a struggling Church. It was not without its martyrs during the Diocletian persecution, and a Church was built in honour of one—St. Demetrius—which, alas, is now a mosque.

Paul's work in Thessalonica was 'not in vain in the Lord'.

THE PAULINE EPISTLES

GROUP 2

1 CORINTHIANS

2 CORINTHIANS

GALATIANS

ROMANS

A.D. 57, 58

The Salvation Epistles

CHRIST AND THE CROSS

The Redeemer

THE PAULINE EPISTLES

GROUP 2

1-2 CORINTHIANS   GALATIANS   ROMANS

A.D. 54-57

The Salvation Epistles

CHRIST AND THE CROSS

The Redeemer

The four groups of Paul's Letters are quite distinctive, due to his circumstances at the time of writing, and to the need of the Churches to which he wrote. During his third missionary journey, A.D. 54-58, he reached the height of his conflict with Judaism and Hellenism, and this is reflected in the Letters he wrote in these years—1-2 *Corinthians*, *Galatians*, and *Romans*. Lightfoot points out that the evil of Judaism was *bondage*, and of Hellenism, *licence*, and that the gospel of the Cross was the answer to them both. In 1-2 *Corinthians* the Apostle teaches, '*not licence, but liberty*'; in *Galatians* he teaches, '*liberty, not bondage*'; and in *Romans* both these truths are taught. Religious belief and moral change are shown in their relation to Christ's work on Calvary, and to one another.

When Paul wrote these Letters he had been evangelizing for twenty years, and *Romans* is the quintessence of his teaching.

CORINTH

Corinth, fifty miles west of Athens, was the capital of Achaia. It was a flourishing commercial city with a cosmopolitan population.

The history of the city began in the 11th century B.C. In the wars between Alexander's successors it remained a stronghold of great importance, and changed hands several times. In 146 B.C. the Roman general, Mummius, burnt the city and carried off its art treasures. For a century the site was deserted, and then Caesar founded a colony there.

The city owed its importance to its situation.

ACHAIA

MAP 31

CORINTH

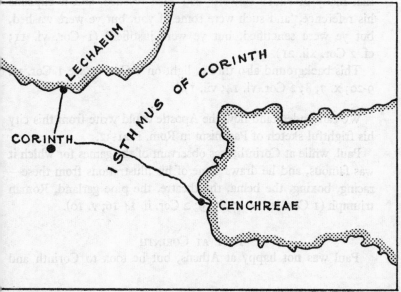

MAP 32

It had two ports, Cenchreae and Lechaeum which gave it complete control over the traffic across the isthmus of Corinth. Cenchreae was 8¾ miles from Corinth, and Lechaeum was 1½ miles from the capital. Across this isthmus—'bridge of the sea' (Pindar)—was the quickest way from Rome to Asia. It was a perilous thing for vessels to round Cape Malea, the southernmost promontory of Greece, because of its treacherous tides. A proverb said: 'When you round Malea, forget your home' and, 'Before sailing round Malea, make your will.' Because of this danger it was customary for ships to be hauled on rollers across the isthmus, there being no canal as there is to-day.

Corinth at this time was characterized by wealth and wickedness and these were closely related. Farrar says that this city "was the Vanity Fair of the Roman Empire, at once the London and the Paris of the first century after Christ." It was conspicuous for its depravity "even amid the depraved cities of a dying heathenism." A thousand prostitutes were consecrated to the service of Impurity in the infamous Temple of Aphrodite Pandemos on Acrocorinthus. Its profligacy was abysmal. Impurity prevailed to such an extent that 'to live like a Corinthian' was the equivalent of 'to commit fornication.' Chrysostom termed it 'a city the most licentious of all that are or ever have been.' It was from such corruption that many of Paul's converts had been rescued, and it explains his reference, 'and such were some of you, but ye were washed, but ye were sanctified, but ye were justified' (1 Cor. vi. 11; cf. 2 Cor. xii. 21).

This background also throws light on 1 Cor. v (see 1 Cor. vi. 9-20; x. 7, 8; 2 Cor. vi. 14; vii. 1).

We can understand how the Apostle could write from this city his frightful sketch of Paganism in Rom. i. 21-32.

Paul, while at Corinth, was observant of the games for which it was famous, and he draws some of his illustrations from these— racing, boxing, the bema, the theatre, the pine garland, Roman triumph (1 Cor. ix. 24-27; iv. 9; 2 Cor. ii. 14-16; v. 10).

PAUL AT CORINTH

Paul was not happy at Athens, but he took to Corinth and

'sat down' (*kathizō* cf. Matt. xiii. 48) there for 18 months (Acts xviii. 11).

He passed from a free Greek city to a Roman colony, from a quiet provincial town to the busy metropolis of a province, and from the seclusion of an ancient university to the seat of government and trade (Conybeare and Howson).

The change, Rackham says, was like passing from Oxford to London. 'It was into the midst of this mongrel and heterogeneous population of Greek adventurers and Roman bourgeois, with a tainting infusion of Phoenicians—this mass of Jews, ex-soldiers, philosophers, merchants, sailors, freedmen, slaves, tradespeople, hucksters, and agents of every form of vice—a colony "without aristocracy, without traditions, without well-established citizens" —that the toilworn Jewish wanderer made his way' (Farrar).

That eighteen months in Corinth made spiritual history which has affected the Christian Church for nineteen hundred years.

In God's good providence the missionary made the acquaintance in the city of another Jew who was also a Christian and a tentmaker. With Aquila and his wife Priscilla Paul abode, and they worked together at their craft.

The Apostle was entitled to temporal support from those to whom he ministered, but he would not take this lest it be said that he preached for gain (1 Cor. ix. 1-19). Even so, the Apostle was often in need. How poignant a passage is 2 Cor. xi. 7-12!

Chrysostom says: 'St. Paul, after working miracles, stood in his workshop at Corinth, and stitched hides of leather together with his hands, and the angels regarded him with love, and the devils with fear' (cited by Wordsworth, on Acts xviii. 3). No higher example can be found of the possibility of combining diligent labour in the common things of life with the utmost spirituality of mind.

Paul was not unopposed in Corinth (2 Thess. iii. 1, 2), but he had eminent success. Nowhere did he make more converts. By miracles (2 Cor. xii. 12) and messages he won Justus, and Crispus, and Stephanas, and Fortunatus, and Achaicus, and Erastus, and Gaius, and Quartus, and Tertius; and the reference to "churches" in Rom. xvi. 16 indicates that Christian communities were formed in other places.

It is not known for certain how often Paul visited Corinth. Two visits are quite definite—those recorded in Acts xviii. 1-17, and in xx. 2, 3. But there are references which seem to indicate that there was a third visit, and that this was made during the period of his residence in Ephesus (Acts xix.) Luke, in the Acts, says nothing about such a visit, but 2 Cor. ii. 1; xii. 14, 21; xiii. 1, 2 must be explained. If the visit of Acts xx. 2, 3 is the third visit there must have been a second, and it was not the visit of Acts xviii. There may be another way of explaining these references, but at least they suggest a second visit. This second visit is supported by Lightfoot, Conybeare and Howson, Schmiedel, Alford, Bernard, Rendall, Bleek, Findlay, Robertson, Plummer and others; but it is not supported by Edwards, Paley, Stanley, Zahn, Beza, Grotius, Farrar, Lewin and others. Perhaps absolute *proof* of such a visit cannot be claimed, but it is more than probable.

After the eighteen months at Corinth in A.D. 52-53 Paul returned to Antioch in Syria by Jerusalem in A.D. 54. In the same year he set out on his third missionary journey which lasted for about four years, most of which time was spent at Ephesus, and it was during this period that the Apostle's Letters to Corinth were written.

1 CORINTHIANS
A.D. 54

What is called the *first* letter to Corinth was not the *first*, for in it we read of a previous one: 'I wrote unto you in an epistle' (v. 9). This epistle is lost.

It would appear that Paul wrote to Corinth four times at least: *first*, 1 Cor. v. 9; *second*, 1 Corinthians; *third*, 2 Cor. ii. 3, 4; vii. 8, 9; a severe letter; and *fourth*, 2 Corinthians (or part of it).

It has been thought that 2 Cor. vi. 14-vii. 1, is part of the lost letter of 1 Cor. v. 9, but this is purely hypothetical. It should be said, however, that to omit this section and pass from vi. 13 to

vii. 2 makes good sense. Also it may be said that the section vi. 14-vii. 1 comes into chapter vi abruptly, whereas it is naturally related to 1 Cor. v. 9, 10. But there is no MS. evidence that any copy of 2 Corinthians ever lacked the passage.

The writing of 1 Corinthians had a double occasion: (a) a letter which the Church wrote to Paul (vii. 1), and (b) a report which the Apostle had received from certain persons who were 'of the household of Chloe' (i. 11).

Relative to this last point, the persons in question were probably slaves of Chloe. She, in all likelihood, lived in Ephesus, and her slaves, who appear to have been Christians, had visited Corinth. This is more probable than that members of the Church at Corinth had become informants.

How much of the letter relates to the inquiries which Paul had received from the Church, and how much to the report which certain persons had brought to him, is not easy to say; but these two factors account for the letter.

Between an Introduction and a Conclusion the Epistle has five main parts as follows.

CHART 156

1 CORINTHIANS					
	I i. 10–iv. 21	II v–vi	III vii. 1–xi. 1	IV xi. 2–xiv. 40	V xv
	DISSENSIONS	DISORDERS	DIFFICULTIES	DECORUM	DOCTRINE
INTRODUCTION i. 1-9	1. The Fact i. 10-17	1. Indiscip- line v. 1-13	1. Marriage and Celibacy vii. 1-40	1. Women and Veiling xi. 2-16	THE RESURRECTION 1. The Belief 1-11
	2. The Evil i. 18-iv. 5	2. Lawsuits vi. 1-8	2. Christian Liberty viii. 1-xi. 1	2. Profanation of the Lord's Supper xi. 17-34	2. The Denial 12-19
	3. The Appeal iv. 6-21	3. Impurity vi. 9-20		3. Manifesta- tion of the Spiritual Gifts xii-xiv	3. The Fact 20-28
					4. The Reality 29-34
					5. The Nature 35-49
					6. The Hope 50-54
					7. The Triumph 55-58

(right margin: CONCLUSION xvi)

Two things closely related must be clearly apprehended by anyone who would understand this Epistle, namely: the composition of the Church at Corinth, and the condition of it at the time that Paul wrote.

The Composition of the Church

It was constituted of Jews and Gentiles, and of more Gentiles than Jews. Of these, few were of the educated, influential, or well-connected classes.

> 'Why, look at your own ranks, my brothers; not many wise (that is, judged by human standards), not many leading men, not many of good birth, have been called' (i. 26).—*Moffatt.*

Paul does not say 'not any,' but 'not many' (cf. Acts xviii. 8; Rom. xvi. 23).

A century later it was a common reproach that Christianity was a religion of the vulgar.

The Condition of the Church

From what we have said about life in Corinth (p. 64) it will be seen that most of the converts had been rescued from appalling moral and social conditions, and the influence of these things does not leave one at the time of conversion. The spirit of dissension, uncleanness, the neglect of moral discipline, quarrelsomeness, unseemliness, irreverence, and self-assertiveness are all reflected in this Letter.

These Church members were 'daily living in the great wicked streets, among the cunning, crowded merchants, in sight and hearing of everything which could quench spiritual aspirations and kindle carnal desire; when the gay common life went on around them, and the chariot-wheels of the LORD were still afar— it was hardly wonderful if the splendid vision began to fade.'

'Very many—some in shame and secrecy, others openly justifying their relapse by the devil-doctrine of perverted truth— had plunged once more into the impurity, the drunkenness, and the selfishness, as though they had never heard the heavenly calling, or tasted the eternal gift' (Farrar).

In the light, then, of the composition and condition of the Church at Corinth this Letter must be read.

Dissensions (i. 10-iv. 21)

Cliques and coteries in a Church are disastrous. There were four factions in this Church—the Paul party, the Apollos party, the Cephas party, and the Christ party. These partisanships rent asunder the Church's unity, and ruined its testimony. Sectarianism and denominationalism are disruptive. The Apostle's appeal is summarized by Dr. Plummer in this way:

> 'My aim in all this is to correct party-spirit and conceit. Do compare your self-glorification with the humiliation of your teachers. This admonition comes from a father whom you ought to imitate. I really am coming to you. Is it to be in severity or in gentleness?' (iv. 6-21).

The seriousness of schism in the Church and in the churches is indicated by the attention which Paul gives to the matter—a quarter of the whole Epistle (i. 10-iv. 21).

He shows that the dissensions in the church at Corinth were due to a two-fold misapprehension:

(1) As to the true nature of the Gospel of Christ (i. 17-iii. 4);

(2) As to the place and office of the Christian minister (iii. 5-iv. 21).

The Gospel is not human wisdom (i. 17-ii. 5), but divine (ii. 6-iii. 4); and Christian ministers are 'stewards of the mysteries of God', and not rival teachers. One plants and another waters; one lays foundations, and others build thereon. Had this been believed in the Corinthian Church they could never have said, 'I am of Paul; and I of Apollos; and I of Cephas; and I of Christ' (i. 12; iii. 4-10; iv. 6).

Disorders (v-vi)

Of these there were three—indiscipline, lawsuits, and impurity.

1. INDISCIPLINE
(v. 1-13)

The case is that of a member of the Church who had his stepmother as his concubine, a crime so monstrous as to be condemned even by heathen. It is not improbable that the reason for the Church's inaction was because the offender was a person of means and therefore of service to the Church. At any rate they did nothing about it. Their sin was that they *tolerated* a gross evil in their midst. This is the charge brought against the Church in Pergamos. (Rev. ii. 12-17).

'Thou hast there some that hold the teaching of Balaam'. The toleration of evil is participation in it. 'A little leaven leaveneth the whole lump' (6). This is true alike of conduct, and creed (Gal. v. 9).

It is to be feared that in the Churches of to-day discipline is almost unknown; but where evil is tolerated in the interests of charity, charity becomes a crime.

In a letter now lost Paul had bidden the Corinthian Christians not to company with fornicators, and they had taken this to mean anyone who was a fornicator, but Paul meant only those who were Christians! He gives no advice to non-Christians (9-13).

2. LAWSUITS
(vi. 1-8)

Paul was not against the Law Courts (Rom. xiii. 1-7), but he was against Christians taking Christians to these for the settlement of disputes among themselves.

> 'Have things come to such a pass that, among the whole of you, there is not a single person who is competent to arbitrate between one Christian and another, but that, on the contrary, Christian goes to law with Christian, and that too before unbelievers?'

This principle is still applicable. Christian affairs should be settled by Christians.

3. IMPURITY
(vi. 9-20)

Fornication, sexual intercourse between unmarried persons, was common in Corinth, and the Christians there were exposed to it, and some of them were guilty of it. Even by civilised worldly standards sexual impurity is wrong, but Paul takes high ground when he declares that the Christian's body belongs to God and is a temple of God, so that fornication is taking from Christ what is His property and giving it to a harlot.

What was true then is true now.

Difficulties (vii-xi. 1)

In chapters i-vi the Apostle has dealt with complaints which had reached him about the state of the Corinthian Church. In chapters vii. 1-xi. 1 he deals with matters about which the Corinthians had written for his advice (vii. 1; viii. 1). Of these there are two, and they are of importance far beyond the Church at Corinth—*Marriage and Celibacy*, and *Christian Liberty*.

1. MARRIAGE AND CELIBACY

(ch. vii)

Christianity did not create this problem, but it had to take it into account. Of old the Jews extolled marriage, but after the return from Babylon asceticism became prominent.

'We infer,' says Dr. T. C. Edwards, 'that the Apostle in this chapter discusses, not an isolated question, but a widespread and prominent tendency of the age, not originating always in a definite theory, much less occasioned by separate instances of celibacy, but presenting to Christianity a great moral force which it must either subdue or assimilate, and undoubtedly to be connected with the doctrine that all contact with matter was essentially evil.'

The same writer analyses the chapter as follows:

1. A general statement (1-7).
2. The case of a Christian who has not been married or who is in a state of widowhood (8, 9).
3. The case of a Christian married to a Christian (10, 11).
4. The case of a Christian married to an unbeliever who is willing to cohabit with the believer (12-14).
5. The case of a Christian married to an unbeliever who refuses to cohabit with the believer (15, 16).
6. A digression in reference to circumcision and slavery (17-24).
7. The case of virgins (25-35).
8. The case of widows (39, 40).

The whole treatment of this problem is most illuminating. Swete, writing on Rev. xiv. 4, says, 'No condemnation of marriage, no exclusion of the married from the highest blessings of the Christian life, finds a place in the New Testament.'

2. CHRISTIAN LIBERTY
(viii. 1-xi. 1)

Whether or not a Christian should eat meat that had been offered to an idol was a live question in Paul's time, but it is no longer so, at any rate in the West. The Apostle's answer to the inquiry of the Corinthians is detailed and profound. He shows that to eat such meat is a matter of indifference, and then he shows that it is not a matter of indifference.

He speaks, not of the practice only, but of the principle. He distinguishes between strong and weak Christians. He discriminates between what a Christian is free to do, and what it is unwise for him to do. He supports his arguments by his own example, and from past history he shows that idolatry is always dangerous. He illuminates his advice by illustrations from the Isthmian or Olympic games; and he concludes by bidding the Corinthians to follow him in so far as he followed Christ.

An idol is a nonentity, therefore to an enlightened Christian the meat problem does not arise (viii. 1-6), but all Christians are not enlightened, and so one's actions must be determined, not by liberty, but by love (viii. 7-13; cf. Rom. xiv).

On this love-principle the Apostle himself acted (chapter ix). By participating in idol-feasts the Corinthians exposed themselves to grave danger, as the example of the Israelites shows (x. 1-14). He who would partake of the Table of the LORD should have nothing to do with the table of demons (x. 15-22).

'Now to sum up what we are saying' (Heb. viii. 1, R.V. *m.*), 'here is my advice,' says Paul (x. 23-xi. 1).

Decorum (xi. 2-34).

1. WOMEN AND VEILING
(xi. 2-16)

The reference here is not general or domestic, but relates to procedure at public worship. The discussion sounds strange to us to-day, and to what extent it is applicable and obligatory it is difficult to say.

On a broad foundation of the divinely ordained order of creation (8-12) the Apostle speaks of decorum and custom in respect of men and women and the veil, and the wearing of the hair long and short.

In Corinth, in a religious connection, all harlots went unveiled —the Greek *Hetaerae*—and this in itself was a reason why Christian women should be veiled in their religious services. But there were other reasons. For the women members of the Church at Corinth to discard the customary head covering at public worship indicated a spirit of revolt against order and decorum.

The true understanding and use of this section lies between pushing it aside as of no significance to-day, and making a literal and rigid application of it to all religious assemblies.

2. PROFANATION OF THE LORD'S SUPPER
(xi. 17-34)

It should be understood that in the early Church two meals were combined, what was called the '*Agapē*,' or 'Love-Feast,' and the *Lord's Supper*, variously called the *Holy Communion*, and the *Eucharist*. The earliest record of this is in Acts ii. 46. The celebration of the Supper was part of a common daily meal, the regular substantial meal of the day, which was held in the evening after sunset. At this meal rich and poor Christians met, and the former were expected to provide for the latter. Early in the second century the '*Agapē*' and the *Lord's Supper* were separated, and the latter became more and more a distinct sacred ordinance.

The situation about which Paul writes is that in which the religious and the social elements were united, and he severely condemns the shocking way in which the Corinthians conducted this double meal. 'The rich brought their luxurious provisions, and greedily devoured them, without waiting for any one; while the poor, hungry-eyed Lazaruses—half-starved slaves, who had no contribution of their own to bring—watched them with hate and envy as they sat famishing and unrelieved by their full-fed brethren' (Farrar).

Worse still, there were those who drank until they became drunk (20, 21). What was designed to be a sacred fellowship had become a senseless orgy, and, in consequence, judgment was visited upon them (30-32).

From this disgraceful display we see that 'even apostolic times were no golden ages of purity and primitive simplicity' (Plummer)

3. THE MANIFESTATION OF THE SPIRITUAL GIFTS
(xii-xiv)

The highest level of thought and truth in this Epistle is reached in these chapters; but, alas, the scope of the present work does not allow of a detailed exposition of them.

The whole section treats of the *Spiritual Gifts*, and the Apostle speaks, in the first place, of the *Variety and Unity* of them (xii); then, of the *Greatest* of them (xiii); and, finally, of the *Superiority of Prophecy over Tongues* (xiv).

The subject of chapter xii is the rich endowment of the Gifts; of chapter xiii, it is the ruling energy of them; and of chapter xiv, the right exercise of them.

The possession of *Spiritual Gifts* was one of the characteristics of the Apostolic age, but it is not restricted to the Church of that age. Dr. Edwards has well said that the 'vindication of these extraordinary manifestations of power rests on the two supernatural elements in the Church. The one is the Divine purpose in the creation of the Church, which is the exaltation of Jesus as Lord. The other is the presence in the Church of a Divine worker, the Spirit of Christ, who will bring this purpose to pass'. Christ is the external standard, and the Spirit is the inward power.

Chapter xii is the *locus classicus* on this great subject, and it cannot be studied too carefully, nor followed too diligently (cf. Rom. xii. 3-8).

Whether all these Gifts were intended to be possessed and used throughout the Christian age, and whether in fact they have been manifested at times and in places, are matters for research and contemplation.

The *charismata* in this chapter (xii. 4, 9, 28, 30, 31) are grace-gifts from God to Christians, and they are called *pneumatika* (xii. 1) because they are bestowed by the Spirit of God.

The Rich Endowment of the Spiritual Gifts (xii)

After a challenging introduction (1-3) the *diversity*, *unity*, and *purpose* of the Gifts are set forth (4-11); and then these truths are illustrated by the analogy of the human body (12-31).

The one essential characteristic of the Gifts is diversity in unity—diversity in their action, unity in their origin; diversity in relation to the Church, unity in relation to God; diversity making them useful, unity proving them to be Divine (Edwards).

Various classifications of the Gifts have been suggested, and, perhaps, the best of them is that which places them in five categories.

I. GIFTS OF INTELLECTUAL POWER:
    1. The Word of Wisdom (8).
    2. The Word of Knowledge (8).

II. GIFTS OF MIRACULOUS POWER:
    3. Faith (9).
    4. Healing (9).
    5. Miracles (10).

III. GIFT OF TEACHING POWER:
    6. Prophecy (10).

IV. GIFT OF CRITICAL POWER:
    7. Discerning of Spirits (10).

V. GIFTS OF ECSTATIC POWER:
    8. Kinds of Tongues (10).
    9. Interpretation of Tongues (10).

The literal human body and the mystical spiritual body are compared, and to great effect.

The statement reveals that every member has and is a gift; that all the gifts are not of commensurate value; but that they are all necessary and interdependent.

If that had been believed and acted upon throughout the Church's history, uncountable grievous events would never have occurred. The situation at Corinth which the Apostle is addressing is an illustration of this (see chapter xiv).

The Ruling Energy of the Spiritual Gifts (xiii)

This is one of the sublimest passages in world literature. Harnack has spoken of it as 'the greatest, strongest, deepest thing Paul ever wrote.'

It belongs in a class with chapter xv, Rom. viii. 31-39, and Heb. xi.: 'On each side of this chapter the tumult of argument and remonstrance still rages; but within it, all is calm; the sentences move in almost rhythmical melody; the imagery unfolds itself in almost dramatic propriety; the language arranges itself with almost rhetorical accuracy' (Stanley).

The chapter is really a digression, yet it is vitally relevant to what immediately precedes and follows it (xii, xiv). It contains, Wesley affirmed, the whole of true religion.

Love here is not defined, but just described and displayed. 'There are times,' it has been well said, 'when definition is destruction. Whoever questioned the beauty of the sunset? But who can define it? The astronomer can give us the mathematics of it . . . but there is no sunset glory in the mathematics. There is a chemistry of colours, but there is no wistful healing light in that chemistry. Beauty defined is beauty destroyed.'

There are two words for 'love' in the New Testament—*agapaō* is the love of character and principle, and *phileō* is the love of feeling and emotion. The former is used of the love of God and Christ, and is the word used in this chapter xiii. The significance of these words is well illustrated in John xxi. 15-17.

The 'love' of our chapter is spiritual, divine, and indestructible; the subject being treated in three parts as follows:

> The Pre-eminence and Value of Love (1-3);
> The Prerogatives and Virtues of Love (4-7);
> The Permanence and Victory of Love (8-13).

See the writer's *The Love Life*.

What this chapter shows is that the use of the Gifts is safe when inspired by love, and the next chapter shows that it is not safe without it.

The Right Exercise of the Spiritual Gifts (xiv)

In this illuminating chapter the Apostle deals with the subject of TONGUES, and we should follow carefully what he says.

'Tongue' is the translation of two words in the New Testament, *dialektos*, and *glōssa*, and the latter is the more frequent. Two passages only concern us here—Acts ii. 1-13 and 1 Cor. xii-xiv.

The word *dialektos*, which occurs six times, and in the Acts only, means a language, a known tongue. The word *glōssa* is used of the physical organ, of speech, of languages, and of a spiritual gift. In Acts ii. 1-13 both these words occur. From verses 6 and 8, where *dialektos* and *glōssa* occur, it is evident that they both refer to known languages.

This, however, is not the meaning of *glōssa* in Mark xvi. 17; Acts x. 46, xix. 6; and in 1 Cor. xii-xiv. In these passages the word refers to a spiritual gift, and not to any known language. It is never used of preaching the gospel, but only of prayer addressed to God (xiv. 2, 28). The words spoken were not understood by any who heard them until they were interpreted (xiv. 2, 5, 9, 14). The gift of 'tongues' and of 'interpretation' were both miraculous (xii. 10, 30; xiv. 13), and he who spoke in 'tongues' was in a state of ecstasy (xiv. 2), and might be thought to be speaking the language of angels (xiii. 1). The writer knows of some who went to China in the belief that when they got there God would enable them at once to preach in Chinese. They soon came back.

A view less foolish, but as erroneous is that 'speaking in tongues' is the proof that one has received the baptism of the Spirit. There is no Scripture warrant for such an idea. A spurious and emotional Pentecostalism has brought incalculable harm to individuals and communities.

See the writer's *The Baptism of the Spirit, and Speaking with Tongues.*

The Corinthians gave priority, and prominence to the gift of tongues because it was exciting and spectacular, but Paul puts at the bottom what they put at the top. In the evaluation of the gifts priority is given to those which were most useful. For this reason, the Apostle says, prophecy, inspired utterance for edification and comfort (xiv. 3), is far superior to speaking in 'tongues.'

Doctrine (xv)

This is the only chapter in the Epistle on doctrine, and it has been spoken of as 'the earliest Christian doctrinal essay.'

The subject of the Resurrection was not one of the matters about which the Corinthians had asked Paul to write to them— such as Marriage, and Meats—but it was one of the matters reported on by some of Chloe's slaves (i. 11; xi. 18). This is the greatest utterance in the Bible on the Resurrection, as chapter xiii is the greatest utterance on Love, and as Hebrews xi is on Faith.

It should be noticed that this Epistle begins with the subject of Christ Crucified (i. 13; ii. 2), and ends with the subject of Christ Risen (xv). These are the two facts on which the Gospel rests, and without them there could have been no Church, and no Christianity.

We cannot here enter upon a detailed exposition of this great chapter, but would indicate only the sequence of the argument. There are seven sections.

1. The Gospel of the Resurrection, and the teaching of the Apostles (1-11).
2. The Denial of the Resurrection, and its logical consequences (12-19).
3. The Fact of the Resurrection, and its sublime consummation (20-28).
4. The Reality of the Resurrection involved in certain existing practices (29-34).
5. The Nature of the Resurrection, and its mode defended (35-49).
6. The Resurrection body adapted to the condition and duration of the new life (50-54).
7. The Conclusion of the matter in triumph and exhortation (55-58).

One might almost be grateful for the denial of the resurrection at Corinth which eventuated in such a pronouncement as this. Much truth has been brought to light by heresy!

Clement of Rome, and friend of Paul (Phil. iv. 3), wrote to the Corinthian Church about A.D. 97, and a comparison of his letter with the Apostle's is interesting and instructive. Clement's letter shows acquaintance with Paul's on the subjects of schism, the gifts, love, order in worship, and the resurrection, but it is lacking in the forcefulness which characterizes the Apostle's letter. Clement's letter would apply to any Church, and was read in many churches, but Paul's belongs to a situation which—let us hope—was not found anywhere else.

The great passages in the Epistle are those on: the true 'Sign' and 'Wisdom' (i. 17-ii. 16); Planting and Building (iii. 6-15); the Apostles (iv. 9-13); the Lord's Supper (xi. 23-26); the Gifts (xii); Love (xiii); and the Resurrection (xv).

Samples of the many striking utterances in the Epistle are:

'Do not form any premature judgments—but wait until the Lord comes back. For he will light up the darkness that now hides things and show what the motives in people's minds are, and then everyone will get from God the praise he deserves' (iv. 5).

'Love is what builds up character' (viii. 1).

'We will stand anything rather than put any hindrance in the way of the good news of Christ' (ix. 12).

'That is the way you must run, so as to win' (ix. 24).

'In evil be babies, but mentally be mature' (xiv. 20).

'Devote yourselves to the Lord's work, for you know that through the Lord your labour is not thrown away' (xv. 58).

'Be on the watch. Stand firm in your faith. Act like men. Show yourselves strong. Do everything with love' (xvi. 13, 14).

(The translation is that of E. J. Goodspeed).

Great indeed is this (1st) Letter to Corinth; great in its sweep, its frankness, its insight, its wisdom, its ethics, its theology, its assurance, its sense, and its friendliness.

For a list of words which occur in 1 Cor. only of Paul's Epistles, see the writer's *Know Your Bible*, vol. 2, pp. 131-132.

THE PAULINE EPISTLES

GROUP 2

2 CORINTHIANS

A.D. 57

Much interest attaches to this Letter for various reasons—its tenderness, its severity, its structure, its autobiographical material, its occasion or occasions, its design, and more besides.

The most casual reader must recognize the sharp contrast between chapters i-ix and x-xiii, and this change of tone must be accounted for in some way.

Is the Epistle a unity, or are there here combined two or more letters in whole or in part? What letters are referred to in 1 Cor. v. 9; 2 Cor. ii. 3, 4; vii. 8, 9, 12; x. 9, 10?

The scope of this book does not require that we answer or attempt to answer these questions in detail, but it will be well, very briefly to state views which are held on the subject.

Of these there are in the main two: (*a*) the view that the Epistle is a unity notwithstanding the contrast between i-ix and x-xiii; and (*b*) the view that chapters x-xiii are a part of the severe letter mentioned in ii. 3, 4; vii. 8, 9.

In support of (*a*) it is claimed that chs. i-ix are addressed to a submissive majority, and chs. x-xiii, to an impenitent minority of the Christians. Also, that grave news from Corinth reached Paul after he had dictated i-ix.

Also that had chs. x-xiii been another letter there would have been some Manuscript evidence of the fact; but there is none.

In support of (*b*) it is urged that no circumstances in the course of dictating a letter could arise which would make possible so violent a change of tone.

Also that the tender congratulations of chs. i-ix could not, in the same letter, turn to the severe condemnation of x-xiii.

Also that no one after appealing for money for the Jerusalem

Church, and saying 'Thanks be to God for His unspeakable Gift,' could turn and rend the people to whom he had appealed.

Also that having spoken of a severe letter (ii. 4; vii. 8, 12), which cannot be 1 Corinthians, it is as easy to believe that chs. x-xiii is that letter in part as to assume that it is lost.

If it be granted that x-xiii is the part of the severe letter referred to in ii. 4; vii. 8, 12, it follows that the order of these two divisions of the Epistle should be reversed. One can understand complaint being followed by conciliation, but not these in reverse as in this Epistle. But again, be it said, there is no Manuscript authority for such a change.

The programme of Paul in relation to Corinth may have been as follows:

1. Paul ministers at Corinth for eighteen months (Acts xviii. 11).
2. Paul returns to Syria, and later settles at Ephesus (Acts xviii. 18, 19).
3. He sends a letter to Corinth condemning fornication (1 Cor. v. 9). This letter is lost. FIRST LETTER.
4. Bad news reaches Paul from Corinth by members of Chloe's household (1 Cor. i. 11).
5. The Corinthians write a letter to Paul asking for advice. The matter was conveyed by Fortunatus, Stephanas, and Achaicus (xvi. 17).
6. Paul writes 1 Corinthians to answer inquiries, and to rebuke irregularities (vii. 1; viii. 1). SECOND LETTER.
7. Paul pays a hasty visit to Corinth from Ephesus (2 Cor. ii. 1; xii. 14; xiii. 1).
8. Trouble arises in the Church. The Apostle's authority is doubted or denied (2 Cor. x. 7-18).
9. Paul sends a severe letter to Corinth (ii. 3, 9; vii. 8-12; chapters x-xiii. 10). THIRD LETTER.
10. Titus meets Paul at Troas and reports that the crisis in Corinth is over (ii.; vii. 6-16).
11. The Apostle writes 2 Cor. i-ix to the Church (viii. 16-24). FOURTH LETTER.
12. Paul reaches Corinth and remains there for three months (Acts xix. 21; xx. 3), during which time he writes 'Galatians' and 'Romans'.

If this programme is correct Paul wrote *four letters* to Corinth, two of which have come down to us, one is wholly lost (but see 1 Cor. v. 9 with 2 Cor. vi. 14-vii. 1), and one may be preserved in part in 2 Cor. x-xiii. 10. Also the Apostle paid at least three visits to Corinth.

The analysis given here follows the one-letter theory, but the two-letter theory would place Part III before Parts I and II.

CHART 157

INTRODUCTION i. 1-11	2 CORINTHIANS			CONCLUSION xiii. 11-14
	Part I	Part II	Part III	
	i. 12-vii. 16	viii-ix	x. 1-xiii. 10	
	CONSOLATION	SOLICITATION	VINDICATION	
	1. The Minister of The Gospel An Explanation i. 12-ii. 11	1. Macedonian Liberality viii. 1-5	1. Paul's Divine Authority x. 1-18	
	2. The Ministry of The Gospel An Exposition ii. 12-v. 21	2. Appeal for Generosity viii. 6-15	2. Paul's Manifest Apostleship xi. 1-xii. 10	
		3. Commendation of Delegates viii. 16-24	3. Paul's Faithful Admonition xii. 11-xiii. 10	
	3. The Ministered unto by The Gospel An Exhortation vi. 1-vii. 16	4. Incentives to Giving ix. 1-15		

The view one takes of chapters x-xiii. 10 will determine several matters of importance. For example, they who regard the Epistle as a unity assume that the offender of ii. 2-11; vii. 12, is the same as the one of 1 Cor. v. 1. But the former is one who had wronged Paul himself, which the incestuous person had not done.

In reading 2 Corinthians, chapters x-xiii. 10 should be read first, and then chapters i-ix. In this way we shall see that the severe letter had produced the desired effect, and on the notes of commendation and thanksgiving the Apostle's correspondence with Corinth ended.

THE SEVERE LETTER
(x. 1-xiii. 10)

Assuming that this is the letter referred to in ii. 3, 9; vii. 8-12, it seems unlikely that we have the whole of it. But there is enough to indicate what the trouble was and how it affected Paul.

Certain Judaisers, probably from Jerusalem, had reached Corinth and were trying to persuade the Church that Paul was not a true apostle, and that the authority he claimed was not valid; and this was the occasion of the severe letter. But why should Paul feel so strongly about this denial of his apostleship and consequent authority? The answer is—because his whole life and ministry were based on the fact that he had been converted, called, and commissioned by God (Gal. i. 15, 16).

Had he not seen the risen Lord? (1 Cor. ix. 1; xv. 8). Was he not as truly an apostle as Peter and James? (Gal. ii. 7-9). Had he not the signs of an apostle?—the power of binding and of working miracles, the laying on of hands, and founding of churches. He was recognized as an apostle by Peter and James, and he taught apostolic doctrine.

If these Judaisers were right Paul's claim for his twenty years of ministry was false. The matter was of the most vital importance especially to Gentile Christians. For this reason, then, Paul argues and proves that his apostleship and authority are of divine origin (x. 1-18).

1. PAUL'S DIVINE AUTHORITY
(x. 1-18)

First of all he *appeals to the Church* (x. 1-6). He had been charged with cowardice, but he could show them that they were mistaken. He could and would fight, but not with weapons of the world.

Then, *he answers his critics* (x. 7-11).

They had spoken of the Apostle in contemptuous terms. They had said he could write well, but, for the rest, he was ineffective, that he wrote forcibly, and acted feebly; but he would show them that his correspondence and his conduct were consistent.

And definitely he stands by *his appraisement of claims* (x. 12-18). He treats with sarcasm those who were commending themselves, and claims that his glorying does not go beyond legitimate limits, that he does not take credit for what others have done. God had given Corinth to him as a sphere of labour, and they owed to him, instrumentally, their existence as a Church.

Paul had 'an intense sympathy with the purpose of God that the Gospel should be preached to every creature; and an intense scorn for the spirit that sneaks and poaches on another's ground, and is more anxious that some men should be good sectarians, than that all men should be good disciples' (Denney).

2. PAUL'S MANIFEST APOSTLESHIP
(xi. 1-xii. 10)

Turning now to his *apostleship* Paul declares that it is demonstrated by his conduct, his sufferings, and his visions.

The Witness of his Conduct (xi. 1-15)

Paul indulged in a little foolish boasting, and expected the Church to be as tolerant of him as it was of his detractors (1-6), whom he calls 'those pre-eminent apostles of yours' (5), but whom he knew to be self-asserting impostors.

Paul admits that he might be a poor speaker, but at least he knew what he was talking about. Of what use is eloquent ignorance! And as to his maintenance—he earned his bread by hard work at tent-making so that no one could ever say that he sponged on the Church at Corinth (7-15). He preached without payment (to which he was entitled, 1 Cor. ix. 6-17), and would continue to do so, even though at times he was short of money (9). Others, however, his converts at a distance, had helped him (II Cor. xi. 8, 9; Phil. iv. 10-17).

Is the honest freedom of preachers affected by the fact that those to whom they preach pay them a salary? The writer's freedom was once challenged by his being told 'we pay you'!

The Witness of his Suffering (xi. 16-33)

Paul could be very sarcastic, and often was. Here he says: 'You can afford to bear with fools, and do so with pleasure; you are so wise yourselves. In your sublime tolerance you bear with any of these impostors, no matter what he does; if he makes slaves of you, if he devours your substance, if he entraps you, if he gives himself airs, if he strikes you in the face. It may be a disgraceful confession to make, but I really have not been equal to acting in that way' (19-21).

There is a place for sarcasm in a Christian's literary arsenal (cf. 1 Kings xviii. 27), but it must be used with care.

The great passage in this section is Paul's catalogue of his sufferings (23-33). He had spoken of these before (1 Cor. iv. 11-13; 2 Cor. iv. 7-10; vi. 4-10), but not so specifically as here. It should be remembered that this catalogue does not include any suffering after A.D. 57, so that must be added: his physical weakness and frequent illnesses (Gal. iv. 12-15; 2 Cor. xii. 7-10); his escape from Corinth (Acts xx. 3); the sorrow of his farewell visits (Acts xx. 5-xxi. 14); his arrest at Jerusalem (Acts xxi. 27-36); his imprisonment at Caesarea (Acts xxiv); his trials (Acts xxiv-xxvi); his shipwreck on the way to Rome (Acts xxvii); his imprisonment at Rome (Acts xxviii); his trials at Rome (2 Tim. iv. 6-18), and his execution.

About all these sufferings very little is said in the Acts, and Paul himself only summarizes them. Surely these records place Paul at the top of the list of sufferers in all time. The catalogue in Hebrews xi. 32-38 is sad enough, and so were the sufferings of the martyrs from Nero's time until to-day; but, probably, these agonies were of brief duration, but Paul's lasted for thirty years (A.D. 37-67). No other has ever suffered so much and so bravely. And let us keep in mind that it was as an Apostle that he did so.

The Witness of his Vision (xii. 1-6).

Paul gives as another evidence of his apostleship the 'visions and revelations' which had been granted to him. These he had received fourteen years before, and as he wrote this Epistle in A.D. 57, these visions must have been in A.D. 43, while he was in Tarsus (Acts ix. 30); but this is the only reference to them. 'It is idle,' says Denney, 'to exploit a passage like this in the interest of apostolic psychology.' Paul had other visions later on (Acts

xvi. 9; xviii. 9; xxii. 17f.), but this one stands by itself mysterious and marvellous. That the experience cannot be explained does not make it of no consequence. It affected the whole life of Paul.

It is of consequence also for the more specific reason that it is connected with a trouble which followed him through life. He calls it 'a thorn in the flesh' (xii. 7). It has been conjectured that this was epilepsy, ophthalmia, malarial fever, hysteria, and other ailments; but after all the resources of imagination have been exhausted we must come to the conclusion that we do not know what it was. The trouble was not spiritual, or moral, but physical. The Apostle prayed that he might be delivered from it, but his prayer was not answered (8, 9).

From this incident we may learn that sickness is not necessarily due to the sin of the sufferer (cf. Job); that healing is not always God's will for the afflicted; that it is not true that if one is not healed it is due to a want of faith; that every prayer is not answered, even when delivered by most devoted Christians; that if God declines to answer earnest prayer He compensates by giving abounding grace to carry on (9, 10). Paul was never so great as in this crisis.

3. PAUL'S FAITHFUL ADMONITION
(xii. 11-xiii. 10)

He again refers to his disinterested service for the Corinthians (xii. 11-18); of his haunting fears lest he should find them as he would not have them to be (xii. 19-21); and he tells them that for the *third time* he is coming to them, and warns them that he will not spare them, even as he did not on his second visit (the unrecorded one) (xiii. 1-10).

If xiii. 11-13 belongs to the severe letter, with these few affectionate sentences the Apostle brings his storm-tossed letter into a haven of love and peace (Plummer).

In this conclusion are exhortation (11, 12), salutation (13), and benediction (14), the greatest of Paul's benedictions.

THE FINAL LETTER
(i-ix)

The writer of these notes feels, rightly or wrongly, that the weight of internal evidence is on the side of the theory that in 2 Corinthians there are two letters. That chapters x-xiii are the letter referred to in ii. 3, 4; vii. 8, 9; and that in time it precedes chapters i-ix which reflect the result of what, for convenience, is called the severe letter.

Front line scholars are on both sides of the problem, and the strongest argument of those who claim that the Epistle is a unity is that there is no Manuscript evidence for the two-letter theory.

The matter will be debated while time lasts, but here we follow the two-letter theory.

This theory makes chapters i-ix a distinct letter, written after Paul had learned from Titus what the effect had been in Corinth of the letter (chapters x-xiii); and it is the last which the Apostle wrote to that Church.

It is in two distinct parts: chapters i-vii, and viii-ix. In the first part the Apostle reveals his heart to his converts; and in the second part he appeals for a liberal money-offering for the needy Jerusalem Church.

This letter is the least systematic and the most emotional of all Paul's letters, as Romans is the most systematic and the least emotional.

Paul's movements and experiences are clearly indicated—the troubles at Ephesus (i. 8); the anxiety at Troas (ii. 12, 13); the comfort in Macedonia (ii. 12; vii. 5-8); and the prospect of visiting Corinth again (ix. 4, 5).

After the storm comes the calm. The vehement indignation, scathing irony, strong denunciation, and commanding authority, now give place to satisfaction, sympathy, commendation and appeal.

The Severe Letter is on a very human level. Paul is speaking of himself, and he does not always claim divine authority for what he says (xi. 17). But the Final Letter is quite different. Although Paul must still speak about himself, in relation to the previous troubles, it is not to himself that he calls attention, but to the glory of the Christian Gospel and the privilege of proclaiming it.

2 CORINTHIANS

PART I.   Chs. i-vii

THE INTRODUCTION
(i. 1-11)

This consists of a *Salutation* (1, 2), and *Thanksgiving* (3-11); and the Thanksgiving is in two parts: it is first for *Divine Comfort* (3-7), and then, for *Divine Deliverance* (8-11).   In verses 3-7 the idea of comfort occurs ten times: *paraklēsis* six times, and *parakaleō* four times.   In chapters x-xiii, the Severe Letter, the word does not occur at all.   Recall that *Paraklētos* is used of the Holy Spirit Who is the Comforter.

Paul does not say from what trouble he had been delivered (8-11), but it was something that happened in Asia, and, probably, in Ephesus, the capital (see Acts xix).   'Deliver' is the word here, as is 'comfort' in verses 3-7.

After this Introduction the subject to the end of the first division (i. 12-vii. 16) is *The Gospel*; and Paul writes first of all of himself as the messenger of it (i. 12-ii. 11); then, of the message he had to proclaim (ii. 12-v. 21); and finally, of the Corinthians who had been the recipients of it (vi. 1-vii. 16).   The first of these parts is an explanation; the second, is an exposition; and the third, is an exhortation.

1. THE MINISTER OF THE GOSPEL
(i. 12-ii. 11)

Paul first of all appeals to the Corinthians for understanding and sympathy (i. 12-14).   The reason for this follows.

In verses i. 15-ii. 4 *the Apostle explains his change of plan.* Apparently the plan was: to cross from Ephesus to Corinth; to go from Corinth to Macedonia; and finally to return from Macedonia to Corinth, and from there to sail for Jerusalem.   This plan, it would seem, was made known to the Church, perhaps by Timothy (cf. 1 Cor. iv. 19), but Paul changed it and went to Macedonia first (1 Cor. xvi. 5-7).

Evidently the Corinthians thought that he had broken his promise, and in this passage (i. 15-ii. 4) he explains and defends his action.

Between writing 1 Corinthians and 2 Cor. i-ix something had happened. In ii. 3, 9, Paul says: 'I wrote as I did,' and by this he cannot refer to 1 Corinthians, nor to 2 Cor. i-ix; but the matter is clear if he is referring to the Severe Letter (x-xiii).

Also, *the offender of* ii. 5-11 cannot be the incestuous person of 1 Cor. v, for two reasons: (*a*) he had injured Paul in some way (5), which the other offender had not; and (*b*) Paul forgives him (10) as he had not the right or power to forgive the incestuous person. The offender of ii. 5-11, not identified, was, probably, the ringleader in the Church against Paul's apostleship and authority. It was because of him and those who agreed with him that Paul had written the Severe Letter (chapters x-xiii).

Changing circumstances may necessitate the change of plans. Paul had paid these people one painful visit and did not wish to pay them another such (ii. 1 cf. xii. 14; xiii. 1).

There is here no warrant or excuse for ministers, or other people, lightly and needlessly to cancel appointments they have made. As far as it is possible we should fulfil every promise.

2. THE MINISTRY OF THE GOSPEL
(ii. 12-v. 21)

This is a very rich portion, containing: Praise for good news (ii. 12-17); the Source of satisfaction and sufficiency (iii. 1-6); two ministries contrasted (iii. 7-18); ministering the Gospel (iv. 1-6); the frailty of the messengers (iv. 7-15); the preacher's hope, here and hereafter (iv. 16-v. 10); and the minister's devotion to his message (v. 11-21).

Praise for Good News (ii. 12-17)

These verses are of great interest as revealing Paul's emotions. In 12-13 we see a man racked with anxiety and torturing suspense. Paul had a fine missionary opportunity at Troas but could make no use of it because of severe tension of spirit. The reason is that he had expected Titus to meet him at Troas and tell him how his severe letter had been received at Corinth; but Titus had not come, and Paul became the victim of painful depression.

Have you ever felt unable for your work because of depression? Should a Christian ever be depressed like this? Should we ever have unnerving anxiety? How psychologically ignorant we are! How little we know of the impingement of a tired body and taut nerves on our spirits!

ii. 14-17. That Paul's trouble was physical and mental and not spiritual is evident from what immediately follows.

Nothing more is said of Titus until vii. 5-7, but his arrival in Macedonia had such effect upon Paul that he burst out into a hymn of praise.

> 'Thank God! He always leads me in His triumphal train, through Christ, and spreads the perfume of knowledge of Him everywhere through me as His censer-bearer' (14).

'Wherever Christ's servants are, there should be fragrance. A Christian without this redolence is as impossible as incense whose presence is unfelt by those who come near to it' (McFadyen)

Paul speaks of some who, as to their preaching, are vendors, hucksters, peddlers, adulterators of God's word. No doubt such are in view in x. 12, 18; xi. 12, 13, 20; xii. 14, and throughout x-xiii.

The Source of Satisfaction and Sufficiency (iii. 1-6)

The underlying thought of this portion is *writing* (2, 3, 6). In 2, 3 Paul speaks of living writing, and in 6, of dead writing. 'Ink' can write anything, and it can be blotted out (Exod. xxxii. 33) or washed off (Num. v. 23), but what the Spirit writes abides, because He writes not on parchment but in people.

He does this instrumentally, but Paul disclaims any self-sufficiency for such a work.

Living Letters—Christians. The Author—Christ. The Amanuensis—Paul. The Tablets—hearts. The Agency—not ink, but the Spirit. The Substance—new life. The Readers—all men.

Two Ministries Contrasted (iii. 7-18)

The dominating word here is *splendour* (glory, *doxa*, *doxazō*), and it occurs thirteen times.

What Paul says is that the old ministry was splendid, but that the new ministry is more splendid. How wonderful is the contrast: Moses and Christ; Mosaism and Christianity; Death and Life; on Stone and in the Heart; Letter and Spirit; Condemnation and Righteousness; Passing and Permanent; Face Veiled and Unveiled; Bondage and Freedom; Transience and Transformation.

There are at least ten points of contrast between the Old and the New Dispensations. Christianity is not a glorified Judaism; it is something entirely new. There is a fundamental difference between the Law and the Gospel (cf. John i. 17).

The great verses 17, 18 are rhythmical and rhetorical.

> 'Now the Lord is the Spirit;
> And where the Spirit of the Lord, there is freedom.
> But we all with unveiled face,
> The glory of the Lord reflecting,
> As in a mirror
> Into the same image are changed
> From glory to glory
> Even as from the Lord Spirit.'

Ministering the Gospel (iv. 1-6)

It is not difficult to recognize in these verses charges denied which had been made, and these surely are related to the chapters x-xiii. When Paul speaks of 'disgraceful and underhand ways,' of 'practising cunning,' of 'tampering with God's word,' and of preaching himself (5), he implies that he had been charged with these things; and, also, that there were those in Corinth of whom these things were true (1, 2).

The Gospel is veiled—as Moses' face had been—to them that are blinded by the god 'of this age.' To such 'the radiancy of the glad tidings of the glory of the Christ cannot beam forth.'

What Paul preached was 'Jesus Christ as Lord,' and he was glad to be a 'slave' to the Corinthians 'for Jesus' sake' (5).

Mark what Plummer calls 'the stately series of genitives'—

'the light of the knowledge of the glory of God in the face of Christ' (6, cf. 4).

Plummer points out that verses 1-6 run in couplets: the glory of the new ministry (1, 2); the condition of those who are too blind to see the glory of the Gospel (3, 4); the source of the glory (5, 6).

The Frailty of the Messengers (iv. 7-15).

Paul had been charged with boastful self-sufficiency (5) and in this section he slays that slander. He had just spoken of the glory of the gospel, and he continues: '*But* this glory has another side,' and from this he bursts out in a most wonderful passage which is half poetry and half prose.

Better than any comment one might offer on verses 7-12 are some translations of them.

'This illuminating power is entrusted to unattractive and worthless persons, as treasure is stored in earthen jars, in order that it may be patent to all that the excellence of power which we exhibit is God's gift, and does not emanate from us.

'In our conflicts we suffer heavily, but are never utterly defeated. Often hard pressed, yet not driven to surrender; in desperate plight, yet not in despair; chased from the field, yet not left to the mercy of the foe; beaten to the earth, yet not killed outright; always carrying about in the body the imminent danger of dying as Jesus died, in order that by the continual escapes and deliverances of our bodies it might be manifest to the world that Jesus is still alive.'   (Plummer).

'We have a treasure, then, in our keeping, but its shell is of perishable earthenware; it must be God, and not anything in ourselves, that gives it its sovereign power.

'For ourselves, we are being hampered everywhere, yet still have room to breathe; are hard put to it, but never at a loss; persecution does not leave us unbefriended, nor crushing blows destroy us; we carry about continually in our bodies the dying state of Jesus, so that the living power of Jesus may be manifested in our bodies too.'
                                                        (Knox).

'But I have this treasure in a mere earthen jar, to show that its amazing power belongs to God and not to me. I am hard pressed on every side, but never cut off; perplexed, but not driven to despair; routed, but not abandoned; struck down, but not destroyed; never free from the danger of being put to death like Jesus, so that in my body the life of Jesus also may be seen.'   (Goodspeed).

'But we have these jewels in clay pots, that the wonderful greatness of the power may be not ours but God's.

'We are hard pressed on every side, but not cut off; in difficulty, but not in despair; persecuted, but not helpless; struck down, but not destroyed; everywhere we carry about in our bodies the dying of Jesus, that the life of Jesus may be seen in our bodies.'

(Williams).

'This priceless treasure we hold, so to speak, in a common earthenware jar—to show that the splendid power of it belongs to God and not to us. We are handicapped on all sides, but we are never frustrated; we are puzzled, but never in despair. We are persecuted, but we never have to stand it alone; we may be knocked down but we are never knocked out! Every day we experience something of the death of the Lord Jesus, so that we may also know the power of the life of Jesus in these bodies of ours.'   (Phillips).

'A treasure of price is this message; yet I bear it in a frail vessel of clay-ware, so proving that not from me, but from God is derived its all-prevailing efficacy.

'On every hand hard-pressed am I—yet not crushed! In desperate plight am I—yet not in despair! Close followed by pursuers—yet not abandoned by Him! Beaten to the earth—yet never destroyed! Evermore bearing about in my body the imminence of such a death as Jesus died, so that the life, too, of Jesus may be shown forth in this body of mine.'   (Way).

'What we bring you is a treasure of great value; but we who bear it are but vessels, and that of fragile earthenware, in order that it may be evident that the irresistible power of the Gospel does not originate with us, but is of God.

'We are hard pressed incessantly, but never cornered; we are frequently at a loss, but never in despair; frequently persecuted, but never abandoned to our persecutors; hurled to the ground, yet ever rising undestroyed. Always, and everywhere we go, in the deadly perils that beset us, we accept death as really as the Lord Jesus accepted it, in order that in our deliverances the resurrection of Jesus may be clearly reproduced.'   (Isaacs).

'Howbeit we have this treasure in earthen vessels, that the surpassing greatness of the power may be of God, and not from ourselves. On every side pressed hard, but not hemmed in. Without a way, but not without a by-way, pursued, but not abandoned, thrown down but not destroyed.

'At all times the putting to death of Jesus in our body bearing about, in order that the life also of Jesus in our body may be made manifest.'

(Rotherham).

This is one of the great passages of the Pauline literature, and a classic on how a Christian should regard trouble.

Dr. Dale of Birmingham said to D. L. Moody:

'Mr. Moody, I cannot see any connection between you and your success!' But God connected the two.

The Christian's Hope Here and Hereafter (iv. 16-v. 10).

Hope in the New Testament is not a 'perhaps' or a 'peradventure' but a certainty, a glad assurance.

Chapter iv. 16-18 is a profound passage on spiritual renewal. How striking are its contrasts!

Outward nature and inward nature; wasting away and being renewed; light and weight; momentary and eternal; not looking and looking; things seen and things unseen; transient and eternal.

In fifty-three words Paul tells of the blessing, the method, and the condition of spiritual renewal.

As to the *Blessing*: spiritual renewal is a great reality, a gradual process, and a glorious triumph.

As to the *Method*: affliction is a common experience, a converting energy, and the true Christian can estimate it.

As to the *Condition*: Paul speaks of the habit of, the reason for, and the effect of looking at the unseen.

In chapter v. 1-10 the Apostle thinks aloud about his present and future estate, and says what he is resolved to do about it.

He speaks of his physical body as a 'tent' in which he dwells. This is interesting seeing that he was a tent-maker. Then he speaks of his future body as a 'house,' and he desires earnestly that there shall be no time between his 'tent' home and his 'house' home during which he would be 'naked,' not having any body (3). The Apostle teaches that in our present condition we are in exile from the Lord, and that it would be, and will be, better to be with the Lord. Meanwhile, he says, 'We are of good courage' (6, 8).

> Here in the body pent
> Absent from Him I roam,
> Yet nightly pitch my moving tent
> A day's march nearer home.

Paul 'makes it his aim to please Christ' (9), and an impelling motive is that 'all Christians must appear before Christ's judgment seat' (10).

This judgment is for Christians only, and it is not a penal judgment, but one of rewards. Study the parables of the Talents, and the Pounds. The way to avoid loss and to make sure of gain in that day, is to make it our ambition and aim to please Christ now.

The Minister's Devotion to his Message (v. 11-21).

The *devotion* is in verses 11-15, and the *message* is in verses 16-21.

Paul declares that in his ministry he is 'controlled by the love of Christ' (14).

'Paul's thought of the Cross is the overwhelming sense that the Divine heart suffers in and for the sin of the world, and that this Divine suffering is rooted in Divine love' (Strachan).

In chapter v. 17-21 is, perhaps, the greatest passage in Paul on *reconciliation*. The word occurs here five times. The reconciliation of God and man is needed, purposed, offered, and proclaimed.

The great ideas in v. 17-21 are: 'Christ' (17, 19); 'a new creation' (17); 'reconciliation' (18); 'from God, through Christ' (18); 'not counting their trespasses against them' (19); 'ambassadors for Christ' (20); 'God making His appeal through us' (20); 'God made Him to be sin Who knew no sin' (21); 'in Him we might become the righteousness of God' (21).

3. THE MINISTERED UNTO BY THE GOSPEL
(vi. 1-vii. 16)

Paul sets forth in vi. 1-10 *the method and condition of apostolic ministry*. As in other parts of this Epistle there is a rhythmic swing in what the Apostle says. WAY calls it a 'Hymn of the Herald of Salvation'. WAY's other hymn designations are: 'Hymn of the Change' (iii. 18). 'Hymn of Tribulation' (iv. 8-11). 'Hymn of the Home Eternal' (iv. 16-v. 10). 'Hymn of the New Life' (v. 14-17).

In these verses (vi. 1-10) Paul speaks of his conduct and experiences as God's ambassador, and as a minister to whom had been entrusted the message of reconciliation (v. 20). It is the second of three descriptions in this Epistle of Paul's sufferings (cf. iv. 8-11; xi. 23-28). What a catalogue! Afflictions, sore straits, privation, scourgings, prison-cells, riots, toils, night vigils, and fastings. And throughout all the Apostle exhibits purity, illumination, longsuffering, kindness and love.

'He was praised and defamed. Branded as a deceiver—vindicated as true. Ignored by men—recognized by God. Ever at the point to die—yet lo, he lives on. Chastened by suffering, yet never done to death. Sorrowing ever, yet evermore glad. Poor himself, yet bestowing riches on thousands. Having nothing, yet holding all things in sure possession.'

In the light of all this Paul in vi. 11-13 appeals to the Church. 'Corinthians, Corinthians! to you my lips are unlocked, my heart is opened wide. Not, oh, not in me is there any narrowness; the narrowness is in you, in your own hearts. Requite my love— I appeal to you as my children—open wide your hearts too' (WAY).

It is not likely that after writing like this Paul would have added chapters x-xiii.

The Moral Demands of the Christian Gospel (vi. 14-vii. 1)

This is another illustration of what WAY calls hymns, and it is a 'Hymn of Consecration.'

Some critics regard the passage as an interpolation, and they connect it with 1 Cor. v. 9, the lost letter. About this only three things need be said: (*a*) chapters vi. 13 and vii 2 connect naturally; (*b*) chapter vi. 14-vii. 1 belongs to the subject of 1 Cor. v. 9; (*c*) there is no evidence in MS., or version, or quotation, that any copy of the Epistle ever lacked this passage. There we must leave it.

What matters, of course, is what the passage says, and not how it fits into its context.

Five questions are followed by a series of quotations, and an exhortation.

There is such a thing as moral incongruity. No right thinking person can reconcile 'righteousness and iniquity,' 'light and darkness,' 'Christ and Belial,' 'faith and infidelity,' 'true worship and idolatry' (14-16).

'Righteousness and iniquity' are in the realm of conscience and conduct. 'Light and darkness' belong to thought and feeling. 'Christ and Belial' are leaders of two conflicting hosts. 'Believer and unbeliever' relate to religious persuasion and conviction. 'The temple of God and idols' point to true and false worship, to the true and the counterfeit church.

'As God said' (16-18) does not refer to any one passage (cf. Lev. xxvi. 11, 12; Jer. vii. 23; xi. 4; xxiv. 7; xxx. 22; xxxi. 1, 33; xxxii. 38; Ezek. xi. 20; xxxvi. 28; cf. II Sam. vii. 14).

What are reasonably the scope and limits of 'be not mismated with unbelievers' it is not quite easy to say. It is generally referred to marriage, but there can be other mismatements: in friendship, in business, in some kinds of sport; yes, and in religious alliances which are incompatible and incongruous. Such alliances are popular to-day, but they lead only to apostasy.

It is not popular to 'come out' from what is falsely popular; but a Christian should not ask 'Is it popular?' but 'Is it right?'

It should be noticed that in vii. 1 are two operations. One of them is instantaneous, 'cleanse (aorist); and one is progressive, 'perfecting' (pres. part.). We cannot 'cleanse' progressively, and we cannot 'perfect' instantaneously.

The unclean spirit must be turned out of the heart, but the place must be occupied by the Holy Spirit, or the evil will return (cf. Matt. xii. 43-45).

The Object and Effect of a Previous Letter (vii. 2-16)

This passage speaks of a Letter (8, 12), and of an offender (12). What Letter? Which offender?

Following what has already been said, the Letter will be the 'severe' one (x.-xiii. see page 83 ff.); and the offender will be the ringleader of the group that denied Paul's apostleship and authority (cf. ii. 1-11).

This section is in four parts: (a) an appeal for the confidence of the Corinthians (2-4); (b) the longing Paul had had for the arrival of Titus, and the comfort which his coming had brought (5-7; cf. ii. 12, 13); (c) the Letter and the offender (8-12); and (d) joy because of Titus and his report (13-16).

How could an inspired apostle 'regret' what he had written (8)? Perhaps we must distinguish between 'regret' and 'repent'.

Of this passage (vii. 2-16) Plummer says: 'The Apostle "lets himself go," and can hardly find language in which to express his appreciation of the present attitude of the Corinthians towards himself and Titus, and his consequent joy over them and over the joy which they have produced in Titus.

Words expressive of comfort, rejoicing, glorying, boldness, and courage occur with surprising frequency, as if he could not repeat them too often.'

Parakaleō occurs 4 times; *paraklēsis* 3 times; *chairō* 4 times; *chara* twice; *kauchēsis* twice, and *kauchaomai*, *parrēsia*, and *tharreō* once each; *zēlos* twice; *spoudē* twice; *metanoia* twice; *phobos* thrice and *hupakoē* once.

It is preferable to read x-xiii before i-vii than after. Only a great soul can be severe and tender as the circumstances require. Severity only is cruel, and tenderness only is maudlin.

2 CORINTHIANS

PART II. Chs. viii-ix

CHRISTIAN GIVING FOR CHRISTIAN USES

These chapters are the *locus classicus* on this subject, and the importance that Paul attached to what, in the churches, is called the 'collection,' or 'offering' (there is a difference) is marked by his references to it in addition to these two chapters (Acts xxiv. 17; Gal. ii. 10; Rom. xv. 26, 27; 1 Cor. xvi. 1-4).

In speaking of the 'offering' Paul uses nine words: *logia*, collection (1 Cor. xvi. 1, 2); *charis*, grace (1 Cor. xvi. 1, 3; 2 Cor. viii. 4); *koinōnia*, fellowship (2 Cor. viii. 4; ix. 13; Rom. xv. 26);

diakonia, service (2 Cor. viii. 4; ix. 1, 12, 13); *hadrotēs*, abundance (2 Cor. viii. 20); *eulogia*, blessing (2 Cor. ix. 5); *leitourgia*, ministration (2 Cor. ix. 12); *eleēmosunē*, alms (Acts xxix. 17), and *prosphora*, offerings (Acts xxiv. 17).

Paul did not think it to be a bathos to say, 'Now concerning the collection for the saints' (1 Cor. xvi. 1) after he had spoken sublimely of Christ's resurrection and the believer's (ch. xv.).

On the background of Macedonia's liberality the Apostle urges the Corinthians to give generously (viii. 1-7). He points to the example of the Lord Jesus Christ, and indicates the proportion to be observed in contributing (viii. 8-15). He tells the Corinthians that Titus and two others will be in charge of this service (viii. 16-24). In view of his intention to visit Corinth soon the Apostle expresses the hope that the offering will have been raised (ix. 1-5), and that it will have been generous (ix. 6-15).

There is nothing here of the frantic and sensational appeals which to-day are so frequent. Paul's treatment of the subject is a universe away from modern ways of 'raising the wind.' Chicken suppers, whist drives, dances, raffles, conjuring and pierrots are among methods employed to increase the finances of many a modern church. But this is not only not Christian giving, it is not giving at all; and it is an insult to Almighty God.

Over against all that, hear Paul:

'A wealth of liberality overflowed from the churches of Macedonia, notwithstanding their extreme poverty' (viii. 2).
'These people begged earnestly for the favour of taking part in the relief of the saints' (viii. 4).
'The Lord Jesus Christ, though He was rich, became poor, that by His poverty we might become rich' (viii. 9).
'What one can afford to give is acceptable, and more is not expected' (viii. 12).
'The raising of such a fund is "gracious work," and is for "the glory of the Lord"' (viii. 19).
'He who sows sparingly will also reap sparingly, and he who sows bountifully will also reap bountifully' (ix. 6).
'No one should give reluctantly, or under compulsion, for God loves a cheerful giver' (ix. 7).
'He who gives generously will not be impoverished thereby because God will provide him with every blessing' (ix. 8-11).
'Thanks be to God for His inexpressible Gift' (ix. 15).

Love so amazing, so Divine,
Demands my soul, my life, my all.

On this note Paul's correspondence to Corinth ends.

For the 171 words which occur in this Epistle, and in none of Paul's other Letters, see the writer's *Know Your Bible*, vol. 2, p. 145.

No one can read this Epistle without realizing that the Apostle's mind was agitated by intense emotions. There is not the constructiveness and smoothness which are observable in his other Letters. It is not unlikely that there were intervals between the writing of different parts of the Epistle, which would account for a certain disjointedness. Paul's mental anxiety, physical weakness, and his journeys in Macedonia easily explain the phenomena. This divinely used man was very human.

THE PAULINE EPISTLES

GROUP 2

GALATIANS

A.D. 57

As we turn to this Epistle two difficulties confront us, namely, its *destination*, and its *date*. Though in some ways related, these problems are distinct.

DESTINATION

What is meant by GALATIA has been, is, and is likely to be a subject of much controversy. The name was used in two senses— geographically, and politically. When used geographically it signified the northern part of the central plateau of Asia Minor; and when used politically it embraced a much larger area, including what is spoken of as South Galatia. (See Map 22 The Drama, Vol 2, p. 408).

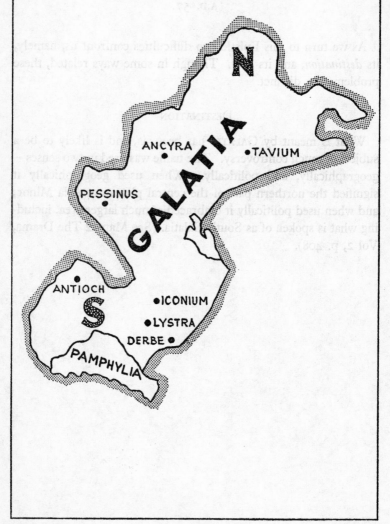

NORTH GALATIA
AND
SOUTH GALATIA

N

GALATIA

ANCYRA •
• TAVIUM

PESSINUS •

ANTIOCH
S
• ICONIUM
• LYSTRA
DERBE •

PAMPHYLIA

MAP 33

The name 'Galatia' originated between B.C. 278-232 when a horde of Gauls from Europe invaded Western Asia Minor. They settled in what is called North Galatia, or Galatia proper with the city-centres of Pessinus, Ancyra, and Tavium. (See Map 33). Later, under Rome, what is called South Galatia was added to this Province. The Map 22 shows the whole extent of the ultimate 'Galatia'.

The point of controversy as to the *destination* of the Epistle, is in the question—in what sense is the name used in the New Testament?

The references are:

Acts xvi. 6 -	-	'They went through the region of Phrygia and Galatia.'
Acts xviii. 23	-	'Through the region of Galatia and Phrygia.'
1 Cor. xvi. 1. ⎫ Gal. i. 2 ⎭	-	'The churches of Galatia.'
2 Tim. iv. 10	-	'Crescens has gone to Galatia.'
1 Peter i. 1 -	-	'To the dispersion in Galatia.'

Lightfoot says that 'Galatia' refers to the North, and that the Churches were at Pessinus, Ancyra, and Tavium; and *Ramsay* says that it refers to the South, and that the Churches were at Antioch, Iconium, Lystra, and Derbe; and each of these scholars is followed by a host of others.

Our view of the matter must be based on the facts and probabilities of the case, and this is an intricate problem.

Even Lightfoot, who supports the 'North Galatian' theory, says: 'It is strange that while we have more or less acquaintance with all the other important Churches of St. Paul's founding, with Corinth and Ephesus, with Philippi and Thessalonica, not a single name of a person or place, scarcely a single incident of any kind connected with the Apostle's preaching in Galatia should be preserved . . . in either the history (i.e., Acts) or the Epistle —unless Acts xvi. 6; xviii. 23, and xix. 1 refer to the North.'

On the other hand, we know that Paul visited South Galatia twice at least (Acts xiii. 14; xiv. 1, 6, 7; xv. 36, 41; xvi. 1; Gal. iv. 13), and founded Churches in Antioch, Iconium, Lystra, and Derbe; and in the Epistle he refers to his ministry among these people (iv. 12-20); to the Gospel that he preached (i. 6-9); and to his apostolic authority (i. 11-ii. 10).

If 'Galatia' refers to the Northern Province, Paul's ministry there is a blank; but if to the Southern Province, the record in the Acts and Epistle is full and circumstantial.

There are many full discussions of this problem—for example, Moffatt's, in his 'Introduction to the Literature of the New Testament' (pp. 90-101), but the controversy sways to and fro like a rugby scrum.

DATE

As to the *date* of the Epistle there is an even greater variety of conjecture than as to destination. It has been placed by different critics as the earliest and as the latest of all Paul's Epistles, and at intermediate positions. Also the place of writing is variously affirmed—at Antioch, at Ephesus, in Macedonia, on the journey between Macedonia and Achaia, and at Corinth.

These matters of destination, date, and place of writing remain undetermined, but here we lean toward the 'South Galatian' theory, and to the view that the Epistle was written either in Macedonia, or, more probably, at Corinth in A.D. 57 (Acts xx. 2, 3), between the writing of 2 Corinthians and Romans.

It is, of course, the case that many scholars who hold the South Galatian theory consider that the Epistle was written before the Jerusalem Council decrees of Acts 15 (A.D. 50), or Paul would have made some reference to them. These scholars generally believe that the Apostle wrote the Epistle either in Antioch or *en route* to the Council.

The thing that matters, of course, is that the letter was written, and what it says was not only for those who first read it, but is also for Christians in every generation and everywhere.

We should note that this Epistle is one of two which Paul sent to a group of churches—the other being Ephesians, which without doubt was a circular Letter.

This fact is not affected by the North or South Galatia theory. The address is 'To the *Churches* of Galatia' (i. 2).

But, unlike 'Ephesians,' this Letter confronts a definite situation and the Apostle challenges it.

Placing Galatians between 1-2 Corinthians and Romans is neither fanciful nor arbitrary because it has striking resemblances to both.

It is likely that the Epistle belongs to the Second of Paul's Four Groups of Letters. Group One has 1-2 Thessalonians, and Group Three has Ephesians, Philippians, Colossians and Philemon, and with neither of these Groups has Galatians any noticeable affinities; but, with 1-2 Corinthians and Romans it is intimately related in style, matter, tone and treatment; and from this it is reasonable to conclude that it belongs to the same period and circumstances which gave birth to these.

Compare:

GALATIANS	1 CORINTHIANS
iv. 13	ii. 3
v. 9	v. 6
v. 6	vii. 19
vi. 15	vii. 19

Compare also:

GALATIANS	2 CORINTHIANS
i. 6	xi. 4
i. 9	xiii. 2
i. 10	v. 11
iii. 3	viii. 6
iii. 13	v. 21
iv. 17	xi. 2
v. 21	xiii. 2
vi. 7	ix. 6
vi. 15	v. 17

In addition to these references there are some words which occur only in 2 Corinthians and Galatians of Paul's epistles: *confirm* (κυρόω), Gal. iii. 15; 2 Cor. ii. 8: *perplexed* ('ἀπορέομαι), Gal. iv.20; 2 Cor. iv. 8: *contrariwise* (τοὐναντίον), Gal. ii. 7; 2 Cor. ii. 7: *devour* (κατεσθίω), Gal. v. 15; 2 Cor. xi. 20.

But most striking are the parallels between Galatians and Romans; so striking and numerous are these as to force the conclusion that both these Epistles were written about the same time, when the Apostle's mind and heart were full of the themes which they both emphasize. Examples of these parallels are:

GALATIANS	ROMANS
ii. 16	iii. 20
ii. 19	vii. 4
iii. 6	iv. 3
iii. 7	iv. 11
iii. 8	iv. 17, 18
iii. 9	iv. 23, 24
iii. 10	iv. 15
iii. 11	iii. 21; i. 17
iii. 12	x. 5
iii. 15-18	iv. 13, 14, 16
iii. 22	xi. 32
iii. 27	vi. 3
iii. 29	ix. 8
iv. 5, 6	viii. 14-17
iv. 28	ix. 7
v. 14	xiii. 8-10
v. 6	viii. 1
v. 17	vii. 13-25
vi. 2	xv. 1

The height of the Judaistic controversy is reached in 2 Corinthians and Galatians. It has scarcely begun in 1 Corinthians, and it has almost faded away in Romans, but in 2 Corinthians and Galatians are blended opposite emotions—tenderness and severity, remonstrance and sarcasm, autobiography and theology, commendation and rebuke.

It is not easy to describe how the four Letters of the Second Group are related to one another, but the relation is intimate and vital, and is best felt if the order 1 Corinthians, 2 Corinthians, Galatians, and Romans is accepted. In the first of these four Letters the storm is threatening; in the second and third it is at its height; and in the fourth it has subsided.

Galatians 'is the rough sketch of which the Epistle to the Romans is the finished picture' (Farrar).

In Galatians the emphasis is on *freedom*, and in Romans it is on *justification*, yet both these subjects are in each of these Epistles.

The occasion of this Epistle was the same as that which led to the writing of 2 Cor. x-xiii. After Paul had left Galatia—emissaries of the Judaizing party went from Judaea to the Galatian Churches—whether North, or South—with the definite purpose of discrediting Paul and his ministry.

The two outstanding items in their programme were: (*a*) to deny the apostleship of Paul (i. 1, 11, 12), and (*b*) to insist on the circumcision of the Gentiles as being necessary to Christian faith (cf. vi. 12, 13; also v. 2, 3; ii. 3 with Acts xv. 1, 5; xi. 1-3).

This meant that a man could not become a perfect Christian without becoming a partial Jew; for the Gentiles to become true believers they must conform, as far as might be, to the rule and usage of the Church in Jerusalem.

It will be seen that of the two lines of attack one was *personal*, and the other was *doctrinal*, and it is this double attack which Paul combats and refutes in this Epistle.

Chapters i-ii, iv. 12-16 deal with the personal matter, and chapters iii-v. 10, with the doctrinal matter. The personal part is vehement, and the doctrinal part is cogent.

Dean Farrar said: 'More than any book which was ever written these few pages marked an epoch in history'. Paul's words were and are battles.

Prof. Sabatier said: 'There is nothing in ancient or modern language to be compared with this Epistle. All the powers of Paul's soul shine forth in its few pages. Broad and luminous view, keen logic, biting irony, everything that is most forcible in argument, vehement in indignation, ardent and tender in affection, is found here, combined and poured forth in a single strain, forming a work of irresistible power'.

Martin Luther said: 'The Epistle to the Galatians is my Epistle. I have betrothed myself to it. It is my wife'.

It is the battle-axe which Luther brought down with terrific and telling force upon the helmets of his foes.

The Epistle is the Magna Charta of spiritual emancipation; the bulwark of Protestantism.

The content of the Epistle is clear and concise. Between an *Introduction* (i. 1-10) and a *Conclusion* (vi. 11-18) there are three Divisions. The first is a *Personal Narrative* (i. 11-ii. 21); the second is a *Doctrinal Argument* (iii.-v. 1); and the third is a *Practical Exhortation* (v. 2-vi. 10).

THE INTRODUCTION
(i. 1-10)

THE ADDRESS (1, 2)

Note the abruptness of it, and compare Rom. i. 1-7. Paul was going to defend his apostleship, so he begins by affirming it.

THE BLESSING (3-5)

The substance of it—'grace and peace'. The source of it— 'God the Father and our Lord Jesus Christ'. The sacrifice in it— Christ's death, occasioned by 'our sins'; voluntarily imposed, 'Who gave Himself'. The purpose of it—our deliverance; and the appointment of it—the will of God the Father.

This is a profound theological statement.

THE OCCASION (6-10)

The apostasy of the Galatians (6, 7). The perverters were well-known persons. The anathema on the heretics (8, 9). The Apostle's authority (10).

There is only one true Gospel, and all other claims are a denial of it.

There are times when intolerance is a duty.

I. THE PERSONAL NARRATIVE

(i. 11-ii. 21)

CHART 158

GALATIANS No. 1		
INTRODUCTION i. 1–10	PART I	
	i. 11–ii. 21	
	PERSONAL NARRATIVE	
	1. Claim to Divine Illumination ..	(i. 11, 12)
	2. Conduct before Conversion ..	(i. 13, 14)
	3. Commission at Conversion ..	(i. 15, 16*a*)
	4. Course after Conversion ..	(i. 16*b*, 17)
	5. Contact with the Apostles ..	(i. 18–ii. 10)
	6. Controversy with Peter ..	(ii. 11–16)
	7. Conclusion of the matter Justification is by Faith ..	(ii. 17–21)

The Apostle received the Gospel which he preached by Divine revelation (i. 11, 12). On this fact his apostolic authority rested.

Before his conversion Paul was learned and zealous, but he was wrong, and quite sincerely persecuted those who were right (i. 13, 14).

But he was predestined to his apostolic mission (i. 15-17). Here are election, conversion, revelation, commission, contemplation, and preparation.

As 'Arabia' reached from Damascus to Mount Sinai we do not know where Paul went (cf. iv. 25), nor how long he was there; but it seems certain that he went away, not to preach, but to rethink the Old Testament in the light of the revelation he had received.

What Paul wants to make clear is that he did not confer with anyone about the new situation and its implications.

'*Three Years*' after his conversion Paul went back to Jerusalem (i. 18-24), and remained there for a fortnight as the guest of Peter; during which time he saw James the brother of Jesus.

That must have been a marvellous fortnight for both Paul and Peter; but, for reasons not clearly stated, it was brought to an abrupt close, and Paul went to Syria and Cilicia, where he evangelized for eleven years—if reckoned from his last visit, or fourteen years—if reckoned from his conversion (ii. 1); and Tarsus was his headquarters (Acts xi. 25).

From this record of his movements, and from the fact that for so long Paul was unknown to the churches in Judaea, except by report, he proves that his status and mission were derived in entire independence of the Apostles at Jerusalem.

'AFTER FOURTEEN YEARS' (ii. 1-10)

Several questions arise here which it is not within the scope of our present purpose to examine, but only to state.

1. Are the 'fourteen years' to be reckoned from Paul's conversion, or from the visit of i. 18?
2. Is this visit referred to in the Acts? And if so, is it to be related to chapter xi. 30, or chapter xv?
3. Why was Titus with the Apostle at Jerusalem?
4. Did Paul, or did he not, circumcise Titus?

What, for our present purpose, must be kept in mind is that Paul is proving that his Apostleship was underived from men, and was valid.

On this visit to Jerusalem he had conversation with Peter, James, and John about himself and his work, and the result was that these authorities recognized his Apostleship and his mission to the Gentiles (6-10). Barnabas is included in this recognition.

This is a section of great historical importance.

CONTROVERSY WITH PETER AT ANTIOCH (ii. 11-21)

The narrative is in two parts: first, the clash between Paul and Peter (ii. 11-14) and then, the justification of it because of its implications (ii. 15-21).

If Paul's record is in chronological sequence—though all do not hold it to be so—this incident would have taken place after the Jerusalem Conference and before Paul and Barnabas separated; that is, it falls between verses 35 and 36 of Acts xv.

It is this view which makes Peter's conduct so reprehensible, and Paul's stand so justifiable.

The Jerusalem Conference of A.D. 50 (Acts xv) settled the matter of the relation of Christian Gentiles to the Mosaic Law. Peter and Barnabas had a large share in coming to the decision arrived at (Acts xv. 6-12), and when they returned to Antioch (Acts xv. 30) Peter put the decision into practice by eating with the Christian Gentiles (Gal. ii. 12), a thing he had done before (Acts x. 48; xi. 2-4).

But when 'certain men came from James' Peter withdrew from his fellowship with the Gentiles, 'fearing the circumcision party'. Other Jews and Barnabas did the same (Gal. ii. 12, 13).

This was clearly a case of inconsistency and cowardice, and is an illustration of an old characteristic of Peter—impulsive and erratic Peter.

If it was right for him to eat with the Gentiles it was wrong for him to withdraw; and if it was right for him to withdraw, it was wrong for him to have eaten with them. Peter was on the horns of a dilemma, and evidently he realized this, because he did not argue it out with Paul.

On the contrary, he must have acknowledged his fault, for years after, speaking of his rebuker, he said: 'our beloved brother Paul' (2 Pet. iii. 15).

From this we learn that the best of men may make grievous mistakes; that when such are made it is well to admit them; and that incidents of this sort should never be allowed to break friendships.

Over against Peter's cowardice was Paul's courage. Years before, Paul had been Peter's guest (Gal. i. 18), and it is never easy, especially in public, to rebuke anyone to whom we have been indebted.

Courage was one of Paul's many great qualities, and it is admirable whenever it is exhibited.

The case of Barnabas differed from that of Peter in some respects, and was most regrettable. He had been Paul's fellow-missionary on the first journey, and evidently the two were much attached, and Paul was indebted to him for much (Acts ix. 27; xi. 25, 26).

But he took the wrong road on this occasion, and, maybe, the incident had some bearing on the separation of these two men shortly afterward (Acts xv. 36-39). The friendship, however, remained intact (1 Cor. ix. 6).

People who fall easily apart from one another, and are content for it to be so, are not real friends.

The next paragraph (ii. 15-21) passes from direct address to Peter to an application of the truth for which Paul was contending which is inclusive of the whole Church of God.

This is characteristic of Paul's method and manner. Frequently in his letters, he suddenly soars from the local to the universal, and then comes back to the local. An outstanding illustration of this is Phil. ii. 1-30. From a personal appeal (1-4) he spreads his wings and soars to giddy heights of Christological truth (5-11), and then returns to the local (12-30).

He does the same in the passage before us. From the incident narrated in verses 11-14 Paul breaks out into a statement relative to the Law and the Gospel (15-21) which is the very heart of his theology.

In 130 words or more the Apostle presents 'a whole body of divinity'. Note the words which dominate this utterance: *justification*, 5 times; *law*, 6 times; *faith*, 4 times; *life*, 6 times; *death*, 4 times; and under and over and around all—*Christ*, 9 times.

The affair with Peter was not a mere difference of opinion; it raised the whole question of Christianity. Justification could not be by Law and by Grace; by Moses and by Christ; by Sinai and by Calvary; by Works and by Faith. It had to be by one or the other, but it could not be by both; and Paul declares, here and everywhere, that it is by Grace, by Christ, by Calvary, and by Faith.

Christianity is not a ceremony but a life, and so it brings not bondage but freedom.

Here is summarized the vital distinction between the Old and the New Covenants (O.T., and N.T.).

Paul says that the Christian is crucified, and yet he lives; that he is himself, and yet not himself; that he lives a life in the flesh, and yet a life of faith.

If justification could have been by forms and ceremonies, then Christ died in vain.

With this great utterance the Personal Narrative in this Epistle ends (i. 11-ii. 21), and the way has been prepared for the Doctrinal Argument of iii. 1-v. 1.

2. THE DOCTRINAL ARGUMENT

(iii. 1-v. 1)

The first division of this Epistle (i. 11-ii. 21) proves the *authority* of Paul's Gospel, and this Doctrinal division affirms the *truth* of it.

The Personal and the Doctrinal divisions are united by the profound statement in chapter ii. 15-21.

CHART 159

GALATIANS No. 2	
PART II	
iii. 1–v. 1	
DOCTRINAL ARGUMENT	
I. THE DOCTRINE EXPOUNDED (iii)	II. THE DOCTRINE ENFORCED (iv. 1–v. 1)
1. Past Christian Experience (1–5)	1. Legal Illustration (iv. 1–11)
2. Covenant of God with Abraham (6–18)	
3. General Scope of the Law (19–24)	Parenthesis (iv. 12–20)
4. Present Christian Standing (25–29)	2. Historical Illustration (iv. 21–v. 1)

The connection and contrast of Law and Grace, of the Old and New Covenants, are set forth here with convincing logic.

THE DOCTRINE EXPOUNDED

(Ch. iii)

Paul gives four proofs of the truth of the Gospel which he preached, and the *first* is:

THE PAST EXPERIENCE OF THE GALATIANS (iii. 1-5)

They owed their conversion, not to the works of the Law, but to the death of Christ, Whose crucifixion had been 'placarded before their eyes'.

The Cross is always central in Paul's message of salvation.

He asks, was their possession of the Spirit due to 'works' or to 'faith'? And if to 'faith', why should they return to 'works'?

Furthermore, why had the Galatians suffered for their 'faith' if they owed everything to 'works'? Had their true experience gone for nothing?

The Spirit had worked mightily in and among them, and it was senseless, therefore, for them to turn their backs on all this, yielding to the evil spell of the Judaisers.

If the Christian begins rightly why should he carry on wrongly? We should continue and end on the true principle on which we began. Let us not turn our back on our best past.

Paul's *second* proof of the truth of his Gospel is:

THE COVENANT OF GOD WITH ABRAHAM (iii. 6-18)

Abraham and his spiritual seed were and are justified by faith, not by works (6-9).

Israel's spiritual history began with Abraham, not with Moses; and Abraham's true posterity are those who are justified by faith as he was, Gentiles though they may be.

The negative side of this truth is that the Law does not and cannot justify, but condemns, because no one can fulfil it (iii. 10-12), and the failure to fulfil puts one under a curse.

It is because of this that Christ died, becoming accursed for us that He might ransom us from the curse which the unsatisfied Law imposes (iii. 13, 14).

> When all was sin and shame
> A second Adam to the fight
> And to the rescue came.

Paul concludes this part of his argument by 'an illustration from human life'.

When once a man's 'will' is ratified no one can annul it, or add to it.

In like manner, the Law cannot repeal a Promise which God had made to Abraham 430 years before the Law was given (iii. 15-18). The Promise and Faith go together, as do the Law and Works. Salvation cannot be by both of these, and as it must be by one of them it must be by the Promise as the source and Faith as the agent of the saving blessing.

Paul's *third* proof of the truth of his Gospel is:

THE GENERAL SCOPE OF THE LAW ITSELF (iii. 19-24)

The question would arise—If what avails is the Promise made to Abraham, of what value or need was the Law through Moses?

This is the matter which Paul now deals with, and he has several things to say about it:

(a) The Law was 'interpolated to reveal sin' (19).

(b) The Law was temporary, 'till the Offspring should come' (19).

(c) The Law was mediated through angels and Moses, and came not direct from God (19, 20).

(d) Though the Law differs widely from the Promise it is not antagonistic to it (iii. 21). It 'consigns' everyone to the 'custody of sin,' so that the only way of escape is by faith in the Promise (iii. 22).

(e) The Law, therefore, is a preparation for the Gospel (iii. 23, 24). Paul likens it to 'a slave employed in many families to have general oversight, both disciplinary and protective, over a boy till he has reached the age of maturity.' (Duncan).

In an Oxyrhynchus papyrus a mother writing to her son uses this word *pedagogue*. She says: 'Let it be the care both of you and your *attendant* that you go to a suitable teacher'; and again, 'salute your highly esteemed *attendant* Eros'.

'Pedagogue' is Paul's word (cf. 1 Cor. iv. 15), and the ideas in it are supervision, moral direction, discipline and suppression.

The 'schoolmaster' of the A.V. is misleading; and the idea that the Law brought men to Christ's school for further instruction is wrong.

'It is not as a Teacher that Paul thinks of Christ, but as a Redeemer: the Christian life is not an advanced education, but a deliverance from death unto life' (Duncan).

Not by 'works', then, but only by 'faith' can one be justified.

Paul's *fourth* proof of the truth of his Gospel is in:

THE CHRISTIAN'S PRESENT STANDING (25-29)

Here a threefold relationship is shown.

1. *The Believer's Relation to God in Christ* (iii. 25-27)

He becomes a 'son of God, through faith', and at the time of his 'baptism into Christ'.

This is the sole reference to 'baptism' in the Epistle, and it is of the utmost importance to understand what is meant by what is said.

It is commonly held that the reference is to the rite of baptism, whether with little or much water; but this cannot be, for innumerable devout Christians have not, in this way, been baptized at all.

But let it be seen that the reference is to the Baptism of the Spirit, by which one is incorporated into the mystical Body of Christ, and all is clear.

Every Christian, when he became a Christian, was 'baptized into Christ'. This is the meaning here, and in 1 Cor. xii. 13; Eph. iv. 5.

Immersion in water is a Christian's public confession of his faith in Christ, and of the fact that *he is 'in Christ'*, but the rite does not put him there.

2. *The Believer's Relation to all other Believers* (iii. 28)

All distinctions—racial, social, and sexual—are done away with 'in Christ'. 'If any one is in Christ he is a new creation' (2 Cor. v. 17).

'Of course such distinctions exist in the natural world, but they can no longer be regarded as ultimate.'

What is here said is true of all believers alike, so that what the Judaisers were insisting on had no validity.

'In Christ' is one of the greatest ideas of Divine revelation, and it occurs in the New Testament not fewer than 35 times.

3.   The Believer's Relation to Abraham (iii. 29)

All who are 'in Christ' are Abraham's 'offspring', and 'heirs according to the Promise'. Not to understand this is to misread the Old Testament and the dispensational designs of God.

The doctrine of Justification by Faith in Christ alone which has been *expounded* (chapter iii), is now *enforced*.

THE DOCTRINE ENFORCED

(Chs. iv. 1-v. 1)

This is done by means of two illustrations, one legal, and the other historical, and between these is a parenthesis of a personal character.

(i)   The Legal Illustration (iv. 1-11)

The Apostle refers, first of all, to a legal situation in which an heir is in bondage so long as he is a minor (iv. 1-3). It is not certain what law he has in mind, whether Jewish, Roman, or some other, but the illustration remains valid.

Jews and Gentiles alike in their pre-Christian days were no better than children or even slaves, although God had marked out an inheritance for them; but now that Christ has come the time of bondage ends for all who believe, and they enter into the freedom of sonship (iv. 4-7).

This was true of the believing Galatians, and to some extent they must have understood it. Why then were they turning back from freedom to bondage, and from worship of God to idols, at the instigation of the Judaisers? (iv. 8-11).

The *'elemental spirits'* (στοιχεῖα) of vv. 3, 9 refer either to 'the elements of religious knowledge (Erasmus, Calvin, Goodspeed); or to 'a hierarchy of cosmical agents', world spirit-rulers; or to the heavenly bodies, by which 'days, and months, and seasons, and years' (10) are regulated (Augustine, Chrysostom, Theodoret, Ambrose). (Cf. Col. ii. 8). Let us beware of the peril of relapse (iv. 9) and remember that even an apostle may labour in vain (iv. 11).

Parenthesis (iv. 12-20)

Between the legal and historical illustrations is a parenthesis (iv. 12-20) in which Paul makes a moving appeal to his Galatian converts.

There are two paragraphs: one referring to the past attitude of the Galatians to himself (12-16); and the other to their present attitude towards his opponents (17-20).

His reference to 'bodily ailment' recalls 2 Cor. xii. 1-10 (which see). Divers guesses have been made as to what this 'ailment' was, some of which must be definitely ruled out.

All we know is that it was physical, evident, recurrent, and humiliating.

When ministering to the Galatians, Paul had an attack, and his converts were kind to him (iv. 14).

But now they turned from Paul to his detractors, and it greatly distressed the Apostle.

The whole parenthesis throbs with pathos and passion; it is full of tenderness, perplexity, and anxiety.

It is better to suffer than to cause suffering.

(ii)   The Historical Illustration (iv. 21-v. 1)

This is in two parts, the first being *Two Women and Two Sons* (iv. 21-23), and the second, *Two Covenants and Two Experiences* (24-v. 1).

Throughout this letter Paul has been emphasizing the difference between the Law and the Gospel; between what Abraham and what Moses stood for; between works and faith; and he concludes his argument by what he calls 'an allegory' (iv. 24).

Lightfoot points out that 'corresponds' in verse 25 means literally, 'belongs to the same row or column with', and so the contrasting ideas in this section are best seen when arranged in two rows:

Hagar	Sarah
Slave-girl	Free-born wife
Ishmael	Isaac
Child of Flesh	Child of Promise
Old Covenant	New Covenant
Law	Promise
Earthly Jerusalem	Heavenly Jerusalem
Cast out	Inherit

By the allegorical method, the characters and events of Scripture are regarded as types of spiritual realities.

This method was adopted by Philo, and Origen, and others and it can be suggestive without being fantastic.

The upshot of the whole argument of chapters iii-iv is in chapter v. 1 'For freedom Christ has set us free; stand fast therefore, and do not submit again to a yoke of slavery'.

It would be to little purpose that the Galatians escaped from the slavery of Heathenism if they bowed themselves to the slavery of Judaism.

The Christian Gospel—and there is no other *Gospel*—does not offer alternative slaveries, but perfect freedom from all slavery.

'Make a firm stand then, do not slip into any yoke of servitude.'
(Moffatt).

'Freedom' in contrast to bondage is one of the basic thoughts of this Epistle. It occurs in one or other of its forms eleven times: *eleutheria* (4), *eleutheros* (6), and *eleutheroō* (1).

The freedom that Paul was thinking of was from the bondage of Judaism; and this is by no means a dead issue. Very many Christians have no experience of Christian freedom, but are in bondage to 'wearing and fretting externalism', to fasts and feasts, to times and seasons, to sacerdotal assumptions, to unwarrantable authorities, to denominational prejudices, to shibboleths and badges, to schools and slogans, to 'timorous ritualisms and small ceremonial punctualities', to 'the decaying corpse of obsolete traditions', to priests and postures, and much besides.

Lazarus had life, but he had not liberty (John xi. 44), and, like him, crowds of Christians, are tightly wrapped in grave clothes. Of many it must be said:

> 'They bawl for freedom in their senseless mood,
> But still revolt when truth would set them free;
> Licence they mean when they cry liberty,
> For who loves that, must first be wise and good.'

To all such Paul preaches a gospel of freedom.

> 'Free from the law, oh, happy condition!
> Jesus hath bled, and there is remission!
> Cursed by the law, and bruised by the fall,
> Grace hath redeemed us once for all.'

After the Personal Narrative (i. 11-ii. 21) and the Doctrinal Argument (iii. 1-v. 1) comes

3. THE PRACTICAL EXHORTATION
(v. 2-vi. 18)

It is the good news of liberty that dominates the third division of this Letter, and Paul has four things to say about it, namely: its effective subversion; its higher expression; its abiding secret; and its practical outcome.

CHART 160

GALATIANS No. 3	
PART III	
v. 2–vi. 10	CONCLUSION vi. 11-18
PRACTICAL EXHORTATION	
1. Subversion of Liberty .. .. .. (v. 2–12)	
2. Expression of Liberty .. .. .. (v. 13-15)	
3. Secret of Liberty .. .. .. (v. 16–26)	
4. Outcome of Liberty .. .. .. (vi. 1–10)	

See the author's *Know Your Bible*, vol. 2, pp. 159-161

1. THE EFFECTIVE SUBVERSION OF LIBERTY (v. 2-12)

Paul warns the Galatians of the peril of circumcision (v. 2-6). He tells them that if they yield to Jewish ceremonialism Christ will be of no use to them. Yielding at one point would be yielding at all points (cf. Jas. ii. 10). Bondage and freedom cannot go together.

Why has there been a halt in the race? (v. 7-10) 'A little yeast leavens the whole lump'. Here this is said of belief and in 1 Cor. v. 6 of behaviour.

The Judaisers were saying that Paul himself preached circumcision, and he wants to know—if this is so—why he is persecuted (v. 11, 12).

2. THE HIGHEST EXPRESSION OF LIBERTY (v. 13-15)

This is in 'love', and not in 'snapping at each other, and preying upon each other'. Freedom expresses itself in selfless service.

3. THE ABIDING SECRET OF LIBERTY (v. 16-26)

The 'Spirit' and the 'Flesh', and the 'Spirit' and the 'Law' are contrasted (v. 16-18).

Then follow two catalogues, one bad and one good (19-23).

'The Works of the Flesh' (19-21)

These are in four groups: (a) sensuality; (b) idolatry; (c) dissension; and (d) revelry.

See Romans i. 29 ff; 2 Cor. xii. 20 ff; Eph. v. 3 ff; Col. iii. 5 ff.

'The Fruit of the Spirit (v. 22, 23)

This is in three groups of three each:

In relation to God—'love, joy, peace'. In relation to others—'patience, kindness, goodness'. In relation to oneself—'faithfulness, gentleness, self-control'. 'Against such things there is no law'.

'Works' is plural, but 'fruit' is singular, because evil passions are many and varied, but the fruit of the Spirit is a harmonious whole.

We must die to the flesh if we would live by the Spirit (v. 24, 25); and we must be 'guided' by Him by Whom we 'live' (v. 25).

4. THE PRACTICAL OUTCOME OF LIBERTY (vi. 1-10)

Here, there is first an exhortation to show sympathy (vi. 1-5), and then an exhortation to practise liberality.

We should show sympathy (vi. 1-5)

Nowhere is sympathy among Christians more needed and so little shown as when some are 'overtaken in any trespass' (1). Too often is sympathy not shown, but, alas, the lapse is broadcast. Let us beware, for we may be tempted, and may stand in need of the sympathy which we have failed to show.

The following words on burden-sharing and burden-bearing are profoundly important (2, 5). Two words are used, *baros* (v. 2), for the burden which should be shared; and *phortion* (v. 5), for the burden which cannot be shared.

We all have burdens which others can share with us if they wish to; burdens of sorrow, loss, want, disappointment, failure, fear, and other loads which are not necessarily and essentially our own. Such loads we should help others to carry (2).

But there are other burdens which cannot be shared, such as our personal responsibilities, and our personal obligations. These burdens are a man's pack, a soldier's kit, and each of us has to carry his own. We cannot throw it off, and we cannot transfer it to other shoulders.

The responsibilities which are essentially one's own place each of us in a solitude (see Zech. xii. 12-14). When at last we stand before the Judgment Seat of Christ we shall not have any-one to answer for us. There we shall have to carry our own load.

There is a place between being 'something' and being 'nothing' (3) which it is important to consider (Rom. xii. 3-8).

A hymn says: 'Oh, to be nothing, nothing'. We need another hymn that will say: 'Oh, to be something, something'.

We should practise liberality (vi. 6-10)

Paul's points in this exhortation are: the duty (6); the principle (7, 8); the encouragement (9); and the opportunity (10).

This paragraph on giving temporal assistance is surprising in its context, but it is quite emphatic (vi. 6-10); and it is viewed in a strong light (8, 9). Compare 1 Cor. ix; 2 Cor. viii-ix; Phil. iv. 10-20.

Note two great utterances here:

'Whatever a man sows, that he will also reap' (7).
'Let us not grow weary in well-doing, for in due season we shall reap, if we do not lose heart' (9).

THE CONCLUSION
(vi. 11-18)

Here Paul calls attention to his *autograph* (11), his *adversaries* (12, 13), his *apologia* (14-16), and his *apostleship* (17); and all is crowned with a brief but weighty benediction (18).

Paul was dead to himself, dead to the law, and dead to the world (ii. 19, 20; vi. 14).

Luther said: 'The world and I are well agreed. The world cares not a pin for me, and I, to cry quittance with it, care as little for the world'.

Pericles said: 'It is not gold, precious stones, statues that adorn a soldier, but a torn buckler, a cracked helmet, a blunt sword, a scarred face'.

'I bear branded on my body the owner's stamp of Jesus' (vi. 17).

Paul may have written 'with his own hand' the last paragraph only (11-18); or he may have written the whole letter. Dr. George Duncan says: 'Style and contents alike proclaim that, from first to last, Galatians was not dictated, but came direct from the hand of the Apostle'.

So ends this great personal, polemical, and practical Epistle, for which Protestants must be eternally grateful.

For the words which occur in Galatians, and nowhere else in Paul's Letters, and those which do not occur again in the N.T., see the writer's *Know Your Bible*, vol. 2, pp. 157, 158.

THE PAULINE EPISTLES

GROUP 2

ROMANS

A.D. 58

This is the last of the four Epistles of Group 2, and the greatest of them, and of all Paul's Epistles.

It was written during the three months the Apostle spent in Corinth in A.D. 58 (Acts xx. 2, 3), on his way to Jerusalem for the last time (Acts xxi. 15, 17).

In all likelihood *Galatians* was written at the same time, as a comparison of the two Letters shows (p. 107).

Romans is the most complete and systematic of all the Epistles, and the praise of it from many quarters has not been exaggerated.

ALFORD   -   'The greatest work of St. Paul.'

COLERIDGE -   'The most profound writing extant.'

GODET   -   'The greatest masterpiece which the human mind has ever conceived and realized; the first logical exposition of the work of God in Christ for the salvation of the world.'

LUTHER   -   'The chief part of the New Testament, and the perfect Gospel.'

CALVIN   -   'Every Christian man should feed upon it as the daily bread of his soul.'

MEYER   -   'The greatest and richest of all the apostolic works.'
(H.A.W.)

THOLUCK   -   'A Christian philosophy of human history.'

FARRAR   -   'It is unquestionably the clearest and fullest statement of the doctrine of sin and the doctrine of deliverance as held by the greatest of the Apostles.'

The values of the Epistle are manifold. *Historically* it throws much light upon Christianity and the world of Paul's day. *Intellectually* its form and substance make great demands upon the thoughtful mind. *Theologically* it is profound and compre-

ROME

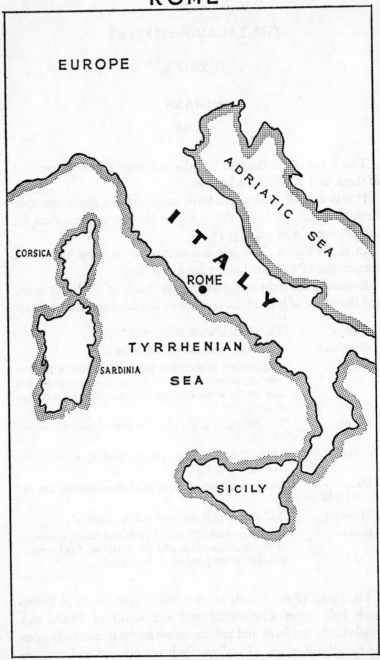

EUROPE

ADRIATIC SEA

ITALY

CORSICA

ROME

TYRRHENIAN

SEA

SARDINIA

SICILY

 MAP 34
128

hensive in its terms and teaching. *Spiritually* it is a great revelation of the scope, secret, and strength of the Christian life. *Practically* its influence upon the believing soul and in the Christian Church is incalculable.

The Epistle was taken to Rome by Phoebe, a member of the Church in Cenchreae, one of the two harbours of Corinth (xvi. 1). Surely no courier ever carried so important a document, and the loss of it would have been a calamitous disaster.

The city to which it was carried was Rome, the world's metropolis, and the centre of the world's intercourse. To this city there flowed and in it there congregated men of every nationality and social status.

It was lauded by poets and orators as 'the Queen of Cities,' 'the Home of the Gods', 'Golden Rome,' and 'the Epitome of the World.'

From the vastness of its extent, the density of its crowds, representative of every race and religion, from its being the natural treasure-house of all that was valuable and curious in the Empire, from its being the centre of political and intellectual life, from its elaborate amusements provided gratuitously for the inhabitants, it fascinated and drew to itself patriots as well as adventurers of all types.

The rich man went to Rome to enjoy himself; the poor, to beg; the new citizen to give his vote; and the citizen who had been dispossessed to reclaim his rights.

The rhetorician from Asia, the Greek philosopher, the Chaldean astrologer, the magician from Egypt, the begging priest of Isis, all jostled each other in the struggle for existence in this Metropolis.

The Rome of Paul's day was, as Farrar says, 'at the epoch of her most gorgeous gluttonies and her most gilded rottenness. No advocacy can silence the awful indictment which Paul writes to the inhabitants of the imperial city' (Rom. i. 20-32). Seneca spoke of Rome as a cesspool of iniquity, and Juvenal pictured her as a filthy sewer into which flowed the abominable dregs of every Achaean and Syrian stream.

Rome was 'crushed under the ignominies inflicted on her by the despotism of madmen and monsters; corrupted by the pol-

lutions of the stage, and hardened by the cruelties of the amphi-
theatre; swarming with parasites, imposters, poisoners, and the
vilest slaves; . . . terrorised by insolent soldiers and pauperised
mobs, the world's capital presented at this period a picture
unparalleled for shame and misery in the annals of the world'
(Farrar).

It was in this city that the Christians were, to whom Paul
wrote this magnificent Epistle; and, it would seem, there was no
central organisation, but rather that the Church consisted of a
number of little groups scattered over the great city, each with
its own rendezvous.

To which of these groups the Letter was taken, and how it
reached the other groups we are not told; but this would be easier
of accomplishment than the distribution of 'Ephesians' to the
churches of Western Asia Minor.

It is very significant that the book of the 'Acts' leaves us at
Rome. This City had been the conscious or unconscious objective
of the Christian Church from the beginning, and not without
reason.

In the great plan of God certain strategic cities were entered
and the standard of the Cross unfurled as Christianity moved
rapidly and surely westward. *Jerusalem* was the starting point,
and *Rome* was the goal, and the great halting places between
were *Antioch* in Syria, *Ephesus*, *Philippi*, and *Corinth*, and there
are profound reasons why these cities were chosen.

In the second century before Christ Jews were beginning to
spread all over the civilized world and, of course, they did not
neglect Rome. Many of them settled in the city for purposes of
business, and these, later on (B.C. 63), were greatly increased in
number by the Jewish captives which Pompey brought to the
city.

From the 'Acts' we learn that about A.D. 52 Claudius issued
an edict for the banishment of all the Jews from Rome (xviii. 2),
and Suetonius attributes it to persistent tumults in the Jewish
quarter 'at the instigation of Chrestus.'

This would seem to indicate that the early preaching of

Christianity in Rome was becoming effective. This expulsion accounts for the presence in Corinth of Aquila and Priscilla, with whom Paul stayed and worked at his and their craft (Acts xviii. 1-4).

From this Epistle to Rome it is clear that many of the Jews became Christians, and these are in view in the many references to the Old Testament, and especially in chapters ix-xi.

Tradition ascribes the founding of the Church in Rome to Peter, and claims that he was bishop there for twenty-five years.

The first of these traditions is almost certainly incorrect, and the second is foolish fable.

Had these traditions been true, surely some reference would have been made to them in 'Romans,' which went to the city, or in 'Ephesians,' 'Colossians,' and 'Philippians' which came from it.

On the contrary Paul says that he did not build on another man's foundation, but went where other apostles had not been (2 Cor. x. 15, 16; Rom. xv. 20-22), and this is given as a reason for his desire to visit Rome (cf. i. 8-15).

It is practically certain that no apostle founded the Church at Rome, but that its beginnings were due to those 'visitors from Rome, both Jews and proselytes' who were converted at Pentecost (Acts ii. 10).

Furthermore, throughout the Roman Empire at this time was great freedom of movement, and among the crowds that went to and fro there must have been Christians, disciples from Antioch, Ephesus, Corinth and other centres which had been reached by the Gospel.

Paul therefore did not go to Rome to found a Church but to find one to which he had written several years before.

The Letter to Rome was not occasioned as were the two to Corinth, by evil of a practical nature; nor as was the Letter to the Galatians, by evil of a doctrinal nature, though, no doubt, both practical and doctrinal evil existed there; but Paul's reasons for writing to Rome were different.

Three reasons may be given, and in the order of relative importance.

1. *Paul wanted to visit Rome*

He plainly says his prayer was that he might have a prosperous journey by the will of God to go to Rome; that oftentime he purposed to go to the Capital; and that he was 'ready to preach the gospel there'; that 'having no more place where he was, and having a great desire through many years' to visit the imperial city, he promised that he would do so on his journey to Spain.

Paul had preached his gospel in the East, and now, from Corinth, he looked towards the West, and to Rome the capital of civilization.

2. *The Relation of the Law to the Gospel*

Paul had just written his Letter to the Galatians, and the subject of the Law and the Gospel, of Judaism and Christianity, of works and faith, and of the relation of believing Gentiles to both, filled his mind and heart, and, guided by the Holy Spirit, he felt constrained to write more fully on this important subject.

The Epistle to the Galatians, therefore, was part of the occasion of the Roman Letter.

3. *The Completion of the Missionary Journeys*

The Apostle had been evangelising for more than ten years, during which time he had made three journeys which had taken him from the Syrian Antioch to Philippi, Athens, and Corinth. When he wrote the Letter to Rome he, probably, was little short of sixty years of age, but having regard for his permanent physical condition, and his many sufferings (2 Cor. xi. 23-29), he might well speak of himself as Paul "the aged" in A.D. 63 (Phile. 9).

There was little likelihood, therefore, that he would travel much more, and he must have felt a holy urge to summarize the substance of his apostolic preaching and teaching during these strenuous years; and this is what he has done in his Letter to Rome.

'The Epistle is the ripened fruit of the thought and struggles of the eventful years by which it had been preceded' (Sanday & Headlam); and this compendium of Christian doctrine would more widely circulate from Rome than from any other city, east or west.

Opinion differs as to the purpose of this Epistle. Some regard it as chiefly *historical*, and others, as chiefly *dogmatic*. Some regard chapters ix-xi as the dominating theme of the Epistle, and others regard these chapters as subordinate, or even as parenthetic, or irrelevant.

Others, again, consider that the Epistle is a unity, and that all its parts are related to the idea of *the Righteousness of God* (i. 16, 17).

In this latter view the Epistle is in three clearly marked divisions: the subject of the first (i. 18-viii. 39) being *The Righteousness of God in Relation to Sins and Sin*; of the second (ix-xi), *The Righteousness of God in Relation to the Calling of Israel*; and of the third (xii-xv. 13), *The Righteousness of God in Relation to Every-Day Life*.

From this we see that the first division is *Doctrinal*; the second is *Dispensational*; and the third is *Practical*. The first treats of *Salvation*; the second, of *History*; and the third, of *Behaviour*.

CHART 161

ROMANS No. 1				
	I	**II**	**III**	
	i. 18-viii. 39	ix-xi	xii. 1-xv. 13	
	DOCTRINAL	DISPENSATIONAL	PRACTICAL	
FOREWORD. i. 1-17	Philosophy of SALVATION	Philosophy of HISTORY	Philosophy of BEHAVIOUR	FINAL WORD. xv. 14-xvi. 27
	1. THE CHRISTIAN MESSAGE	1. ELECTION OF ISRAEL	1. PATHS OF DUTY	
	i. 18-v. 11	ix. 1-29	xii-xiii	
	Summary—v. 12-21	2. REJECTION OF ISRAEL	2. PRINCIPLES OF ACTION	
	2. THE CHRISTIAN LIFE	ix. 30-x. 21		
	vi. 1-viii. 30	3. CONVERSION OF ISRAEL	xiv. 1-xv. 13	
	Summary—viii. 31-39	xi. 1-36		

See the writer's *Know Your Bible*, Vol. 2, pp. 174-175; and *Salvation and Behaviour*

Looking at the Epistle as a whole we cannot but be impressed by the sequence of its parts. Omitting chapters ix-xi for a moment we see that here, as often in Paul's letters (Gal., Eph., Col.,), *creed* and *conduct* are intimately related, and in this order (i-viii; xii-xv). The Law says, Do and you shall live; but the Gospel says, Live and you will do.

The first note in the Pauline theology is not 'work out your salvation,' but 'get salvation, and then work it out,' for no one can 'work out' what is not first 'worked in' (Phil. ii. 12, 13).

It is when *doing* is put before *doctrine* that the saying is true, 'Doing is a deadly thing; doing ends in death.' Paul does not begin to build the house of life from the roof, but he first lays a firm foundation on which a substantial house can safely rest. The Apostle never exhorts men to work *towards* salvation, but always, to work *from* it.

Paul and James are not at variance. Paul says, 'faith should lead on to works,' and James says, 'only works can prove that you have faith.'

DIVISION I

DOCTRINAL (i. 18-viii. 39)

The Righteousness of God in Relation to Sin and Sins

A logical sequence is observable in the Doctrinal division (i-viii). The Apostle's first concern is with the *Christian Message* (i-v), and then, with the *Christian Life* (vi-viii).

Without the Christian Message the Christian Life is impossible. Truth must precede experience. It is the Message that shows the need for Life, and the Life proves the truth of the Message.

CHART 162

ROMANS No. 2	
I. DOCTRINAL. PHILOSOPHY OF SALVATION. i. 18–viii. 39	
1. THE CHRISTIAN MESSAGE	2. THE CHRISTIAN LIFE
i. 18–v. 21	vi. 1–viii. 39
(i) CONDEMNATION. i. 18–iii. 20	**(i) SANCTIFICATION. vi. 1–viii. 11**
(a) Of the GENTILES - - i. 18-32	(a) The PRINCIPLE of It - vi. 1-14
(b) Of the JEWS - - ii. 1-iii. 8	(b) The PRACTICE of It vi. 15-vii. 6
(c) Of the WORLD - iii. 9-20	(c) The PREVENTIVE of It vii. 7-25
	(d) The POWER of It - viii. 1-11
(ii) JUSTIFICATION. iii. 21–v. 11	**(ii) GLORIFICATION. viii. 12-30**
(a) The GROUND of It - - iii. 21-26	(a) The PROMISE of It. - viii. 12-17
(b) The MEANS of It - iii. 27-iv. 25	(b) The EXPECTATION of It viii. 18-27
(c) The EFFECT of It - - v. 1-11	(c) The CERTAINTY of It viii. 28-30
SUMMARY. v. 12-21	**SUMMARY. viii. 31-39**

1. THE CHRISTIAN MESSAGE
(i-v)

There are two dominating notes in the *Christian Message—Condemnation* and *Justification*, and they are struck in this order. There is no need for Justification where there is no Condemnation. Freedom cannot be given where there is no bondage, and life cannot be imparted where it already exists. In the Divine purpose the act of Justification follows on the fact of Condemnation; and the blessing of Justification is as wide as the bane of Condemnation.

'God so loved the world, that He gave His only begotten Son, that whosoever believeth in Him should not perish, but have everlasting life.'

(i) CONDEMNATION (i. 18-iii. 20)

The Apostle shows that under *Condemnation* are all Gentiles and all Jews; that, therefore, all the world is condemned (i. 18-iii. 20).

For a religion to be universally applicable and effectual it must answer to universal need, and it is here shown that the need to which the Christian religion answers is universal. No other religion answers to world-need, and, therefore, no other religion is universal in its scope.

The Condemnation of the Gentiles is dealt with first (i. 18-32), and their responsibility, guilt, and punishment are set forth. Their responsibility is the cause of their guilt, and their punishment is the effect of it.

(*a*) *Responsibility* just means ability to respond, and such ability must always have its roots in knowledge. It is here emphatically declared that the Gentiles have knowledge which makes them responsible (i. 18-20).

Religion is *natural* and *revealed*. By the former we have knowledge of God and of our duty from natural sources; and by the latter, from special and specific revelation, as in Judaism and Christianity. When Paul charges the Jews (chapter ii) he takes his stand on the latter ground; but when he addresses the Gentiles he does so on the former ground.

The material and moral realms are manifestations of Deity. Not only is He revealed in human consciousness, but that consciousness is part of the revelation.

A philosopher has said that there are two wonderful things—the starry world, and the moral law. By the world within we are able to apprehend the world without, and to rise, as Philo said, 'from below upwards, as if by a kind of celestial ladder, guessing at the Creator from His works by probable inference.'

(*b*) *Guilt* is a terrible thing, and the guilt of Paganism has never been stated more terribly than in this passage (i. 21-32).

The Gentiles, and especially the Gentiles of Rome are charged with perverseness (18), irreligion (21*a*), pride (21*b*, 22), idolatry (23, 35), sensuality (24, 26, 27), wrongness—of which there are 21 illustrations—and incorrigibility (32).

This catalogue of evils is simply devastating; and does any of us stand outside of it?

(*c*) *Punishment* follows inevitably on such guilt, and this passage shows the attitude and action of God (18, 24, 26-28, 32).

Thrice it says, 'God gave them up' (24, 26, 28), by which is meant, not only that He lets sinners have their own way, but also that the consequence of their sin is judicially inflicted. 'Those who do such things deserve to die' (32, R.S.V.).

The Condemnation of the Jews follows (ii. 1-iii. 8).

The Jewish critic is in the same position as the Gentile sinner, because God is no respecter of persons (ii. 1-11). Not the hearers of the Law are just before Him, but only the doers of it (ii. 12-16).

True, the Jew has a special revelation, but he has transgressed it (ii. 17-24); and because of his character and conduct his circumcision is of no avail (ii. 25-29).

It is true that the Jew has great advantages, but he cannot be saved by these if he is out of harmony with them (iii. 1-8).

The Condemnation of the whole World is therefore shown (iii. 9-20). The Scriptures declare the universality of human guilt (iii. 10-18); and the Jew is shown that the Law which reveals sin cannot remove it.

It is only when the truth of universal condemnation is apprehended and acknowledged that we are ready for the next part of the Christian Message—the gospel of Justification (iii. 21-v. 11).

(ii) JUSTIFICATION (iii. 21-v. 11)

The Ground of Justification is God's Grace (iii. 21-26)

The statement, 'Justified freely by His grace through the redemption that is in Christ Jesus' (24), is the heart of the Epistle, and of the Christian Message.

What a conjunction of great words and ideas! *'justified,' 'freely,' 'grace,' 'redemption,' 'Christ Jesus.'*

To 'justify' means 'to pronounce righteous,' and here (21-26) we are told that righteousness has its *source* in God, that it is *manifested* or revealed, that it is *independent* of the Law, that it was *predicted,* that it is *bestowed,* that it is *costly,* that it is *atoning,* that it is *ethical,* that it is *effective,* and that it is *final.*

The Means of Justification is our Faith (iii. 27-iv. 25).

Justification cannot be by human merit, neither can it be by faith in our faith, but only by faith in the justifying God. This is shown in the history of Abraham who believed before he was circumcised (iv. 1-12).

The promise made to him was not conditioned by law-keeping but by faith, and this makes all who believe, whether Jew or Gentile, Abraham's spiritual posterity (iv. 13-18).

Abraham's faith, and the Christian's, relate to life from the dead which is consummated in Christ who died for our trespasses, and was raised for our justification (iv. 19-25).

The Effect of Justification is Assurance (v. 1-11)

Assurance as to the past (v. 1); as to the present (v. 1, 2); and as to the future (v. 2).

Afflictions cannot destroy this assurance (v. 3-5), for it is confirmed by God's great love manifested in Christ (v. 6-8); so we may make our boast in God who, through Christ, has vouchsafed to us this reconciliation (v. 9-11).

In a wonderful passage (v. 12-21) all that has preceded is summarized. Condemnation and Justification are traced to their historical sources in Adam and Christ. (See the writer's *Salvation and Behaviour*, p. 27, 28).

2. THE CHRISTIAN LIFE
(vi.-viii.)

As in the Message there were two notes, so here there are two; *Sanctification* relating to the *present* (vi. 1-viii. 11), and *Glorification* relating to the *future* (viii. 12-30).

SANCTIFICATION (vi. 1-viii. 11)

In unfolding the true doctrine of *Sanctification* the Apostle has four things to say; and these relate to the *Principle* (vi. 1-14), the *Practice* (vi. 15-vii. 6), the *Preventive* (vii. 7-25), and the *Power* of Sanctification (viii. 1-11).

This summary is expanded in the author's 'Salvation and Behaviour', pp. 29ff., which reads in part:

'This statement in chs. vi-viii is the classic on the subject of the Christian Life, and cannot be given too close attention. . . . The first five chapters are the *foundation* on which the *superstructure* of chapters six to eight rests. Not only must the *Christian Message* be believed before the *Christian Life* can be lived, but the *Christian Life* is the proof that the *Christian Message* has been believed. There cannot be fruit where there is no root, but the proof of the root is the fruit.

Our Justification is in the Crucified Saviour, and our Sanctification is in the Risen Lord. By the separation of these two subjects in the Church's thinking and teaching, the loss in Christian experience has been incalculable. Justification by faith in Christ is only the beginning of God's purpose for us, and the continuance of that purpose is a life lived according to a revealed pattern. What that pattern is, appears in chapters vi-viii of this Epistle. . . .

In the first place, the *Principle of Holiness* is stated, which consists in the individual's identification with Christ in His death and resurrection (vi. 1-11). . . . This leads to a consideration of the *Practice of Holiness* which is realized in the believer's abandonment to his new relations as a Christian (vi. 12-vii. 6).

But such a life will not go unchallenged, and so the *Preventive of Holiness* is set forth, which is seen to be the activity within of sin and of self (vii. 7-25).

And finally, the *Power of Holiness* is shown to be the unhindered dominion over us of the Holy Spirit (viii. 1-17).

Here nothing is omitted which would help us better to understand and more fully to realize what Christ meant when He said: 'I am come that ye might have life (chs. i-v), and that ye might have it abundantly' (chs. vi-viii. 17). . . .

The Apostle is dealing with that for which we were justified, a life rooted in a principle which, if apprehended and believed, is productive of holiness.

What, then, is this principle? It is the Christian's recognition of his *identification with Christ in His death and resurrection*. . . .

This identification with Christ is the profoundest truth in the

New Testament, and is . . . a challenge to the common experience of Christian people. We who in Adam were 'dead *in* sin' are now in Christ 'dead *to* sin'.

What is here declared *is a fact for faith*, and *not an emotion* for experience, and it is squarely based on the immediately preceding passage concerning the federal headships of Adam and Christ (v. 12-21). Our state by nature is one of sin under the headship of Adam, and our state by grace is one of death to sin under the headship of Christ.

The Greek aorist tense, which denotes a single and completed past act . . . occurs eleven times in the eleven verses, vi. 1-11, with reference to our identification with Christ in death, burial and resurrection. Mark what the passage says: 'We *died* to sin' (2); 'We *were baptized* into His death' (twice, 3); 'We *were buried* with Him into death' (4); 'We *were raised up* from the dead' (4); 'Our old self *was crucified* with Him' (6); 'He who *died* (i.e. Christ, 7); 'We died with Christ' (8); 'Christ *raised* from the dead' (9); 'He died' (i.e. Christ, 10, twice).

These references mean that as definitely as Christ by an act died, and by an act was raised from the dead, so in His death and resurrection every believer died to sin and rose to 'newness of life'. Our 'old self was crucified' when Christ was crucified. All we were and are from Adam, God has rejected, and *judicially*, not *experimentally*, it was put an end to. The crucifixion of self is not something that we can accomplish, for it was accomplished on Calvary. In chs. i-v we are shown that *Christ died for us*, and in ch. vi we are told that *we died with Him*.

Christ died both *for* sin and *unto* it. We could not die *for* it, but in Christ's death we did die *unto* it. Then and there He made His own relation to sin the believer's relation to it, so that we are to 'reckon ourselves dead to sin and living to God.'

We have given detailed attention to this *Principle of Holiness* because of its tremendous importance for an understanding of the innermost significance of being a Christian.

When this great portion of the Epistle is understood and acted upon, schools of teaching on sanctification will disappear, and the Christian will live his life on the God-appointed level.

GLORIFICATION (viii. 12-30)

But the Christian life does not end in this world. It is continued and perfected in the next world (viii. 12-30). What grace commences here, glory will consummate there.

Of this truth, which is one of revelation, Paul speaks of the *Promise* of it (viii. 12-17), the *Expectation* of it (viii. 18-27), and the *Certainty* of it (viii. 28-30).

In this portion of the Epistle occur some of the greatest utterances in all the Bible.

> 'The sufferings of this present time are not worth comparing with the glory that is to be revealed to us' (18).
> 'The Spirit Himself intercedes for us with sighs too deep for words' (26).
> 'We know that in everything God works for good with those who love Him' (28).

Indeed, the whole portion (viii. 12-30) is a lyric of transport and delight.

Following this, and concluding the doctrinal division of the Epistle is a paean of triumph without parallel (viii. 31-39). The Authorized Version cannot be bettered here.

> 'What shall we then say to these things?
> If God be for us, who can be against us?
> He that spared not His own Son, but delivered Him up for us all, how shall He not with Him also freely give us all things?
> Who shall lay any thing to the charge of God's elect?
> It is God that justifieth.
> Who is he that condemneth?
> It is Christ that died, yea rather, that is risen again, Who is even at the right hand of God,
> Who also maketh intercession for us.
> Who shall separate us from the love of Christ?
> Shall tribulation, or distress, or persecution, or famine, or nakedness, or peril, or sword? . . .
> Nay, in all these things we are more than conquerors through Him that loved us.'

(In the A.V. verses 33, 34 are not questions, though almost certainly they should be).

We sinners, from our nadir of despair in chapters i. 18-iii. 20, are lifted to the zenith of triumph in chapter viii, by Him who, while we were yet sinners, died for us and rose again. Hallelujah.

DIVISION II

DISPENSATIONAL (ix-xi)

The Righteousness of God in Relation to the Calling of Israel

To pass from chapters i-viii to chapters xii-xv, from doctrine to practice, is natural and logical, but, on this account, it must not be assumed that chapters ix-xi are an interjection, or are irrelevant. Had these three chapters been omitted Paul's summary of his missionary message would have been sadly defective, for in the redemptive purpose and plan of God the Jews had not only a place, but a primary place.

In this Epistle Paul had already referred to them—in chapters ii-iii. 8, and chapter iv, and necessarily had to do so again if his review of the redemptive process was to be complete.

In the consideration of his theme the Old Testament is not only relevant but vital, and the Old Testament is the record of Israel's place in the outworking of the redemptive design.

CHART 163

ROMANS No. 3		
II. DISPENSATIONAL.	PHILOSOPHY OF HISTORY (ix.-xi.)	
1. ELECTION OF ISRAEL	2. REJECTION OF ISRAEL	3. CONVERSION OF ISRAEL
ix. 1-29	ix. 30-x. 21	xi. 1-36
(i) THE SUBJECTS ix. 1-5	(i) RIGHTEOUSNESS was sought by WORKS and not by FAITH. ix. 30-x. 13	(i) REJECTION is not TOTAL xi. 1-10
(ii) THE VINDICATION ix. 6-29	(ii) OPPORTUNITY and WARNING were NEGLECTED x. 14-21	(ii) REJECTION is not FINAL xi. 11-32
		DOXOLOGY. xi. 33-36
PAST	PRESENT	FUTURE

The significance of the Jew in history is a subject sadly neglected by Christians in general, but this negligence does not and cannot diminish its importance. We are not done with the Jew yet, and will not be, until God's purpose is fulfilled, and not even then.

They are nearer the truth who regard chapters ix-xi as the keystone in the arch of revelation which 'Romans' presents than they are who regard it as simply parenthetic.

The argument of these three chapters follows the line of history. The *election* of Israel relates to the *past*; their *rejection* relates to the *present*; and their *conversion* relates to the *future*.

This division of the Epistle is a true *philosophy of history*. If in the attempt to understand the real significance of history the Jew is recognized only as marginal, error and confusion must result.

1. THE ELECTION OF ISRAEL (ix. 1-29)

(i) *The Subjects of Election* (ix. 1-5)

The matter of *election* is a difficult one, and a degree of mystery will always be attached to it. Two things, however, are true, whether or not we can harmonize them, namely, the sovereignty of God, and the free will of man. Neither of these can cancel out the other. They are both taught in Scripture, and exemplified in experience.

What it is important to notice in this division of 'Romans' is that the election spoken of is not of an individual but of a nation.

Why did God choose the Hebrews, and not the Egyptians, or Assyrians, or Babylonians, or any other race? (Deut. vii. 6-8). And why was world-history associated with the Jordan, and not with the Tigris, or the Euphrates, or the Nile, or the Tiber?

Those who think about this may give different answers, but none can deny the fact.

(ii) *The Vindication of Election* (ix. 6-29)

After deploring the estrangement between Israel and the Messiah (ix. 1-5), the Apostle vindicates God's attitude towards the Jewish race. He shows that

(i) *It is consistent with the Divine Promises* (ix. 6-13):
  (*a*) to Abraham (6-9);
  (*b*) to Jacob (10-13).

    (ii) *It is consistent with the Divine Justice* (ix. 14-18):

        (*a*) The case of Moses (14-16);

        (*b*) The case of Pharaoh (17, 18).

    (iii) *It is consistent with the Divine Authority* (ix. 19-24):

        (*a*) The Absoluteness of it (19-21);

        (*b*) The Exercise of it (22-24).

    (iv) *It is consistent with the Divine Revelation* (ix. 25-29):

        (*a*) Relative to the Gentiles (25, 26);

        (*b*) Relative to the Jews (27-29).

2. THE REJECTION OF ISRAEL (ix. 30-x. 21)

(i) *Righteousness was Sought by Works, not by Faith* (ix. 30-x. 13)

Here the Apostle turns from the consideration of God's sovereignty to that of man's responsibility.

Israel is rejected by God because it rejected God. 'He came to His own world and His own people received Him not' (John i. 11).

The Jews have been rejected because they sought righteousness by works and not by faith; and the Gentiles have been accepted because they sought it, not by works, but by faith (ix. 30-33).

The Jews' pursuit of righteousness, though zealous, has been ignorant (x. 1-4).

This ignorance of the Jews is inexcusable, because their Scriptures declare that righteousness is not by works but by faith, alike for Jew and Gentile (x. 5-13).

(ii) *Opportunity and Warning were Neglected* (x. 14-21)

The universal proclamation of the Gospel has made universal faith possible (x. 14-17).

The Jews' rejection of the Gospel, and the Gentiles' acceptance of it, had been foretold (x. 18-21).

The historical and spiritual strands in this argument are inextricably interwoven.

3. THE CONVERSION OF ISRAEL (xi. 1-36)

This is a passage of great historical and prophetical importance: historical in verses 1-10; and prophetical in verses 11-32.

(i) *The Rejection of Israel is not Total* (xi. 1-10)

Paul's line of argument is that:

> (a) *A Remnant of the Jews is Saved* (1-5a):
>   A personal illustration (1);
>   A historical analogy (2-4);
>   A present fact (5a).
>
> (b) *This Remnant is saved by grace, and not by works* (5b, 6):
>
> (c) *It is a Remnant that is saved, and not the Nation of Israel* (7-10):
>   The Nation's rejection is accounted for (7, 8);
>   The Nation's rejection was predicted (9, 10).

The Apostle now goes on to show that:

(ii) *The Rejection of Israel is not Final* (xi. 11-32)

> (a) The Fall of Israel has brought present blessing to the Gentiles (11-14);
>
> (b) The Restoration of Israel will bring universal blessing (15);
>
> (c) Israel's future is guaranteed by its past (16);
>
> (d) Illustration of the Olive Tree (16-24);
>   A warning to the Gentiles (16-22);
>   A promise to the Jews (23, 24).
>
> (e) Israel's present position and future prospect (25-27);
>
> (f) The Divine programme for Jew and Gentile (28-32).

We have called these three chapters (ix-xi) *dispensational,* and by this is meant a *method* and a *period*; God's dealing with the nation of Israel, and the time—past, present, and future—during which He so deals with them.

This makes it necessary to distinguish between *Jews* and *Gentiles,* and between both, and the *Church* of God (1 Cor. x. 32).

It distinguishes also between the earthly *Kingdom* and the heavenly *Ecclesia.*

Augustine said: 'Distinguish the dispensations and you will understand the Scriptures'; and Dr. David Brown said: 'Those who think that in all the Evangelical prophecies of the Old Testament, the terms "Jacob," "Israel," etc., are to be understood solely of the Christian Church, would appear to read the

Old Testament differently from the Apostle, who, from the use of those very terms in Old Testament prophecy draws arguments to prove that God has mercy in store for the natural Israel.'

The importance of recognizing the distinction between Israel and the Church—between Rom. vi-viii, and ix-xi—can be seen by bringing two passages together:

> 'Nothing *"shall be able to separate us* from the love of God, which is in Christ Jesus our Lord"' (viii. 38, 39).
> 'If God spared not the natural branches, neither will He spare thee.' 'If thou continue (not) in His goodness, *thou also shalt be cut off*' (xi. 21, 22).

The latter statement could not be made of Christians; and the former statement could not be made of Israel.

> O the depth of the riches
> Both of the wisdom and knowledge of God!
> How unsearchable are His judgments,
> And His ways past finding out!
>
> For who hath known the mind of the Lord?
> Or who hath been His counsellor?
> Or who hath first given to Him?
> And it shall be recompensed unto him again.
>
> For of Him (Source), and through Him (Means),
> And to Him (End), are all things.
> To Whom be glory for ever.   Amen.

DIVISION III

PRACTICAL (xii. 1-xv. 13)

The Righteousness of God in Relation to Every Day Life

Christianity is not an *ethic*, nor a *philosophy*, though it is both ethical and philosophical, but it is a *life*. It is not intellectual theory, but energetic character. And because this is so this great Epistle devotes four of its sixteen chapters—a quarter of the whole—to telling Christians how to behave.

This is not an anticlimax, but the crown of Christianity.

The dominating notes of this Division are *Duty* and *Action*; the *Paths* of the one, and the *Principles* of the other are made clear.

CHART 164

ROMANS No. 4

III. PRACTICAL. PHILOSOPHY OF BEHAVIOUR xii. 1-xv. 13	
1. PATHS OF DUTY. xii-xiii	2. PRINCIPLES OF ACTION. xiv. 1- xv. 13

(i) THE VARIOUS SPHERES
      xii. 1-xiii. 7
Religious xii. 1-13
Social   xii. 14-21
Civil   xiii. 1-7
	(i) MUTUAL TOLERATION
	    xiv. 1-12

(ii) THE IMPELLING POWER Love xiii. 8-10	(ii) BROTHERLY OBLIGATION xiv. 13-23

(iii) THE GREAT INCENTIVE
Christ's Return
    xiii. 11-14
	(iii) CHRISTLIKE CONSIDERATION
	    xv. 1-13

1. PATHS OF DUTY (xii-xiii)

This subject is dealt with briefly yet with singular comprehensiveness. It shows in what spheres the Christian's duty lies; what is the impelling power of it; and what is its great incentive.

(i) *The Various Spheres of Duty* (xii. 1-xiii. 7)

The fundamental conditions of Christian living are set forth in two profound verses (xii. 1, 2) from which we learn that the conditions are both outward and inward.

The outward condition is the dedication of the body; and the inward condition is the renewal of the mind.

Relative to the inward condition a *programme* is presented: 'Be not conformed . . . but be transformed'; a *process* is unfolded: 'By the renewing of your mind'; and a *purpose* is revealed: 'That ye may prove what is the will of God, the good, and well-pleasing, and perfect (will).'

This foundation laid, it is now shown that the Christian's duty lies in several spheres which must not be confounded.

Every Christian is living in the *Church* (xii. 3-13), in the *World* (xii. 14-21) and in the *State* (xiii. 1-7), and in each of these his duty lies.

In the Church our responsibility is both *corporate* (xii. 4-8), and *individual* (xii. 9-13).

In the World our duty is manifold; and the Apostle names eleven aspects of it: beneficence, sympathy, harmony, humility, non-self-complacency, non-retaliation, goodness, peaceableness, non-avengement, magnanimity, and conquest. (See the writer's *Salvation and Behaviour* pp. 88-92).

In the State the Christian must recognize properly constituted authority, and be subject to it, as long as such subjection does not violate his duty to God.

(ii) *The Impelling Power of Duty* (xiii. 8-10)

In a few words are two exhortations: one negative—'owe no man anything'; and one positive—'love one another.' Volumes could be written on this.

(iii) *The Great Incentive of Duty* (xiii. 11-14)

This incentive is the Lord's Return. 'The night is far spent; the day is at hand; let us . . . let us . . . let us.' Here *past*, *future*, and *present* are brought together.

Paul says, 'Wake up; dress properly; and walk decently.' 'He that hath an ear let him hear what the Spirit saith.'

2. PRINCIPLES OF ACTION (xiv. 1-xv. 13)

All our actions should be guided by principles, and it will be well for us to know what these principles are. In this part of the Epistle Paul names three: toleration, obligation, and consideration.

(i) *Christians ought to exhibit Mutual Toleration* (xiv. 1-12).

What we should hesitate to do the Apostle does—he classifies Christians as *strong* and *weak*—and, of course, this distinction does exist.

The 'strong' should beware of latitudinarianism; and the 'weak', of obscurantism.

'Weak' Christians are such as are tortured in their conscience about what food to eat (2-4), and what days to keep (5); but Christians who are growing-up will be less and less troubled about these things, because they will be able to distinguish between things indifferent and essential.

The problem of 1 Cor. viii. 7-13 was local, and not universal; but what is written in Col. ii. 16-23 is applicable all the time and everywhere.

One Christian should not laugh at another who eats vegetables only, and the other should not scowl on the one who eats meat also.

Mutual toleration must be exercised also by those who do, and those who do not observe what Keble calls 'The Christian Year.'

The principle here enjoined is applicable to a great variety of matters, and we should relate ourselves to these as they arise, and in the spirit of this passage.

(ii) *Christians should acknowledge Brotherly Obligation* (xiv. 13-23).

Attention is here called to the relative importance of Christian *liberty* and Christian *love*.

It is not always right for us to do all that it would be right for us to do.

There is something greater than *liberty*, and that is *love*. 'There is a great possibility of hurting our fellow-Christians by actions lawful in themselves, and by insisting on rights which God has undoubtedly given to us' (Griffith Thomas).

In actual practice it may be difficult to decide how far one should go in the way of self-denial in concession to the scruples of those who are weak in the faith, but the principle is here plainly set forth.

Love must have the last vote.

(iii) *Christians should exercise Christlike Consideration* (xv. 1-13).

'We that are able ought to bear the weaknesses of the unable, and not to *please* ourselves. Let each of us *please* his neighbour, as regards what is good, with a view to edification. For even Christ did not *please* Himself' (1-3).

Pleasing is obedience with a plus. What we 'ought' to do we should do.

Dr. Griffith Thomas' analysis of verses 1-7 is: 'Obligation (1); Edification (2); Imitation (3); Confirmation (3); Inspiration (4); Supplication (5, 6); Application (7).'

Christ, the Bible, and Prayer will enable us to live as we should in our manifold relations.

From speaking of the weak and the strong the Apostle passes on to the larger subject of the Jew and the Gentile (xv. 8-13). Of this paragraph Sanday and Headlam say:

> 'St. Paul has a double object. He writes to remind the Gentiles that it is through the Jews that they are called, the Jews that the aim and purpose of their existence is the calling of the Gentiles. The Gentiles must remember that Christ became a Jew to save them; the Jew that Christ came among them in order that all the families of the earth might be blessed: both must realize that the aim of the whole is to proclaim God's glory.'

Paul's FINAL WORD (xv. 14-xvi. 27) consists of a number of words. First there are some explanations (xv. 14-21); then, a statement of plans (xv. 22-29); then, a request for prayer (xv. 30-33); then, a number of greetings (xvi. 1-16); then, a warning against false teachers (xvi. 17-20); then, more greetings (xvi. 21-24); and then, a final doxology (xvi. 25-27).

Thus ends the greatest of this Apostle's writings: great historically, dispensationally, philosophically, evidentially, doctrinally, prophetically, spiritually, and practically.

Well did Luther say: 'All wherein true Christianity consisteth . . . is to be found here in such perfection that it is impossible to wish anything more or better. So rich a treasure is it of spiritual wealth that even to him who has read it a thousand times something new will ever be presenting itself.'

> Glory be to the Father, and to the Son,
> and to the Holy Ghost.

THE PAULINE EPISTLES

GROUP 3

COLOSSIANS

PHILEMON

EPHESIANS

PHILIPPIANS
A.D. 61-63

The Prison Epistles

CHRIST AND THE CHURCH

The Lord

THE PAULINE EPISTLES

GROUP 3. A.D. 61-63
COLOSSIANS PHILEMON EPHESIANS PHILIPPIANS

The Divine Life Epistles

CHRIST AND THE CHURCH

The Lord

NOTES

Let us keep before us the fact that the letters of the Apostle Paul fall into four groups, each of which has its distinctive characteristics.

Group 1. 1-2 THESSALONIANS.
            The Second Advent. *Eschatological.*

Group 2. 1-2 CORINTHIANS. GALATIANS. ROMANS.
            The Truth about Salvation. *Soteriological.*

Group 3. COLOSSIANS. PHILEMON. EPHESIANS. PHILIPPIANS.
            Christ and the Church. *Christological.*

Group 4. 1 TIMOTHY. TITUS. 2 TIMOTHY.
            Church Organization. *Ecclesiological.*

These groups are separated from one another in time by about four years: A.D. 52-53; 57-58; 62-63; 67-68. (Chart 147; p. 17).

The differences in theme and style in these groups are due to Paul's outlook at the time, and the changing circumstances of and within the Christian Church in the evangelized areas.

The first and fourth groups present an impressive contrast. The first relates to Christ's Second Advent as not distant; and the fourth envisages an indefinite period before the Advent, necessitating Church organization.

The second and third groups also present sharp contrasts. In the second there is stress and storm, but in the third this gives way to a deep calm. Contest characterizes the second group, but contemplation, the third. In group two there is travail, but in group three this is exchanged for tranquillity. (Chart 149; p. 23).

When group two was written Paul was at the height of his

free ministry. He had been evangelizing for about twenty years, and he was about fifty-eight years of age. But when group three was written Paul was no longer free, but a captive in Rome, though not in the public prison.

It was this captivity that gave the Apostle the opportunity to *think* in a way he could not do when he was travelling long distances.

But for his captivity would these Epistles ever have been written? If Ezekiel had not been a captive abroad, if John had not been exiled on Patmos, and if Bunyan had never been in Bedford gaol, would they ever have given us their immortal writings?

A careful examination of the Prison Epistles will show that they are different in character though all four were written about the same time.

Colossians and Ephesians are a pair, as are Galatians and Romans; and, as we shall see, they treat of two aspects of one subject, namely, *Christ and the Church*.

To what extent Ephesians and Colossians are a pair the following passages will show; placing Ephesians first for the comparison.

CHART 165

COMPARISON OF PRISON EPISTLES			
EPHESIANS	COLOSSIANS	EPHESIANS	COLOSSIANS
i. 4	i. 22	iv. 1	i. 10
i. 7	i. 14	iv. 2–4	iii. 12 ff.
i. 10	i. 20	iv. 15 f.	ii. 19
i. 15–17	i. 3, 4	iv. 18	i. 21
i. 18	i. 27	iv. 22 ff.	iii. 8 ff.
i. 19	ii. 12	iv. 29, 31	
i. 21–23	i. 16–19	iv. 32–v. 1	iii. 12
ii. 1	i. 21	v. 3–6	iii. 5 f.
ii. 5	ii. 13	v. 15 f.	iv. 5
ii. 6	ii. 12	v. 19	iii. 16
ii. 12	i. 21	v. 21–vi. 9	iii. 18–iv. 1
ii. 15	i. 20, ii. 14		
ii. 20	ii. 7	vi. 18–20	iv. 2–4
		vi. 21	iv. 7
iii. 1–3, 5	i. 23–26		
iii. 7	i. 29		
iii. 8 f.	i. 27		

The best explanation—indeed, the only sensible one—is that Paul wrote these two Epistles at about the same time, when his mind and heart were full of the subject which is their common denominator.

There are manifest differences between these Epistles, but the differences are less prominent than their coincidences.

Colossians is polemical, and Ephesians is irenical. In Colossians it is shown that Christ is the Church's Head, and in Ephesians, that the Church is Christ's Body. Colossians is characterized by discussion, and Ephesians, by reflection. In Colossians Paul is the apologist, and in Ephesians he is the theologian. In Colossians he is the soldier, and in Ephesians he is the builder. The destination of Colossians is local, but the destination of Ephesians is widespread. (See Vol. II, p. 489).

Philemon and Philippians differ much from Colossians and Ephesians, and also from one another. Philemon is the only extant example of Paul's private correspondence; and Philippians, though personal in character, was written, not to an individual, but to a Church.

CHART 166

THE PRISON EPISTLES			
Place of Writing: ROME		*Date*: A.D. 61–63	
COLOSSIANS	EPHESIANS	PHILEMON	PHILIPPIANS
Local Assembly Letter	Circular Letter	Private Letter	Local Assembly Letter
DOCTRINAL		ETHICAL	SOCIAL
CHRIST THE CHURCH'S HEAD	THE CHURCH CHRIST'S BODY	MASTER AND SLAVE	AN APOSTLE'S GRATITUDE
Polemical	Irenical	Personal	Affectional
CHRIST IN ALL	ALL IN CHRIST	CHRIST IN THE HOME	CHRIST IN THE ASSEMBLY
Paul's Mind		Paul's Heart	
Apologist	Theologian	Gentleman	Saint
Discussion	Reflection	Mediation	Friendship
Asia	Asia	Asia	Europe
Carried by TYCHICUS iv. 7	Carried by TYCHICUS vi. 21	Carried by ONESIMUS 12-14	Carried by EPAPHRODITUS ii. 25

It will become evident that in Paul's most theological Epistles he is personal, and in his most personal Epistles he is theological.

The destinations of the Prison Epistles will be seen on map 29, p. 20 and map 35, p. 159.

The chronological order of these Epistles is a matter of dispute, and a matter of little importance.

Here we take Colossians first; then the encyclical letter, Ephesians; and as in Philippians, Paul is anticipating release from captivity, we place this Epistle last, though many critics put it first.

Psychological reasons would lead us to the view that Colossians was written before Ephesians; that the calm would follow the controversy.

THE PRISON EPISTLES
COLOSSIANS
A.D. 62-63

Attention has been called to the fact that, in a special way, by both comparison and contrast, Colossians and Ephesians belong to one another, as do Galatians and Romans.

The *comparisons* relate to time and theme. Quite obviously, these Epistles were written about the same time (A.D. 62-63) by the same person (Paul) and at the same place (Rome). Both were sent to Western Asia Minor; and both have for their theme Christ and the Church. Seventy-eight identical phrases appear in both Colossians and Ephesians.

The *contrasts* also are obvious. Ephesians was an encyclical letter, but Colossians was sent to a local Church.

The one has no greetings, and the other has a number (Eph. vi; Col. iv).

Calm characterizes the one, and controversy the other. The theme of the one is treated more fully than that of the other, as Romans is a fuller treatment of Galatians.

The one attacks no heresy, but the other quite clearly does. The one is Ecclesiological, and the other is Christological.

The one shows the Church to be Christ's Body, and the other shows Christ to be the Church's Head.

In Colossians are 55 words which occur in none of Paul's other Epistles, and 34 of these occur nowhere else in the New Testament.

In Ephesians are 42 words which occur nowhere else in the New Testament.

Further comparisons and contrasts are in the Notes on Ephesians. (See the author's *Know Your Bible*, Vol. II, pp. 190, 213, 214).

The view has been ably defended that what are called the Prison Epistles were written, not at Rome, but during Paul's two years' imprisonment at Caesarea. This is not the place to debate this question, but it may be said that the facts point to Rome rather than to Caesarea. (*contra, Bacon, Haupt, Meyer*).

In Philippians, for instance, which is one of this group, Paul anticipates release from captivity; but he had no such hope in Caesarea. On the contrary, he had appealed to Rome, and it was decided that, as a prisoner, he would go there; an event to which he looked forward (Acts xxv-xxvii).

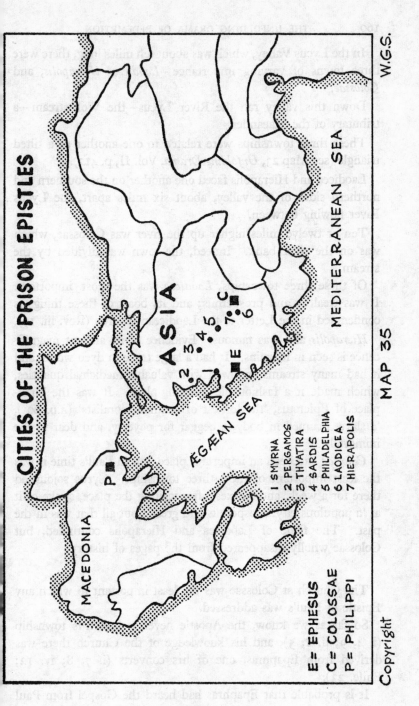

CITIES OF THE PRISON EPISTLES

W.G.S.

MEDITERRANEAN SEA

ASIA

ÆGÆAN SEA

MACEDONIA

1 SMYRNA
2 PERGAMOS
3 THYATIRA
4 SARDIS
5 PHILADELPHIA
6 LAODICEA
7 HIERAPOLIS

E = EPHESUS
C = COLOSSAE
P = PHILIPPI

MAP 35

Copyright

In the Lycus Valley, which was about ten miles long, there were three towns of varying importance—*Laodicea*, *Hierapolis*, and *Colossae*.

Down this valley ran the River Lycus—the Wolf-stream—a tributary of the Maeander.

These three townships were related to one another as a tilted triangle (see Map 23, *Unfolding Drama*, Vol. II, p. 412).

Laodicea and Hierapolis faced one another on the southern and northern sides of the valley, about six miles apart, the Lycus River flowing between.

Ten or twelve miles higher up the river was Colossae, which was on the river bank. Indeed, the town was divided by the stream.

Of these three townships, *Laodicea* was the most important. It was wealthy and prosperous; and its boast of these things is condemned in the Letter to the Laodicean Church (Rev. iii. 19).

Hierapolis also was famous. Evidence of its ancient magnificence is seen in its ruins. It had a large trade in dyed wools, and it had many streams endowed with valuable medicinal qualities, which made it a fashionable watering-place. It was the birthplace of Epictetus, 'the loftiest of heathen moralists' (A.D. 60-), 'a slave, maimed in body, a beggar for poverty, and dear to the immortals'.

Colossae had been an important place, but in Paul's time it was the least important of these three townships. Cyrus sojourned there for a week, and Xerxes, after visiting the place, spoke of it as 'a populous city, prosperous and great'; but all that was in the past. The fame of Laodicea and Hierapolis continued, but Colossae wholly disappeared from the pages of history.

The Church at Colossae was the least important to which any Epistle of Paul's was addressed.

So far as we know, the Apostle never visited this township (i. 4, 9; ii. 1, 5), and his knowledge of the Church there was derived from Epaphras, one of his converts (i. 7, 8; iv. 12; Phile. 23).

It is probable that Epaphras had heard the Gospel from Paul

at Ephesus—a hundred miles from Colossae—and believed it; as did also Philemon and his family (Phile. 19).

Thereafter Epaphras became the leader and teacher of the believers in the Lycus valley (iv. 12, 13).

It ought to impress us greatly that this most wonderful Epistle was sent to a Church and town of such little significance. It reminds us of the fact that the LORD revealed Himself to a loose-living woman by a well in Samaria (John iv).

God's ideas of importance, and ours, are not often in harmony.

What occasioned this Epistle was a visit which Epaphras paid to Paul while he was a captive in Rome, and who, probably by his witness there, was made to share the Apostle's bondage (i. 7, 8; iv. 12; Phile. 23).

It was a long and difficult journey that Epaphras took, for Rome was about 750 miles from Colossae in a straight line, and would be about 1,000 miles by land and sea.

That he took this journey indicates how great and grave was the danger which threatened the Colossian Church, and how urgent it was that the great Apostle should write to them about it.

What the trouble was is made evident in the Letter which Tychicus carried from Rome to Colossae.

Jewish Christians imbued with heathen philosophy were leading the converts astray in two directions, doctrinally and practically, theologically and ethically. On the one hand they were substituting inferior and created beings, angelic mediators, for the Divine Head Himself (ii. 8, 18); and on the other hand, they were insisting on ritual and ascetic observances as the foundation of their moral teaching (ii. 11, 16, 17, 20-23).

Intellectualism characterized the one error, and ritualism, the other; mysticism, the one, and formalism, the other.

The one is known as *Gnosticism*, and the other as *Judaism*; and their common source was the conception of matter as the origin and abode of evil.

Paul has but one answer for both these errors, namely, the supremacy of Christ.

He shows that wrong views as to the true nature of the LORD

mean wrong views about everything else throughout the universe, for Christ is the revelation and manifestation of God.

Paul shows Christ to be the *Creator of all things* (i. 16); the *Head of the Church* (i. 18); and the *Fulness of Deity* (i. 19; ii. 9).

In chapter ii. 9, 10 the whole ground is covered, for here is an authoritative declaration concerning *God*, and *Christ*, and *man*, and their relation and correspondence.

'IN HIM DWELLETH ALL THE FULNESS OF THE GODHEAD BODILY, AND IN HIM YE ARE MADE FULL, WHO IS THE HEAD OF ALL PRINCIPALITY AND POWER.'

'In Him resides all the fulness of the Deity in bodily fashion, and ye are in Him filled full; for He is the Head of every government and authority.'

Gnosticism, which implies the possession of a superior wisdom, which is hidden from others, appeared in the apostolic age in a simple and elementary form only.

Regarding all matter as evil, and that earth could not approach God directly, it postulated a series of successive emanations between man and God, as the instruments of communication and the objects of worship.

'Let no man rob you,' says Paul, 'of your prize by a voluntary humility and worshipping of the angels; . . . which things have indeed a show of wisdom' (ii. 18, 23).

This was not polytheism, for the Gnostics believed in one God only, but it was a theosophic speculation which was contrary to Christianity.

Christ was in the Gnostic scheme, but only as the highest of the *aeons* or *emanations*; not as the Son of God.

It is because of this that Paul insists on the Christian doctrine of the Person of Christ (i. 13-20).

The Christology of this Epistle in no way differs from that of the Apostle's earlier Letters, but here it is stated with greater diecision and fulness.

Whereas John speaks of Christ as the LOGOS, Paul speaks of Him as the PLEROMA; but the main conception is the same.

'The idea of Christ as an intermediate being, neither God nor man, is absolutely and expressly excluded. On the one hand, His humanity is distinctly emphasized. On the other, He is represented as existing from eternity, as the perfect manifestation of the Father, as the absolute mediator in the creation and government of the world' (Lightfoot).

In each of the Prison Epistles is a great Christological passage. In Ephesians it is in chapter i. 19b-23. In Philippians it is in chapter ii. 5-11. In Colossians it is in chapter i. 15-19.

In Ephesians it is *Christ Risen and Glorified.* In Philippians it is *Christ Incarnate, Suffering, and Exalted.* In Colossians it is *Christ Pre-existent and Pre-eminent* (see the author's *Visions of Christ*).

The great Christological passages in the Prison Epistles are: Eph. i. 20-23; Phil. ii. 5-11; and Col. i. 15-20.

In these passages, says Bishop Moule, 'we find Christ's essential and glorious Deity; His eternal Sonship; His immediate action in Creation; His Headship over the Created Universe; His divine free will in Incarnation and Humiliation; His atoning Death; His Resurrection, and Exaltation as the Incarnate, by the Father's power; His Headship over the Church, and animation of it with His Spirit'.

In the Colossian passage, Christ is seen in a threefold relation:

1. *His Relation to God* (i. 15a)

    'WHO IS THE IMAGE OF THE INVISIBLE GOD.'

2. *His Relation to Creation* (i. 15b-17)

    'THE FIRSTBORN OF ALL CREATION; FOR IN HIM WERE ALL THINGS CREATED, IN THE HEAVENS AND UPON THE EARTH, THINGS VISIBLE AND THINGS INVISIBLE, WHETHER THRONES OR DOMINIONS OR PRINCIPALITIES OR POWERS; ALL THINGS HAVE BEEN CREATED THROUGH HIM AND UNTO HIM; AND HE IS BEFORE ALL THINGS; AND IN HIM ALL THINGS CONSIST.'

3. *His Relation to the Church* (i. 18, 19)

'AND HE IS THE HEAD OF THE BODY, THE CHURCH; WHO IS THE BEGINNING, THE FIRSTBORN FROM THE DEAD; THAT IN ALL THINGS HE MIGHT HAVE THE PRE-EMINENCE. FOR IT WAS THE GOOD PLEASURE OF THE FATHER THAT IN HIM SHOULD ALL THE FULNESS DWELL.'

This truly is a fathomless passage. We can almost thank the heresy which caused it to be written!

> Thou art the Everlasting Word,
> The Father's only Son;
> God manifestly seen and heard,
> And heaven's beloved One.
>
> In Thee, most perfectly expressed,
> The Father's glories shine;
> Of the full Deity possessed,
> Eternally Divine.
>
> True Image of the Infinite,
> Whose essence is concealed;
> Brightness of uncreated Light;
> The Heart of God revealed.
>
> But the high mysteries of Thy name
> An angel's grasp transcend;
> The Father only, glorious claim!
> The Son can comprehend.
>
> Throughout the universe of bliss,
> The centre Thou, and sun;
> The eternal theme of praise is this,
> To Heaven's beloved One:
> Worthy, O Lamb of God, art Thou
> That every knee to Thee should bow.
>
> Josiah Conder

Between an Introduction (i. 1-14), and a Conclusion (iv. 7-18), there are three Divisions (i. 15-iv. 6) in this Epistle.

The first is *Doctrinal* (i. 15-ii. 3), and relates chiefly to *Christ*. The second is *Polemical* (ii. 4-iii. 4), and relates chiefly to *the Church*. The third is *Experimental* (iii. 5-iv. 6), and relates chiefly to *the Christian*.

CHART 167

COLOSSIANS		
i. 15–ii. 3	ii. 4–iii. 4	iii. 5–iv. 6
DOCTRINAL	**POLEMICAL**	**EXPERIMENTAL**
Christ	The Church	The Christian
I. THE PERSON OF CHRIST (i. 15–19)	I. THE POSITION OF THE CHURCH (ii. 4–15)	I. SPIRITUAL PRINCIPLES FOR THE INNER LIFE (iii. 5–17)
His Relation to		
1. God (i. 15a) 2. Creation (i. 15b–17) 3. The Church (i. 18, 19)	1. The Threatening Danger (ii. 4–7) 2. The Saving Doctrine (ii. 8–15)	1. Mortification (iii. 5–11) 2. Vivification (iii. 12–17)
II. THE WORK OF CHRIST (i. 20–ii. 3)	II. THE RESPONSIBILITY OF THE CHURCH (ii. 16–iii. 4)	II. SPECIAL PRECEPTS FOR THE OUTER LIFE (iii. 18–iv. 6)
1. The Glorious Purpose (i. 20) 2. The Partial Accomplishment (i. 21–23) 3. The Chosen Instrument (i. 23 b–ii. 3)	1. Negatively (ii. 16–19) 2. Positively (ii. 20–iii. 4)	1. The Home (iii. 18–iv. 1) 2. The Work (iv. 2–4) 3. The World (iv. 5, 6)

INTRODUCTION ch. i. 1-14

CONCLUSION, ch. iv. 7-18

See the writer's *Know Your Bible*, Vol. 2, pp. 193, 194

In the Introduction (i. 1-14), the Salutation (i. 1, 2) should be lingered over. Here two things are outstanding, the Address (i. 2a), and the Blessing (i. 2b).

The Address is: 'to the saints *in Christ in Colossae*'.

The Colossians lived in two environments—as we all do. One was temporal and the other was spiritual. One was in a very finite township, and the other was in the infinite Christ. It means much to Christ that we live where we do. It ought to mean much to the people where we live that we are also 'in Christ'. And it ought to mean much to ourselves that we live in two localities. Think of some instances. John Paton 'in Christ' and in Tanna. Richard Baxter 'in Christ' and in Kidderminster. Mary Slessor 'in Christ' and in Calabar. Frank Crossley 'in Christ' and in Manchester. Mary Reed 'in Christ' and in Chandag. Robert Moffat 'in Christ' and in Kuruman. John Bunyan 'in Christ' and in Bedford. Florence Nightingale 'in Christ' and in Scutari.

Our spiritual locality will help us to live in our temporal locality.

The Blessing. This in Paul's thirteen Epistles is practically. the same—'*Grace to you and peace from God our (the) Father and the (our) Lord Jesus Christ*'. In 1 Thessalonians it is abbreviated to 'Grace to you and peace'. In Colossians 'and our LORD Jesus Christ' is omitted. In 1-2 Timothy, 'mercy' is added, and the title of the Son is 'Christ Jesus our LORD'; and in Titus, it is 'Christ Jesus our Saviour'.

From this we see that the basic blessing is 'grace and peace', words which are full of blessing.

'GRACE' stands for the whole sum of the unmerited blessings which come to men from God the Father, through Jesus Christ. It means the unconditioned, undeserved, spontaneous, eternal, stooping, pardoning love of God. It has its *fountain* in God, its *flow* from God, and its *fulness* in us.

'PEACE.' The content of this, as of 'grace', is threefold—peace with *God*; peace with *ourselves*; and peace with our *fellows*.

We first have *peace with God*; then, the *peace of God*; and finally, the *God of peace*.

'GRACE AND PEACE.' Here the Western and Eastern forms of salutation blend. *Grace* is Greek, and *Peace* is Hebrew, and in combination each is strengthened. 'Grace' is Greek thought Christianised; and 'Peace' is Hebrew thought realized.

The order is never inverted. It is never 'peace and grace', for there must be the expression of grace on God's part before there can be the experience of peace on our part.

These stand related to one another as root to fruit; as spring to stream; as cause to effect; as centre to circumference; as foundation to superstructure.

The blessing is both a prayer and a prophecy.

Paul's Prison Prayers are deeply impressive. There are two in Ephesians, one in Philippians, and this one in Colossians (i. 9-12).

The prayer here is for *Enlightened Behaviour*. It embraces the entire Christian life in the main aspects of it—the *fundamental equipment* (9); the *progressive experience* (10a); and the *manifold expression* (10b-12). (See the author's *Paul's Prison Prayers*.)

Of Creation (i. 15, 16) Christ is the conditional Cause (*en*); the instrumental Cause (*dia*); and the ultimate Cause (*eis*).

The democracy of the Church of God is declared in such a verse as i. 28: 'Warning *every man*, and teaching *every man* in all wisdom, that we may present *every man* mature in Christ'.

Any intellectual or spiritual caste within the Christian Church is pernicious error. Every believer has equal privileges in Christ and fullest access to Him. Jewish exclusivism and Gnostic mysticism were, and in their modern forms are, heresies.

'Touch not, taste not, handle not' (ii. 20-23) are not Christian exhortations but are regulations to be avoided; and, incidentally, they have no more to do with the temperance movement than with our daily dinner.

In both Colossians and Ephesians Christ's work is one of reconciliation (Col. i. 20; Eph. ii. 16).

It is to be feared that many Christians are still living in a dispensation which Christ's Cross ended; dwelling among the 'shadows' instead of glorying in the 'substance' (ii. 13-23). Religious ritual and ceremony, fasts and feasts, forms and formularies are likely to, and often actually do, rob the soul of Christ Himself, and of the freedom wherewith He has made us free (Gal. v. 1-9).

The Christian must never become spiritually inactive, for there are always vices to be 'put off' and graces to be 'put on' (iii. 5-17).

'Words' and 'deeds' are the outward expressions of thoughts and desires; therefore let us look within.

As in Ephesians (v. 21-vi. 9) the Christian's social obligations are here detailed (iii. 18-iv. 1). These statements should be carefully compared, relative to wives, husbands, children, fathers, slaves, and masters.

The close relation of the three Churches in the Lycus Valley is indicated by the greetings at the end of this Epistle (iv. 10-17).

Epaphras, a native of Colossae, 'one of you'. Paul speaks of him deeply and affectionately. He was a convert of Paul, and, probably, was the Pastor of the three Churches.

'A bondslave of Christ Jesus'. 'His prayers'. 'He has worked hard for you' (iv. 12, 13).

In Laodicea, there was a gathering of believers in the house of *Nympha* (or Nymphas. iv. 15). One's house is a good place in which to have a Church.

Onesimus, one of Philemon's slaves, and a bad one, but now regenerated, is spoken of as 'the faithful and beloved brother, who is one of yourselves'. This is a marvellous description, and only Christianity could have made it possible (iv. 9).

The Colossian Letter was read in the other Churches, and the Ephesian Letter was read in all three Churches.

Bishop Lightfoot says: '"Tychicus" was entrusted with copies of the circular letter, which he was enjoined to deliver in the principal Churches of proconsular Asia. This mission would bring him to Laodicea, which was one of these great centres of Christianity; and as Colossae was only a few miles distant, the Apostle would naturally engage him to pay a visit to the Colossians. At the same time the presence of an authorized delegate of St. Paul, as Tychicus was known to be, would serve to recommend Onesimus, who, owing to his former conduct, stood in every need of such a recommendation.'

Of the Father's love begotten
  Ere the worlds began to be,
He is Alpha and Omega,
  He the Source, the Ending, He,
Of the things that are, that have been,
  And that future years shall see,
Evermore and evermore.

O ye heights of heaven, adore Him,
  Angel hosts, His praises sing;
All dominions, bow before Him,
  And extol our God and King;
Let no tongue on earth be silent,
  Every voice in concert sing,
Evermore and evermore, Amen.

A. C. Prudentius, A.D. 348-413.

'CHRIST . . . far above all rule and authority and power and dominion, and above every name that is named, not only in this age, but also in that which is to come.'

THE PRISON EPISTLES

PHILEMON

A.D. 62-63

This is the only strictly personal letter, of all the letters that Paul must have written, which has been preserved.

In the literature of the New Testament it stands alone much as 'Ruth' does in the Old Testament. It is the most perfect specimen in existence of private Christian correspondence; the communication of a perfect gentleman.

'The Epistle showeth a right noble lovely example of Christian love.' (Luther).

'Though he (Paul) handleth a subject which otherwise were low and mean, yet, after his manner, he is borne up aloft to God.' (Calvin).

'The single Epistle to Philemon very far surpasses all the wisdom of the world.' (Franke).

It is 'surpassingly full and significant.' (Ewald).

'We have here only a few familiar lines, but so full of grace, of salt, of serious and trustful affection, that this short Epistle gleams like a pearl of the most exquisite purity in the rich treasure of the New Testament.' (Sabatier).

The Epistle is 'a pattern of tact, fine feeling, and graciousness.' (Holtzmann).

'This exquisite and interesting Epistle, alike a masterpiece of persuasive tact and delicacy, and an enduring model of Christian courtesy.' (Ellicott).

'The Epistle to Philemon stands unrivalled.' (Lightfoot).

Although the Letter is so short—333 or 335 words (according to the text used)—eleven persons are mentioned in it, five at the beginning, five at the end, and throughout is the central figure, the subject and occasion of the Letter—Onesimus.

The Letter was written by Paul in Rome in A.D. 62-63, and was sent to Philemon in Colossae by the hand of Onesimus at the same time that Tychicus conveyed the Colossian Letter to the Church in that town.

Onesimus, which means useful, or profitable, was one of Philemon's slaves. He had robbed his master and escaped to Rome to avoid arrest and punishment, but in the Capital, in God's mercy, he made contact with Paul.

Philemon was one of the Apostle's converts (19), and the Colossian Christians met in his house (2). It is practically certain that Apphia was his wife, and Archippus his son (2).

Epaphras had the spiritual oversight of the Churches in the Lycus Valley (Col. i.7; iv. 12, 13); and because of theological and ethical heresies which threatened these Churches he had gone to Rome to consult Paul, and was held there as a prisoner (23).

We are not told how Onesimus got into touch with Paul, but Epaphras, who knew him well, may have met him in the city and taken him to the Apostle.

What we do know is that as a result of the contact Onesimus was converted, and what followed is told in this Letter.

Speaking of the Colossian Epistle and this private Letter, Dr. Maclaren has said: 'That must have been a great intellect, and closely conversant with the fountain of all light and beauty, which could shape the profound and far-reaching teachings of the Epistle to the Colossians, and pass from them to the graceful simplicity and sweet kindliness of this exquisite letter; as if Michael Angelo had gone straight from smiting his magnificent 'Moses' from the marble mass, to incise some delicate and tiny figure of love or friendship on a cameo'.

Because of the uniqueness and brevity of the Letter the text of the Revised Standard Version is given here, with a detailed analysis.

CHART 168

1-3
INTRODUCTION
I. SUPERSCRIPTION (1, 2) 1. The Writers 2. The Readers
II. BENEDICTION (3) 1. The Blessings 2. The Blessers

PAUL, a prisoner for Christ Jesus, and Timothy our brother,
To Philemon our beloved fellow-worker, and Apphia our sister, and
Archippus our fellow-soldier, and the church in your house:
Grace to you and peace from God our Father and the Lord Jesus Christ.

4-7
COMMENDATION
PAUL'S PRAYERS FOR PHILEMON
I. THANKSGIVING (4, 5, 7) 1. The Cause of it 2. The Motive of it
II. SUPPLICATION (4, 5, 6) 1. The Occasion of it 2. The Purport of it

I thank my God always, when I remember you in my prayers, because I
hear of your love and of the faith which you have toward the Lord Jesus
and all the saints, and I pray that the sharing of your faith may promote
the knowledge of all the good that is ours in Christ. For I have derived
much joy and comfort from your love, my brother, because the hearts of
the saints have been refreshed through you.

8, 9
APPROACH TO THE OBJECT OF THE LETTER
I. PAUL MIGHT ENJOIN (8)   1. His Right   2. His Reason
II. PAUL BUT ENTREATS (9)   1. The Ruling Principle   2. The Personal Plea

Accordingly, though I am bold enough in Christ to command you to do what is required, yet for love's sake I prefer to appeal to you—I, Paul, an ambassador, and now a prisoner also for Christ Jesus—

10-19
DISCLOSURE OF THE OBJECT OF THE LETTER
(*a*) **10-12**
THE REQUEST
I. FATHER AND SON (10)
II. PAST AND PRESENT (11)
III. SENT TO BE RECEIVED (12)

I appeal to you for my child, Onesimus, whose father I have become in my imprisonment. (Formerly he was useless to you, but now he is indeed useful to you and to me).

I am sending him back to you, sending my very heart.

(10-19)
DISCLOSURE OF THE OBJECT OF THE LETTER
(b) 13, 14
THE DESIRE
I. I would have kept, but— (13) II. You had not given (14)

I would have been glad to keep him with me, in order that he might serve me on your behalf during my imprisonment for the gospel; but I preferred to do nothing without your consent in order that your goodness might not be by compulsion but of your own free will.

(10-19)
DISCLOSURE OF THE OBJECT OF THE LETTER
(c) 15-17
THE SITUATION
I. The Way of Providence (15) II. The Slave and Brother (16) III. The Deputy Partner (17)

Perhaps this is why he was parted from you for a while, that you might have him back for ever; no longer as a slave but more than a slave, as a beloved brother, especially to me, but how much more to you, both in the flesh and in the Lord. So if you consider me your partner, receive him as you would receive me.

10-19
DISCLOSURE OF THE OBJECT OF THE LETTER
(d) 18, 19
THE PROMISE
I. I owe you (18) II. You owe me (19)

If he has wronged you at all, or owes you anything, charge that to my account. I, Paul, write this with my own hand, I will repay it—to say nothing of your owing me even your own self.

20, 21
RETREAT FROM THE OBJECT OF THE LETTER
I. THE CLAIM OF LOVE
1. The Favours Requested 2. The Sphere of Fulfilment
II. THE CONFIDENCE OF LOVE
1. In Philemon's Obedience 2. In Philemon's Generosity

Yes, brother, I want some benefit from you in the Lord. Refresh my heart in Christ.
Confident of your obedience, I write to you, knowing that you will do even more than I say.

22
EXPECTATION
PHILEMON'S PRAYERS FOR PAUL

I. PAUL'S HOPE OF LIBERATION
 	
   1. The Source of it
   2. The Ground of it

II. PAUL'S REQUEST FOR ACCOM-
MODATION
 	
   1. His Modesty
   2. His Motive

At the same time, prepare a guest room for me, for I am hoping through your prayers to be granted to you.

23-25
CONCLUSION

I. SALUTATIONS (23, 24)
 	
   1. From one Fellow-prisoner
   2. From four Fellow-labourers

II. BENEDICTION (25)
 	
   1. The Blessing
   2. The Blessed

Epaphras, my fellow-prisoner in Christ Jesus, sends greetings to you, and so do Mark, Aristarchus, Demas, and Luke, my fellow-workers, The grace of the Lord Jesus Christ be with your spirit.

Surely no one who has once felt the charm of this Letter can ever forget it.

The younger Pliny (A.D. 61-113) on a somewhat similar occasion wrote to a friend, and his letter and Paul's may well be compared. Here is the text of it:

'C. PLINIUS to his SABINIANUS, greeting—

'Your freedman, with whom you had told me you were vexed, came to me, and throwing himself down before me clung to my feet, as if they had been yours. He was profuse in his tears and his entreaties; he was profuse also in his silence. In short, he convinced me of his penitence. I believe that he is indeed a reformed character, because he feels that he has done wrong.

'You are angry, I know; and you have reason to be angry, this also I know; but mercy wins the highest praise just when there is the most righteous cause for anger.

'You loved the man, and, I hope, will continue to love him; meanwhile it is enough that you should allow yourself to yield to his prayers.

'You may be angry again, if he deserves it; and in this you will be the more readily pardoned if you yield now. Concede something to his youth, something to his tears, something to your own indulgent disposition. Do not torture him, lest you torture yourself at the same time. For it is torture to you, when one of your gentle temper is angry.

'I am afraid lest I should appear not to ask but to compel, if I should add my prayers to his. Yet I will add them the more fully and unreservedly, because I scolded the man himself with sharpness and severity; for I threatened him straitly that I would never ask you again. This I said to him, for it was necessary to alarm him; but I do not use the same language to you. For perchance I shall ask again, and shall be successful again; only let my request be such, as it becomes me to prefer and you to grant. Farewell.'

The great qualities of this letter are evident, but when compared with Paul's letter we see at once the difference between Paganism and Christianity.

Pliny's letter is for a freedman; Paul's is for a slave. Pliny has doubt about the future good conduct of the freedman; Paul has no doubt about the slave's. Pliny assumes that Sabinianus is and will be angry; Paul does not assume that Philemon is or will be angry. Pliny begs that torture will not be resorted to; Paul asks that the slave be treated as a brother beloved. Pliny severely scolded the freedman; there is no word of Paul scolding the slave. Pliny told the freedman that he would never plead for him again, but said to Sabinianus that he might do so; Paul does not contradict himself. Pliny's letter is frozen kindness; Paul's melts and glows with Christian love.

Faith, hope, and love are notes in the music of this Letter; *faith* in verses 5, 6; *hope* in verses 21, 22; but it is *love* that dominates, because Paul is appealing to Philemon's love—not to his faith (1, 5, 7, 9, 16).

Paul said he would repay what Onesimus had stolen from Philemon. How and when did he do this? In prison he could not work at tent-making. Was it out of money that had been sent to him? (Phil. iv. 10-19.) Or did he work again at his craft after his release from captivity? We do not know, but he certainly did pay, unless Philemon resolutely declined the kind offer, which most probably he did. Or did Onesimus repay the debt?

The Apostle hoped to be a guest in Philemon's home (22): Did he get there? If so, let imagination get to work on what would happen from the moment of his arrival!

In this Letter are several remarks of which there are parallels in the papyri.

When Paul began his letters with '*I thank*' (*eucharisteō*) (1 Thess. i. 2; 2 Thess. i. 3; 1 Cor. i. 4; Rom. i. 8; Col. i. 3; Phile. 4; Eph. i. 16; Phil. i. 3) he was using a secular custom which occurs often in papyrus letters.

When the Apostle speaks of Onesimus as his 'child' (10) and pledges himself financially in terms of a bond, it corresponds to a father's agency for his son, as in the Greek law and Hellenistic law of the papyri.

The reference in verse 13 to Onesimus serving Paul on Philemon's behalf, that is, as his agent, is paralleled in many papyri where the scribe representing an illiterate debtor writes 'for him' (*huper autou*), that is, 'as his agent'.

In a papyrus, now in the Bodleian Library, Oxford, in a letter from Aurelius Archelaus to Julius Domitius, occur the words: 'Already aforetime I have recommended unto thee Theon my friend, and now also I pray lord, that thou mayest have him before thine eyes as myself. For he is such a man that he may be loved by thee'.

With this compare Phile. 17: 'If you consider me your partner, receive him as you would receive me' (17) . . . 'a beloved brother, especially to me, but how much more to you' (16).

'If he has wronged you at all, or owes you anything, charge that to my account' (Phile. 18), has papyri parallels. In one of them two women write to their steward: 'Put down to our account everything you expend on the cultivation of the holding' (Moulton-Milligan *Vocabulary of the Greek Testament*).

A stereotyped formula in the papyri is the promise to pay back borrowed money, 'I will repay'; and all occurrences of it are in the debtor's own hand. With this compare Phile. 19: 'I, Paul, write this with my own hand, I will repay it' (cf. Matt. xviii. 26-29; Luke x. 35).

Attention is called to these parallels to illustrate the fact that the Greek of the New Testament was not classical, but was the vernacular Greek of the period, the language of everyday life, the *Koinē* or common Greek of the Graeco-Roman world.

This short Letter of Paul to Philemon has many values, of which the following may be mentioned:

1. *Its Personal Value.*
   The light which it throws upon the character of Paul.
2. *Its Ethical Value.*
   Its balanced sensitiveness to what is right.
3. *Its Providential Value.*
   Its underlying suggestion that God is behind and above all events.
4. *Its Practical Value.*
   Its application of the highest principles to the commonest affairs.
5. *Its Evangelical Value.*
   The encouragement it supplies to seek and to save the lowest.
6. *Its Social Value.*
   Its presentation of the relation of Christianity to slavery, and to all unchristian institutions.
7. *Its Spiritual Value.*
   The analogy between it and the Gospel Story.

(See the writer's *A Note to a Friend*)

THE PRISON EPISTLES

EPHESIANS

A.D. 62-63

Though Colossians and Ephesians are twin Epistles, each is distinctive. The distinctiveness of Ephesians is evident in several ways.

Two of these relate to its beginning, and its end. Colossians is addressed to a Church (i. 2), but Ephesians is not (see fuller paragraph). In Colossians are personal greetings and the mention of many names (iv. 7-17), but in Ephesians there are no greetings and no names except that of the bearer of the Letter (vi. 21).

Colossians obviously is controversial; a heresy is being attacked and exposed (ii. 8, 9, 18, 19), but in Ephesians there is no such thing; this Epistle is high above *local* controversy and conflict, though it speaks of the Christian's weapons (vi. 10-17).

We may well wonder if there is any explanation of these differences in Letters so closely related and so much alike. The explanation would seem to be in the destination of Ephesians.

Marcion called it 'the Epistle to the Laodiceans', and Basil says that the words 'in Ephesus' were omitted in the most ancient MSS.; which is true of the two oldest MSS. in our hands, the Vatican and Sinaitic. Origen and Jerome also do not recognize the local destination.

The suggestion of Beza and Ussher that the Epistle was intended to be a circular letter completely eliminates the difficulties which otherwise must arise.

The address will then be:

'To the saints . . . those that are indeed faithful in Christ Jesus.'

A space would be left after 'saints' for the name of each Church for which the Letter was intended. As Ephesus would be the first place of call it is easy to see how the Epistle has been addressed 'to the saints which are at Ephesus'.

This explanation is supported by the reference in Colossians

iv. 16, 'See that you read also the letter from Laodicea', which would be this circular Letter called 'Ephesians'. If this be not so, then a Letter which Paul wrote to Laodicea has been lost.

Being a Letter intended for a number of Churches, copies of which would be made from the autograph copy, no subject could be more appropriate than the unity of the Church as the Body of Christ; a unity which in no degree implies uniformity.

The atmosphere, so to speak, of this Epistle is felt in an expression which occurs five times, '*in the heavenlies*' (i. 3, 20; ii. 6; iii. 10; vi. 12); and which, Westcott says, 'describes the supramundane, supra-sensual, eternal order, or, as we should say, generally, the spiritual world, which is perceived by thought and not by sight' (2 Cor. iv. 18).

These '*heavenlies*' relate, in order, to Blessing, Power, Rest, Manifestation, and Victory.

This atmosphere is felt also in such words as '*grace*', '*mystery*,' '*pleroma*,' and '*glory*'. Ephesians is distinctively the heavenly Epistle, pointing us to the things '*far above all*' (i. 21).

The 'Church' of this Epistle is not any local assembly, nor any denomination, but the aggregate of all believers in Christ, disciples of Christ everywhere throughout the Christian age. This 'Church' is not an organization, but an organism, and her one and only Head is the Risen Christ.

She is represented as the House (ii. 20-22); the Body (iv. 12-16); and the Bride of Christ (v. 25-27).

Characterizing the Epistle, Farrar says: 'In the depth of its theology, in the loftiness of its morals, in the way in which the simplest moral truths are based upon the profoundest religious doctrines, the Epistle is unparalleled'.

Excepting the Pastoral Epistles, the Pauline authorship of Ephesians has been more disputed than any other of this Apostle's Writings. We pay no attention here to the subjective speculations of critics such as Von Soden, Baur, Hilgenfeld, Hitzig, Holtzmann, and Weizsäcker. Too much attention has been given to their views, and we lose nothing by ignoring them.

The Epistle is in two main parts of three chapters each. The first part is *Doctrinal* and the second is *Practical*.

This order and proportion are of great importance. Because Christianity is not a theory but a life, it must express itself in terms of conduct, and it must be related to every aspect of human relationship and need.

But Christian conduct must rest on Christian creed, as every superstructure must rest upon a foundation, and so the doctrinal part of the Epistle comes first; and on that great and grand foundation the Christian life rests, and from it it rises.

CHART 169

EPHESIANS No. 1	
DOCTRINAL i–iii	PRACTICAL iv–vi
The Christian Age	**The Christian Life**
INTRODUCTION (i. 1, 2)	
1. THE ORIGIN OF THE CHURCH i. 3–14	1. THE CALLING OF THE CHRISTIAN iv. 1–16
2. THE GLORY OF THE CHURCH i. 15–23	
3. THE CHARACTER OF THE CHURCH ii. 1–10	2. THE CONDUCT OF THE CHRISTIAN iv. 17–vi. 9
4. THE PROGRESS OF THE CHURCH ii. 11–22	
5 THE FUNCTION OF THE CHURCH iii. 1–13	3. THE CONFLICT OF THE CHRISTIAN. vi. 10–20
6. THE FULNESS OF THE CHURCH iii. 14–21	CONCLUSION. vi. 21–24
THE CHURCH—CHRIST'S BODY	

DOCTRINAL. THE CHRISTIAN AGE
(i-iii)

In this Division, which lays the doctrinal foundation, a six-fold statement is made relative to the Christian Church. The subjects are: Her *Origin*; *Glory*; *Character*; *Progress*; *Function*; and *Fulness*. It will at once be seen how vast is the subject, and how divine, 'dark with excess of bright'.

CHART 170

EPHESIANS No. 2					
DOCTRINAL. THE CHRISTIAN AGE. i-iii					
THE CHURCH CHRIST'S BODY					
I	II	III	IV	V	VI
Her Origin	Her Glory	Her Character	Her Progress	Her Function	Her Fulness
i. 3-14	i. 15-23	ii. 1-10	ii. 11-22	iii. 1-13	iii. 14-21
1 THE DIVINE PURPOSE (3-6)	1 OCCASION OF THE PRAYER (15, 16)	1 OUR STATE BY NATURE (1-3) The Past	1 FORMER ALIENATION (11, 12)	THE MYSTERY 1 REVELATION TO MEN (2-6)	1 APPROACH TO PRAYER (14, 15)
2 THE DIVINE PLAN (7-10)	2 OBJECT OF THE PRAYER (17-19)	2	2 PRESENT UNIFICATION (13-18)	2 COMMISSION OF PAUL (7-9)	2 APPEAL FOR PLENITUDE (16-19)
3 THE DIVINE PROCESS (11-14)	3 OUTLOOK OF THE PRAYER (19-23)	OUR STANDING BY GRACE (4-10) The Present	3 ULTIMATE DESTINATION (19-22)	3 INTENTION OF GOD (10-13)	3 ASCRIPTION OF PRAISE (20, 21)

I. THE ORIGIN OF THE CHURCH
(i. 3-14)

Because the thought here is so compact and profound it is not easy to follow it. When translations have done their best we still feel that the unfolding of the truth has left us far behind.

The inspired Apostle calls our attention to the *Divine Purpose* (3-6); the *Divine Plan* (7-10); and the *Divine Process* (11-14).

The first tells of *Election*; the second, of *Redemption*; and the third, of *Salvation*.

The first is by the *Father*; the second is by the *Son*; and the third is by the *Spirit*.

The first is *theological*; the second is *historical*; and the third is *experimental*.

> O Father, Son, and Spirit we
> Extol the threefold care,
> Whose love, whose merit, and whose power,
> Unite to lift us there.

2. THE GLORY OF THE CHURCH
(i. 15-23)

Here is the first of the two great Prayers in this Epistle. In i. 15-23 is the *Prayer for Spiritual Illumination*; and in iii. 14-21 is the *Prayer for Divine Plenitude*. These are exhaustless. We cannot read them too often, know them too well, or experience them too fully. (See the writer's *Paul's Prison Prayers*).

The *occasion* of the Prayer is stated in verses 15, 16; the *object* of it, in verses 17-19a; and the *outlook* of it, in verses 19b-23.

The OCCASION of the Prayer (15, 16) was the news which the Apostle had received of the *faith* of the believers in the churches to which he was writing. Sometimes *love*, and sometimes *hope* also are the occasion of Paul's prayers (Phile. 5; Col. i. 4, 5; 1 Thess. i. 3).

In a papyrus letter, in the British Museum, a sister writes to her brother from Egypt in B.C. 172: 'I continue praying to the gods for your welfare. I am well myself, and so is the child, and all in the house, continually making mention of you. When I got your letter, immediately I thanked the gods.' Here are the terms which Paul uses, '*making mention*', and '*thanks*'.

The OBJECT of the Prayer (17-19a) is first *preparative* (17, 18a), and then *progressive* (18b, 19a). These two ideas are marked by the conjunction 'that' ($\text{\foreignlanguage{greek}{ἵνα}}$), meaning 'in order that' (17), and by the preposition 'for' ($\text{\foreignlanguage{greek}{εἰς}}$) meaning 'with a view to' (18).

What is prayed for in these verses is our spiritual illumination, that we may know 'what—what—what'. These 'whats' refer respectively to brightness of hope, fulness of inheritance, and greatness of power.

The OUTLOOK of the Prayer lifts us into the immensities and infinities (19b-23).

In these living words are presented to our vision the Resurrection (19b, 20a), Exaltation (20b, 21), and Dominion of Christ (22, 23). These verses constitute the climax of the Prayer, and are the very life-breath of our faith, and love, and hope.

Mark the words 'operation' (ἐνέργεια), 'strength' (κράτος), and 'might' (ἰσχύς). All these unite in the display of the Divine 'power' (δύναμις).

Note the five *aorists*: 'He wrought in Christ'; 'He raised Him from the dead'; 'He seated Him in heaven'; 'He put all things under Him'; and 'He gave Him to the Church'.

3. THE CHARACTER OF THE CHURCH
(ii. 1-10)

The Apostle speaks first of our *State by Nature*: the *Past* (1-3): the condition (1); the characteristics (2, 3a); and the consequence (3b).

He then tells of our *Standing by Grace*: the *Present* (4-10).

In these packed verses we are shown: *that* God hath wrought (4, 5a); *what* God hath wrought (5b, 6); *why* God hath wrought (7); and *how* God hath wrought (8-10).

4. THE PROGRESS OF THE CHURCH
(ii. 11-22)

Here also are the same compression and profoundness as hitherto. Attention is called first to *Our Former Alienation* (11, 12); and this in respect of: the *Covenants of Promise* (11); the *Christ of God* (12a); and the *Course of History* (12b).

Secondly, *Our Present Unification* (13-18): the *announcement* of it (13); the *accomplishment* of it (14-16); and the *assurance* of it (17, 18).

A 'wall of hostility' had existed between Jews and Gentiles, but the Cross has broken it down, so that now 'both' are one (cf. Gal. iii. 28).

Thirdly, *Our Ultimate Destination* (19-22), and this in respect of: the *City* (19a); the *Household* (19b); and the *Sanctuary* (20-22).

In the City we have *freedom*. In the Household we have *fellowship*. In the Sanctuary we have *fulness*.

5. THE FUNCTION OF THE CHURCH
(iii. 1-13)

It is important to see that this is a digression. The Apostle said, '*For this cause*', and then his mind and heart thrilled at the thought of the Gospel he had been called to preach, and for which he now was a prisoner, and he turns aside from what he had begun to say, and does not resume it until verse 14 is reached, which repeats the words 'for which cause'.

Only overflowing minds can make such excursions. 'Dr. Thomas Chalmers *wrote* his sermons, because he could never *reach the end* of any great subject without the curb of a manuscript, so strong was the impulse to diverge into the rich fields beside the road' (H. C. G. Moule). For the same reason, when Dr. John Smith was at Berwick-on-Tweed, his office-bearers asked him to write and read his sermons, as otherwise he never finished what he began.

But grateful we must be that the thought of the Apostle Paul was so often parenthetic.

The digression is about what he thrice calls '*the mystery*' (3, 4, 9). This word in the New Testament always means a secret, undiscoverable except as revealed.

First of all the Apostle speaks of:

The Revelation to Men concerning the Mystery (2-6)

This revelation was not made to the saints of the Old Testament dispensation (5). Blessing for Gentiles was often predicted, but those references were not to the Christian Church, but to a time yet to come, when 'the times of the Gentiles' will be consummated (cf. Rom. ix-xi).

To the Apostle Paul truth was revealed which none before him had known (3, 4, 9. cf. Rom. xvi. 25, 26). He was the agent chosen by God to make known the calling and composition of the Christian Church.

Unless we distinguish between the Kingdom and the Church we shall not understand this and kindred passages.

The wonder of 'the mystery' revealed to Paul is in that Gentiles are, by faith, together with Abraham's believing posterity, 'co-heritors, co-members, and co-partners of the promise of life in Christ' (cf. Gal. iii. 6-14).

Now follows a statement relative to

The Commission of Paul to Preach the Mystery (7-9)

The Apostle could not get over the wonder that God in grace had called *him* to preach this great truth. This commission was recognized by the Apostles in Jerusalem (Gal. ii. 7-9). He had Divine authority for his evangelistic ministry, and he was divinely equipped for it (7, 8).

Finally, the Apostle discloses what is

The Intention of God by Means of the Mystery (10-13)

Mentioned first of all is the wonder that to celestial intelligences the wisdom of God is being made known 'through the Church' (10). This brings two worlds into relation and intercourse. How great a mystery is this, and one of which we are profoundly ignorant!

All this is but the exhibition and fulfilment of an 'eternal purpose' which has been accomplished 'in Christ Jesus our Lord' (11). Note the fulness of the title. 'Jesus' tells of His humanity; 'Lord' of His Divinity; and 'Christ' of the mission of the God-Man.

6. THE FULNESS OF THE CHURCH (iii. 14-21)

These words present the second of the two Prayers in this Epistle, and for fervency, comprehensiveness, and sublimity, they are unsurpassed. These two Prayers reach the loftiest language of human worship not uttered by the Lord Himself.

The digression is ended, and the Apostle continues from where he broke off in verse 1, in the words 'for this cause'.

The Approach to Prayer (14, 15)

We should observe that the *occasion* of it is in all that has gone before, which may be summarized as the need of men, and the provision of God.

At this point the Apostle's emotion leads him to 'kneel' (14).

Seldom is the attitude of kneeling in prayer mentioned in the New Testament.

It is the 'Father' who is addressed; not only Christ's, but also ours.

The compass of the prayer is indicated by the words 'the whole family', or, better perhaps, 'every family in heaven and on earth'. All orders of intelligent beings, human and angelic, are held together by their common Head, the Divine Father.

The Appeal of the Prayer (16-19)

This is for Plenitude. The heart and crown of this wonderful prayer is in the words:

'*That ye may be filled unto all the fulness of God*' (19).

As what precedes is directed towards this end (16-19a) and as what follows shows that the desired end is practicable (20, 21), our mind and heart should concentrate on the meaning of '*the plērōma of God*'.

This word, verb and noun, is prominent in the Pauline vocabulary. See Eph. i. 10, 23; iii. 19; iv. 10, 13; v. 18; Phil. i. 11; ii. 2; iv. 18, 19; Col. i. 9, 19, 25; ii. 9, 10; iv. 12, 17. In some places it refers to Christ, and in others to the Church.

This ideal of 'fulness' is to be attained 'in Christ . . . through the Church'. The greatness and glory of it are seen in such passages as Eph. i. 10, 20-23; iii. 10, 19, 21; iv. 10, 13; Col. i. 15-20; ii. 9, 10.

In Paul's Prayer the *conditions* of fulness are the empowering of the Spirit (16), and the indwelling of Christ (17).

The *purpose* of it are apprehension and knowledge (18, 19a).

The *measure* of it is—immediately 'into', and eternally 'unto', 'according to the riches of His glory' (16).

God's measures are measureless.

What we are to 'apprehend' and 'know' is 'the breadth, and length, and height, and depth' of God's love. This is the geometry of the Divine love.

Its 'breadth' is its extent. It is inclusive and universal.

Its 'length' is its duration. It is everlasting; without beginning, pause, or end.

Its 'height' is its transcendence. It is lofty, sublime, and infinite.

Its 'depth' is its condescension. It is the love of the 'Hound of Heaven', which chases us out of all our hiding places.

In God's love we are to be 'rooted and grounded' (17). His love is the *soil* in which our life must have its roots; and it is the *rock* on which our faith must ever rest.

The Ascription of Praise (20, 21)

Just when we are feeling how utterly impossible of realization all this is, the Spirit says:

'Now unto Him who is able to do:' to do what we ask; to do what we think; to do all that we ask or think; to do above all that we ask or think; to do exceeding abundantly above all that we ask or think, 'according to the power that worketh in us'.

Here are the object of our worship; the strength of our confidence; the reason of our gratitude; and the duration of our thanksgiving.

> Through the meadows, past the cities, still the
> brimming streams are roll'd,
> Now in torrent, now expanding into silver
> lakes and gold,
> Wafting life and increase with them,
> wealth and beauty manifold.
>
> Whence descends the ceaseless fulness,
> ever giving, never dry?
> Yonder, o'er the climbing forest, see the
> shining Cause on high—
> Mountain-snows, their watery treasures
> pouring everlastingly.

Here the Doctrinal division of the Epistle ends, and the Apostle passes on to the fruit in Christian life of all this truth (iv-vi).

PRACTICAL. THE CHRISTIAN LIFE
(iv-vi)

The subject of the first three chapters of this Epistle is the *Church*; and the subject of the last three is the *Christian*. The first is an institution, and the second is an individual. The Church must look to its creed, and the Christian to his conduct. One's conduct cannot be right if his creed is wrong; and one's creed, however right, is of no use if it does not issue in corresponding conduct. This truth is loudly proclaimed in the teaching of the LORD, and of his Apostles.

The subject, then, of chapters iv-vi is the *Christian*—his calling, his conduct, and his conflict.

CHART 171

EPHESIANS No. 3		
PRACTICAL. THE CHRISTIAN LIFE. iv-vi		
I. CALLING OF THE CHRISTIAN iv. 1–16	II. CONDUCT OF THE CHRISTIAN iv. 17–vi. 9	III. CONFLICT OF THE CHRISTIAN vi. 10–20
1 GROUND OF OUR GREATNESS (1–6)	1 PERSONAL CONDUCT (iv. 17–32)	1 THE CHRISTIAN WARRIOR (10, 11)
2 VARIETY OF OUR GIFTS (7–13)	2 SOCIAL CONDUCT (v. 1–21)	2 THE CHRISTIAN WARFARE (12)
3 SECRET OF OUR GROWTH (14–16)	3 DOMESTIC CONDUCT (v. 22–vi. 9)	3 THE CHRISTIAN WEAPONS (13–20)

I. THE CALLING OF THE CHRISTIAN
(iv. 1-16)

Ground of Greatness (iv. 1-6)

The key of this division (iv-vi) is *'the calling to which you have been called'* (iv. 1). The Christian life is not a vacation, but a vocation.

The word 'calling' (κλῆσις) in the New Testament, occurring ten times, always refers to the call of God.

Archbishop Leighton, writing on 1 Pet. ii. 9 says of the word: 'It is an operative word, that effects what it bids. God calls man; He works with him indeed as a reasonable creature; but sure He likewise works as Himself, as an almighty Creator. His call . . . doth, in a way known to Himself, twine and wind the heart which way He pleaseth'.

So, 'Whom He *called*, them He justified, and . . . glorified' (Rom. viii. 30).

A Christian's 'calling' begins at the moment of his conversion, and it continues throughout his life. Every Christian is a 'called' person.

But 'called' persons do not inevitably live a 'called' life; so Paul says: 'let your conduct correspond to your calling' (1). 'Worthily' means suitably, fittingly, agreeably.

There should be no schism between our profession and our practice.

Pursuing this idea of the Christian's 'calling', the Apostle declares that, notwithstanding endless natural diversities, all believers are 'one' in Christ.

'One LORD, one faith, one baptism, one God and Father of all' (5, 6).

Denominationally, it is not true that there is 'one baptism'. Some use much water, and some, less. Some baptize infants, and some, adults. Some say that baptism is regenerative, and some say it is not. An Anglican thinks in terms of infant baptism; and some others in terms of believer's baptism.

All this must be eliminated from the passage before us, and the reference be understood of the *baptism of the Spirit*. Only so interpreted is it true that for all Christians there is 'one baptism'.

Westcott says: 'We might naturally have looked for a reference to Holy Communion in which, as the Apostle shows elsewhere, "the one bread" is the pledge that "the many" are "one body" (I Cor. x. 17. R.V. marg.). But the Apostle is speaking of the initial conditions of Christian life. Holy Communion belongs to the support and development of it'.

Variety of Gifts (iv. 7-13)

Having spoken of unity in diversity, Paul now speaks of diversity in unity; and relates it to both special (7-11) and common service (12, 13).

The 'gifts' bestowed upon the Church by the Risen Christ are: 'Apostles, Prophets, Evangelists, Pastors and Teachers' (11). These in their diversity of functions are given by the Ascended Lord for the varied and harmonious development of His Church (cf. Rom. xii. 6ff.; I Cor. xii. 28).

Elsewhere, Paul speaks of bishops, presbyters, and deacons (I Tim. iii. 1, 8; v. 17. cf. I Cor. xii. 28).

There are those who believe that the offices and institutions of the Church are fixed by the New Testament; but others believe that these were never intended to limit development.

We may assume that *development* was intended and inevitable, but the later introduction of offices and institutions which in no sense are a development, but an imposition, cannot claim the warrant and authority of the New Testament.

An ecclesiastical hierarchy, organized priesthood in successive grades, is foreign to the New Testament. In the Epistles, Pauline and Catholic, there is no reference whatever to an office of *priest*. The word does not occur, except in Hebrews, where the references are historical.

The present-day office of priest within the Church is not a *development* of any New Testament office, but is a denial of the priesthood of all believers (I Pet. ii. 9; Rev. i. 6).

Also, the changing of the idea and function of any New Testament office, for example, that of a bishop, is not a *development* but an intrusion.

For what end are the 'gifts' bestowed on the Church? The answer is: '*With a view to the perfecting of the saints for a work of ministry*'.

Well has Westcott said: 'However foreign the idea of the spiritual ministry of all "the saints" is to our mode of thinking, it was the life of the apostolic Church'.

Secret of Growth (iv. 14-16)

Here confronts us the character of the Christian Community. What is true of the Body as a whole must be true of the members that constitute it.

'The Christian Body is one which is always growing towards an ideal whose great features are an adult and well-grounded fidelity to the revealed Gospel; such as to resist and throw off the assaults of subtle error, while yet maintaining a spirit of love, full of the love of God' (H. C. G. Moule).

> To know, to do, the Head's commands,
>   For this the Body lives and grows;
> All speed of feet and skill of hands
>   Is for Him spent, and from Him flows.

II. THE CONDUCT OF THE CHRISTIAN
(iv. 17-vi. 9)

This section covers a wide area of conduct—personal, social, and domestic—and shows how comprehensive and potent is the Christian Gospel.

Personal Conduct (iv. 17-32)

The Apostle refers, first of all, to contrasted principles of life (iv. 17-24); and then to contrasted practice in living (iv. 25-32).

The old life (17-19) and the new (20-24) are brought into sharp contrast. The old must be 'put off', and the new must be 'put on'.

Here are contrasted evil and good, darkness and light, wrong and right, error and truth, heathendom and Christianity.

The 'old man' and the 'new man' are not the same as the 'flesh' and the 'Spirit'. The latter are contiguous and continuous (Gal. v. 16, 17), but the 'old man' is to be definitely and altogether quitted, and the 'new man' definitely and altogether entered.

In chapter iv. 25-32 are set forth contrasted practices: falsehood and truth; righteous and sinful anger; dishonesty and honesty; evil and edifying talk; bitterness, clamour, slander and malice, on the one hand, and kindness, tenderheartedness, and a spirit of forgiveness on the other hand.

Christianity is not a refined paganism, but an entirely new thing.

Social Conduct (v. 1-21)

Christianity requires that love should exclude lust (1-5); that light should exclude darkness (6-14); and that wisdom should exclude folly (15-20).

Christ's self-sacrifice and man's self-indulgence are contrasted (1-5). Lust is from beneath; love is from above.

Believers 'were once darkness'; not merely in the dark, but impregnated with it. But now we 'are light'; not merely in it, but identified and filled with it, so that we are light's children (7, 8).

Darkness and *works* are associated; also light and *fruit* (9-11. cf. Gal. v. 19-22).

Darkness and light are moral qualities (cf. 1 John i. 5-7; Matt. v. 14-16).

Much emphasis is laid upon the Christian's 'walk'. The word occurs in Ephesians eight times, with the meaning of conduct; manner of life.

Noteworthy is v. 19. '*Psalms*' may refer to instrumental accompaniment as well as to psalms from the Psalter. '*Hymns*,' the noun, occurs here and in Col. iii. 16 only. '*Songs*' occurs in Col. iii. 16; Rev. v. 9; xiv. 3; xv. 3.

These terms are not interchangeable, but indicate a variety of vocal musical expression of which we have little trace.

This singing was not in public only, but also at social gatherings. It was not in the heart only, but with the voice.

A non-singing religion is self-condemned.

Domestic Conduct (v. 22-vi. 9)

It should be observed that Paul says nothing here of civic relations. That is done in Rom. xiii.

Christianity is nowhere more distinctive than in its creation of true family life. It puts an end to the once degradation of women and neglect of childhood.

The Apostle specifies the three relations which normally constitute a family; beginning in each case with the weaker. *Wives and husbands* (v. 22-33). *Children and parents* (vi. 1-4). *Slaves and masters* (vi. 5-9).

The order of these specifications is significant. *Wives and husbands* are the foundation of ordered human life. Naturally, *children and parents* follow; and then, completing family equipment, are *slaves and masters*.

What is required of the first are submission and love; of the second, obedience and discipline; and of the third, dutiful service and fair dealing.

The Apostle deals with each of these relationships on the highest level. Wives and husbands are likened to the Church and Christ. Children should obey 'in the LORD', and because it is 'right'; and the discipline and instruction of parents are to be 'of the LORD'. Slaves are to act as serving the LORD; and masters are to remember that they too have a Master.

Read Spitta's hymn, '*The Christian Household*', which is quoted by Bishop Moule in his 'Ephesian Studies', pp. 318-319.

III. THE CONFLICT OF THE CHRISTIAN
(vi. 10-20)

From the ordered life of a Christian home the Apostle takes us to the field of battle. Life is not a picnic but a conflict. Armour, as well as arm-chairs, is needed. The family must fight.

'*Finally*' (10. *tou loipou*) refers to the *future*. It is translated 'henceforth' in Gal. vi. 17; Heb. x. 13.

It is necessary that we anticipate the days before us.

In approaching the subject of the Christian's conflict the Apostle again uses the words 'powerful', 'strength,' 'might' (cf. i. 19; Col. i. 11). These have shades of meaning which must be preserved.

In this momentous passage, attention is called to the Christian warrior (10, 11); the Christian warfare (12); and the Christian weapons (13-20).

The Christian Warrior is told what he should do, and why he should do it (10, 11). 'The armour of God' and 'the wiles of the devil' are contrasted, as, indeed, are 'God' and the 'devil' (11).

Duality runs through all Scripture, and is prominent in the writings of the Apostle John.

The Christian warrior is to 'stand' and 'withstand' (11, 13).

The devil is methodical in his work. The only occurrences of *methodeia* in the New Testament are here and in chapter iv. 14; and in both instances the word means fraudulent artifice, a trick, a strategem.

If Christians were as methodical in resisting the devil, he would have fewer victories.

The Christian Warfare (12)

The foes we have to contend with are not human but super-human (12). These unseen intelligences are not the creation of Jewish fancy, but are objects of revelation.

'Principalities, Powers, Rulers of the darkness of this world, and Spiritual Hosts of Wickedness in the heavenly places' are personal forces; vast in number and highly organized. They may and do work through human agencies (John xiii. 2; Acts v. 3), but they are our real foes (cf. i. 21; iii. 10; Col. i. 16; ii. 15). Do we ever give them a thought?

The Christian Weapons (13-17)

Superhuman enemies cannot be defeated by human means, and so provision is divinely made. It is spoken of here as 'the armour of God' (11, 13); that is, God supplies it.

For engagements there must be equipment; and so the pieces of the Christian's armour are specified. Of these there are six: Girdle, Breastplate, Sandals, Shield, Helmet, and Sword (14-17).

The first five of these are defensive, and the sixth is offensive; and there is no piece for the back.

These pieces of armour represent: Truth, Righteousness, the Gospel of Peace, Faith, Salvation, and the Word of God (cf. Isa. lix. 14-19).

These pieces of armour are related figuratively to the loins, the breast, the feet, the body, the head, and the hand.

William Gurnall, in 1845, published a volume on verses 10-20, and gave it the title, *The Christian in Complete Armour*. The pages are 6 inches long, and nearly 4 inches wide, and there are 827 of them. There are, on an average, 62 lines to a page, and 15 words to a line, which means 930 words to a page; that is, about 770,000 words in all. There were no penny pamphlets on big subjects in those days!

'In all prayer and supplication praying at every season in the Spirit, and watching thereunto in all perseverance and supplication for all the saints' (18).

'All prayer' is not another weapon, but it is part of the soldier's equipment because every warrior must be 'watchful'.

> Restraining prayer, we cease to fight;
> Prayer makes the Christian's armour bright;
> And Satan trembles when he sees
> The weakest saint upon his knees.

The prayer required is *manifold*, 'all prayer'; *incessant*, 'at every season'; *spiritual*, 'in the Spirit'; *watchful*, 'watching'; *persevering*, 'in all perseverance'; and *comprehensive*, 'for all saints'.

The 'Word of God' and 'all prayer' are the foci round which, as in an ellipse, the Christian life must move.

It is the greatness of this Epistle which makes its meaning so difficult to apprehend. Its thoughts are too big for its words. Language staggers beneath the load.

Bishop Ellicott says that the thought of the Epistle (especially of chapter i), is 'so great and so deep that the most exact language and the most discriminating analysis are too poor and too weak to convey the force or connection of expressions so august, and thoughts so unspeakably profound'.

THE PRISON EPISTLES

PHILIPPIANS

A.D. 63

The Prison Epistles are a distinct group, and were written during Paul's first captivity in Rome in A.D. 61-63. Yet they are definitely distinctive; more so than any of the other groups.

Colossians and *Ephesians* are very like one another, but the first was sent to a local Church, and the second was sent to a group of Churches.

Philemon is entirely a personal Note, about a domestic matter, and is the only preserved example in the New Testament of this kind of correspondence.

Philippians is entirely different from the other three. It is sent, not to an individual, as is *Philemon*, but to a Church; and to a Church in Europe, not in Asia.

It is not written to combat any heresy, theological or ethical, as was *Colossians*; nor is it doctrinal in tone as are *Colossians* and *Ephesians*; though there is in it one great doctrinal passage (ii. 5-11).

It has been described as 'the most letter-like of all letters'; and as 'the most beautiful of all the Pauline Epistles'; and as presenting 'the noblest reflection of St. Paul's personal character and spiritual illumination'.

'The most perfect kind of letter-writing is that which comes nearest to good conversation; and of all the Pauline Epistles, none comes nearer to that than the Letter to the Philippians' (Plummer).

'Its infinite charm rests in its exquisite spontaneity' (Farrar).

A great scholar gives 16 pages of his Commentary to defend the view that Philippians was the first to be written of the four Prison Epistles. Other great scholars regard it as having been the last of the four.

It is not of much importance, but there are weighty reasons for the latter view. Moffatt says much in small compass in the words: 'The relations between Philippi and Paul pre-suppose an interval of time which cannot be fairly compressed within a few months'.

Look intently at Map 36 until the distance of Troas from Philippi, and its proximity to it, are fixed in the mind. The distance from Troas to Neapolis, the port of Philippi, was 125 miles—about the distance from London to Bristol—and Philippi was another 10 miles inland. Thus, the distance from Asia to Europe, from Eastern to Western civilization, was only 135 miles.

In Paul's day the journey from port to port took two days in good weather (Acts xvi. 11), and the 10 miles further on to Philippi, made on foot, might take half a day. This $2\frac{1}{2}$ days' journey could be made now by plane in three quarters of an hour.

The progress of Christianity in the Apostolic age has two outstanding features—the proclamation of the Gospel to Gentiles as well as to Jews, and the carrying of the Gospel from Asia to Europe. Both of these are momentous events.

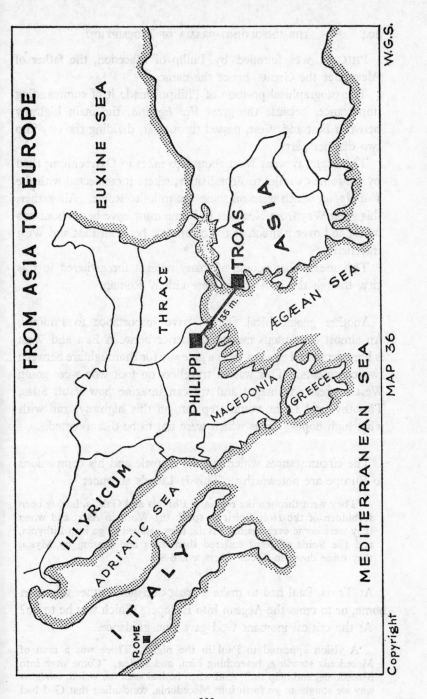

FROM ASIA TO EUROPE

EUXINE SEA

THRACE

TROAS

ASIA

135 m.

PHILIPPI

ÆGEAN SEA

MACEDONIA

GREECE

ILLYRICUM

ADRIATIC SEA

ITALY

ROME

MEDITERRANEAN SEA

W.G.S.

MAP 36

PHILIPPI was founded by Philip of Macedon, the father of Alexander the Great—hence the name.

The geographical position of Philippi made it of commanding importance, because the great *Via Egnatia*, the main highway between East and West, passed through it, dividing the city into two distinct parts.

This highway went West about 240 miles to Dyrrachium; then by sea some 95 miles to Brundisium; where it connected with the *Via Appia*, which went on some 320 miles to Rome. Altogether, this great Way from Neapolis to Rome must have been about 700 miles, and over it much of the commerce between East and West travelled.

This meant that people of many nations foregathered in this city, though the inhabitants were chiefly Roman.

Another geographical feature gave importance to Philippi. An almost continuous mountain barrier between East and West is here depressed so as to form a gateway for thoroughfare between two continents. This was to travellers on foot who were going West a great advantage; and we can imagine how Paul, Silas, Timothy, and Luke would step out on this highway, and with what high hopes; hopes which were not to be disappointed.

The circumstances which led the Apostle and his companions to Europe are noteworthy. This is Luke's account:

'They went through the region of Phrygia and Galatia, having been forbidden of the Holy Spirit to speak the Word in Asia; and when they were come over against Mysia, they assayed to go into Bithynia, and the Spirit of Jesus suffered them not; and passing by Mysia, they came down to Troas' (Acts xvi. 6-8).

At Troas, Paul had to make a great decision—either to return home, or to cross the Aegean into Europe. Which was he to do? At the critical moment God gave him guidance.

'A vision appeared to Paul in the night. There was a man of Macedonia standing, beseeching him, and saying, "Come over into Macedonia, and help us." And when he had seen the vision, straight-way we sought to go forth into Macedonia, concluding that God had called us for to preach the Gospel unto them' (Acts xvi. 9, 10).

This is a great passage on Divine Guidance; a blessing with which Paul was familiar from the day that the LORD appeared to him outside the wall of Damascus.

In the above passage the occurrence of 'we' and 'us' should be noticed. This association of Luke with Paul continues to xvi. 17. It is then dropped, and reappears in xx. 6, and from there it is more or less continuous to the end of Acts (xxviii. 16).

Prof. Ramsay, and others, take the view that it was at Troas, and on this occasion, that Luke first met Paul; but surely this is most unlikely.

The strong lead that he took in this crisis, and afterward, does not suggest that he was a recent convert, or that he had not known Paul before this time. We do not know when these two men first met—it may have been at Tarsus—but in A.D. 52 they seem to be intimate.

Ramsay thinks that Luke was a native of Philippi. If so, it would account for his eagerness in directing Paul's steps towards Macedonia; the vividness of his narrative of events in Philippi; and his close and continuous connection with the Church there.

When Paul left Philippi in A.D. 52 (Acts xvi. 40) Luke did not go with him, and he is seen to be there five years later—A.D. 58 (Acts xx. 6).

Paul's ministry in Philippi was brief but very effective. As was his custom he sought out the Jews first, but as there was no synagogue in the city they must have been few in number.

However, the missionaries attended a prayer meeting by the River Gangites on their first Sabbath in Philippi. This was held in a simple enclosure called a *Proseuchē*.

There do not appear to have been any men at this gathering (xvi. 13) unless there were slaves, who would not be referred to (xvi. 15).

Among the devout women was one named *Lydia*, who was engaged in business in Philippi (Acts xvi. 14). She was not a Jewess, but was of the God-fearing class, and when she heard the Gospel she and others believed and were baptized; so at the riverside prayer-meeting Paul made his first converts in Europe.

Lydia must have been well-to-do, for after the meeting she 'constrained' the four missionaries to make her house their home while they remained in the city (Acts xvi. 15, 40); and there also the believers met who constituted the growing Philippian Church.

Lightfoot has pointed out that the three converts who are mentioned in connection with Paul's brief ministry in Philippi are representative of different races—Lydia, an Asiatic; the slave-girl, a Greek; and the gaoler, a Roman. The first was a business woman; the second, a social chattel; and the third, a government official.

Surely here is illustrated the great truth of Christianity that in Christ 'is neither Jew nor Greek, neither bond nor free, neither male nor female'.

The order of these conversions is also significant: first the proselyte, then the Greek girl, and finally the Roman. This sequence symbolizes the progress of Christianity throughout the world.

Other things which these conversions and the results illustrate are the two great social revolutions which Christianity has effected in the status of women (cf. iv. 2), and the abolition of slavery.

After his conversion did the gaoler give up his appointment and devote himself to spiritual ministry? Was he Epaphroditus? (Phil. ii. 25-30; iv. 18.)

It is of the ministry in Philippi that we first read of whole households being converted—Lydia's and the gaoler's—all of them old enough to believe and be baptized (Acts xvi. 15, 33). We do not know that Lydia was a widow, or that she had ever been married; nor is there any suggestion that there were infants in the gaoler's household.

Paul must have visited Philippi frequently (Acts xvi; xx. 1, 3), and it is more than likely that he wrote to the Church there letters other than the one which has been preserved. (Phil. iii. 1).

He was very dear to them. as they were to him. Several times they sent him monetary help—which no other Church did (Phil. iv. 14-20).

Indications of their mutual affection are seen in i. 7-9, 25, 26; ii. 2, 12, 17, 18, 28; iv. 1, 14-17.

It is strange that the Church in Syrian Antioch, which was Paul's missionary base, never gave him, as far as we know, any temporal help!

Without considering the theories that this Epistle was written in Caesarea, or in Ephesus, we proceed on the assumption that it was written in Rome, in A.D. 63.

Because of the definitely personal character of the Epistle it does not lend itself readily to formal analysis; yet an undesigned outline may be discerned.

CHART 172

PHILIPPIANS			
I	II	III	IV
i. 1–26	i. 27–ii. 30	iii. 1–iv. 1	iv. 2–23
The Joyful Repose of the Christian Life	**The Lofty Ideal of the Christian Life**	**The Devout Energy of the Christian Life**	**The Grand Uniqueness of the Christian Life**
Introduction i. 1, 2			1. Its Selflessness
1. Repose in the Promise of the Past i. 3–11	1. The Standard Appointed i. 27–ii. 16	1. Christianity is opposed to Judaism iii. 1–16	iv. 2–7
			2. Its Spirituality iv. 8, 9
2. Repose in the Purpose of the Present i. 12–18	2. The Standard Approached ii. 17–30	2. Christianity is opposed to Antinomianism iii. 17–iv. 1	3. Its Sufficiency iv. 10–20
3. Repose in the Plan of the Future i. 19–26			*Conclusion* iv. 21–23

See the author's *Know Your Bible*, Vol. 2, pp. 227-228.

This Epistle is about the Christian life as God intends it normally to be lived, life by Christ, in Christ, and Christlike. This is a life joyful, lofty, devout, and unique; it is a life restful, steadfast, energetic, and serene.

Paul is a captive, but he remembers his converts; praising their

progress in the Christian life, and praying for still greater things
(i. 3-11).

Though the Apostle is a prisoner he does not regard his captivity as a disaster, but believes that it will serve the advance of the
Gospel; that 'out of the eater will come forth meat, and out of the
strong, sweetness' (i. 12-14).

There are those who wish him ill, but he has no ill-feeling
towards them.   These foes preached Christ, only to annoy
Paul, but he says: 'What of that?   So long as it is Christ that is
proclaimed, I'm glad' (18).

This is to 'beat a sword into a ploughshare'.

In a noble paragraph, Paul speaks about living and dying
(i. 19-26).   He believes that he will be released from his captivity (19, 24-26) yet, should that not happen, all will be well,
for 'to die will be gain' (21).

Calvin says that this statement is fatal to the view that the
intermediate state is one of sleep and unconsciousness.

What Paul means in verse 21 is not that Christ is life to him,
but that to him life means Christ.   He cannot think of life except
in terms of Christ.

He is 'hard pressed' between two strong desires—to live on
and continue to be a means of blessing to his converts, and 'to
depart and be with Christ which would be very much better'
(22, 23).

Other believers must have similar conflicting ideas, especially
those who have suffered much, and are over sixty years of age,
as probably Paul was!

Not all Christians can serenely look death in the face (see
Heb. ii. 14, 15; 1 Cor. xv. 54-57).

The Apostle exhorts the Christians to steadfastness in suffering
(i. 27-30); to unity and humility (ii. 1-11); and to the effectiveness
that comes of energetic effort (ii. 12-16).

These qualities are not merely idealistic, but were being
exhibited in himself (ii. 17, 18), in Timothy (ii. 19-24), and in
Epaphroditus (ii. 25-30).

Paul's exhortation to humility is supported by a reference to

Christ which is as profound as anything in the New Testament about Him (ii. 5-11). This is one of the greatest of the Christological passages, and is quite exhaustless.

Von Soden has said in his *Early Christian Literature*: 'A purely practical motive has led the Apostle to hand down to us one of the loftiest expressions of his faith in Christ'.

(ii. 5-11)

'Reflect in your own minds the mind of Christ Jesus. Be humble, as He also was humble. Though existing before the worlds in the Eternal Godhead, yet He did not cling with avidity to the prerogatives of His divine majesty, did not ambitiously display His equality with God; but divested Himself of the glories of heaven, and took upon Him the nature of a servant, assuming the likeness of men. Nor was this all. Having thus appeared among men in the fashion of a man He humbled Himself yet more, and carried out His obedience even to dying. Nor did He die by a common death: He was crucified, as the lowest malefactor is crucified. But as was His humility, so also was His exaltation. God raised Him to a pre-eminent height, and gave Him a title and a dignity far above all dignities and titles else! For to the name and majesty of Jesus all created things in heaven and earth and hell shall pay homage on bended knee; and every tongue with praise and thanksgiving shall declare that Jesus Christ is Lord, and in and for Him shall glorify God the Father.'

(Bishop Westcott).

This magnificent statement is in two parts. The first tells of the *Humiliation of the Son of God* (5-8), and the second, of the *Exaltation of the Son of Man* (9-11).

The following analysis of these parts is given in detail because of the very great importance of the passage.

I. THE HUMILIATION OF THE SON OF GOD
(5-8)

1. THE PRE-EXISTENCE OF CHRIST. IN HEAVEN (6):

   (i) *His Divine Nature* (6a):
   - (a) He subsisted in the Form of God (Essence);
   - (b) He was on an Equality with God (Attributes);

   (ii) *His Redemptive Resolve* (6b):
   - (a) Not a Sovereign Assertion ⎫
   - (b) But a Gracious Surrender ⎬ of Prerogatives.

2. THE INCARNATION OF CHRIST. FROM HEAVEN TO EARTH (7, 8a):

    (i) *The Condescending Act* (7a):
        (a) It was Complete: 'Emptied';
        (b) It was Decisive: (aorist);
        (c) It was Voluntary: 'Himself'.

    (ii) *The Conditioning Means* (7b-8a):
        (a) 'Having-taken' (aorist part.);
            'Form.' 'Bondslave.'
        (b) 'Having-become' (aorist part.);
            'Likeness.' 'Men.'
        (c) 'Having-been-found' (aorist part.);
            'Fashion.' 'Man.'

3. THE SELF-ABASEMENT OF CHRIST. ON EARTH (8b):

    (i) *The Course He Pursued*:
        (a) His Decisive Act
            'He humbled Himself' (aorist);
        (b) His Continuous Attitude.
            'Becoming obedient' (aorist part.).

    (ii) *The Issue He Accepted*:
        (a) He Suffered Death;
        (b) He Despised Shame.

II. THE EXALTATION OF THE SON OF MAN
(9-11)

1. A WORK PERFORMED (9a): 'God highly exalted Him':

    (i) *The Nature of It*:
        (a) Resurrection;
        (b) Enthronement.

    (ii) *The Significance of It*:
        (a) A Recognition of Christ's Self-Emptying.
            'Wherefore'.
        (b) A Reward for Christ's Subordination.
            'Also.'

2. AN HONOUR CONFERRED (9b): God 'gave Him the Name.'

    (i) *The Nature of It*:
        (a) Elevation of JESUS to Pre-eminent Rank;
        (b) Presentation to JESUS of the Mystic Name.

    (ii) *The Significance of It*:
        (a) A Man is on the Throne of the Universe;
        (b) The Worship due to the Father is due also to the
            Son.

3. AN END DECREED (10, 11). 'That.'

    (i) *The Nature of It*:
        (*a*) The Universal Acknowledgment of the Lordship of Jesus.
        (*b*) The Glorification of the Father in the Acknowledgment of the Lord.

    (ii) *The Significance of It*:
        (*a*) The Ultimate Overthrow of Evil;
        (*b*) The Ultimate Triumph of Grace.

Four tremendous aorists are in this passage: 'He *emptied* Himself' (7); 'He *humbled* Himself' (8); 'God *highly-exalted* Him, and *bestowed* on Him the Name . . .' (9).

These indicate *not processes, but acts*.

Out of the words, 'He emptied Himself', has arisen the '*kenōsis*' controversy, which by some has been interpreted to mean what must have been far from the Apostle's mind.

The idea that Christ 'emptied Himself' of knowledge and became fallible contradicts the facts.

The idea of the fallibility of Christ's pronouncements—on the Old Testament, for example—and the idea that He accepted limitation of knowledge (Mark xiii. 32) during His manifestation on earth, are not the same things, but surely neither idea is in Phil. ii. 7.

'*The exact meaning of this is beyond us*. Attempts to explain the union of Godhead and manhood are inevitably failures' (Dr. Plummer: the italics are his).

'Any attempt to commit Paul to a precise theological statement of the limitations of Christ's humanity involves the reader in a hopeless maze . . . Christ's consciousness of Deity was not suspended during His earthly life. He knew that He had glory with the Father before the world was, and would receive it back' (Dr. Marvin Vincent).

'He divested Himself, not of His Divine nature, for this was impossible, but of the glories, the prerogatives, of Deity. This

He did by taking upon Him the form of a servant. He stripped Himself of the insignia of majesty' (Bishop Lightfoot).

'It was a laying aside of the mode of Divine existence' (John i. 14. Bishop Westcott).

'That awful and benignant "Exinanition" placed Him indeed on the creaturely level in regard of the reality of human experience of growth, and human capacity for suffering. But never for one moment did it, could it, make Him other than the absolute and infallible Master and Guide of His redeemed' (Bishop H. C. G. Moule).

'He emptied Himself of that effulgence which flesh could not behold and live.'

'He did not cease to be what He was; but He emptied Himself in becoming another; He became man while He was God; a servant while He was Lord of all.'

'God conferred upon Him the Name which is above every name, so that in the Name of Jesus every knee should bow . . .' (9, 10).

The Name referred to is not JESUS, which He received when He was humbled, not when He was exalted, but the incommunicable Name, the Tetragrammaton of the Old Testament, Y.H.V.H., the Great I AM; the supreme Name, translated JEHOVAH in the R.V.

In chapter iii. 1, Paul begins to conclude his Letter, and then his mind kindles again, or he may have been interrupted, and before finishing he must write about some other matters (iii. 2-iv. 7), and then again he begins to conclude, 'Finally' (iii. 1, iv. 8. cf. Eph. iii. 1, 14).

The Apostle's reference to himself is noteworthy (iii. 3-11).

The Philippians are warned against two opposite evils: against *Judaism*, i.e. legal bondage (iii. 2-11); and against *Antinomianism*, i.e. moral laxity (iii. 12-iv. 1).

There is no evidence that these evils were actually in the Church at Philippi, but, perhaps, they were not distant perils; and, in any case, both churches and individual Christians are always in need of these warnings, for, in principle, these evils are always present.

Want of harmony between individuals in a church can gravely injure the whole Church (iv. 2, 3).

At Philippi women were the first converts, and some the first contendents (Acts xvi. 14; Phil. iv. 2).

Every Christian assembly should be characterized by unity and harmony. Paul says: 'Let each of you look not only to his own interests, but also to the interests of others'. 'In humility count others better than yourselves.' 'Agree in the Lord' (ii. 4, 3; iv. 2).

Partisanship is condemned by Paul's repeated 'all' which negatives egotism (i. 1, 4, 7, 8, 25; ii. 17, 26).

Paul's final words to the Philippians are full of pathos (iv. 8-20). His 'thank you' for a gift sent to him by Epaphroditus is heartfelt and dignified. During the twenty-six years of his ministry he had learned many lessons (iv. 11).

The learning was hard, but the knowledge was great.

Paul was grateful for supply through Christians, but his satisfaction was in Christ. For Christians who have, to share with Christians who have not, is the privilege of the former, and should never impair the independence of the latter.

A Christian's attitude towards money is a fair index of his spiritual state.

Two references in the Epistle are of considerable importance: 'the whole praetorian guard,' and 'those of Caesar's household' (i. 13; iv. 22).

'THE PRAETORIAN GUARD.' Of the several meanings given to this term, perhaps the most likely is that which regards it as signifying a body of men who formed the imperial guards.

To one of these praetorian soldiers Paul was chained day and night; he was never left alone (cf. Acts xxviii. 16; Phile. 1, 9; Eph. iii. 1; iv. 1; vi. 20; Col. iv. 3). As the guards were constantly changed they all heard the Gospel, but with what result is not recorded.

'CAESAR'S HOUSEHOLD.' This term embraces not only the most powerful courtiers of the Palace, but also all persons in the Emperor's service, whether slaves or freedmen. Probably Paul's reference is to Christian retainers of the Palace (cf. Rom. xvi. 3-15; and Lightfoot).

'Rejoice' is the keynote of this Epistle. The word occurs in some form 16 times (i. 4, 18, 19, 25; ii. 2, 17, 18, 28, 29; iii. 1; iv. 1, 4, 10).

'Joy' is part of the 'fruit of the Spirit' (Gal. v. 22), and is not the same as happiness. The latter depends on what happens, but joy does not. Happiness is like the calm or rough on the sea's surface, according to the weather, but joy is like the still water deep down.

There is no better illustration of this than that of Ignatius, the martyred Bishop of Antioch. About A.D. 115 he was summoned to Rome for trial, and he set forth from Antioch with gladness.

On the way he halted at Smyrna for some days, and there met its Bishop, Polycarp, who himself was to suffer martyrdom forty years later. From Smyrna he went on to Philippi where he was kindly entertained and escorted on his way by members of the Church.

The route he followed from Philippi to Rome must have been via the Egnatian and Appian Ways (See Vol. II, p. 366, map 21). Ignatius was tried before Trajan, and was condemned to be devoured by beasts; and it is reported that on hearing his sentence he cried out with joy:

> 'I thank Thee, O Lord, that Thou hast vouchsafed to honour me with a perfect love towards Thee, and hast made me to be bound with iron chains, like Thy Apostle Paul.'

'Having spoken thus, he then, with delight, clasped the chains about him; and when he had first prayed for the Church, and commended it with tears to the LORD, he was hurried away by the savage cruelty of the soldiers, like a distinguished ram, the leader of a goodly flock, that he might be carried to Rome, there to furnish food to the bloodthirsty beasts' (Donaldson and Crombie: *Apostolic Fathers*, p. 293).

Polycarp, Bishop of Smyrna, wrote a letter to the Church at Philippi (of uncertain date), in which he mentions Paul several times. It is instructive to compare Paul's and Polycarp's Letters.

With Philippians ends the Prison Epistles, and the next Letters from Paul are what are called the Pastoral Epistles—1 Timothy, Titus, and 2 Timothy. The difference between these and what preceded them is obvious to all. The circumstances, style and outlook are quite different. The reason for this we will refer to in our consideration of Paul's fourth group of letters.

THE PAULINE EPISTLES

GROUP 4

1 TIMOTHY

TITUS

2 TIMOTHY
A.D. 65-67

The Pastoral Epistles

CHRIST AND THE CONGREGATION

The Authority

THE PAULINE EPISTLES

GROUP 4
A.D. 63-68

1 TIMOTHY   TITUS   2 TIMOTHY

The Pastoral Epistles

CHRIST AND THE CONGREGATION

The Authority

The Epistles in this group differ greatly from those of the other three groups, and present problems which the others do not; problems historical, literary, doctrinal, and ecclesiastical.

These problems raise the questions of authorship and date; and in view of the close similarity of the three Epistles to one another it has been and is felt that, in these matters, and in others also, they stand or fall together.

It is outside the scope of this book to consider these matters in detail, but they cannot be altogether by-passed.

1. THE HISTORICAL PROBLEM relates to the place of the Pastoral Epistles in the record of Paul's ministry. An examination of the book of the Acts makes it clear that there is no place in it for the situation which these Epistles disclose. There are references in the Acts to *Ephesus* (xix), to *Troas* (xvi. 8; xx. 6), and to *Crete* (xxvii. 12, 13, 21); but the mention of these places in 1 Tim. i. 3; 2 Tim. iv. 13; Tit. i. 5 is not related to the former. The circumstances of the Pastoral references cannot be fitted into Luke's record.

This may well lead one to ask if these three Letters are the Apostle Paul's.

When Paul chose to appear before Caesar (Acts xxv. 12; xxvi. 32) he was sent to Rome as a prisoner, and was there in custody for some time (Acts xxviii. 16, 30). The reference to 'two whole years' implies that at the end of that time something happened; and it would be easy to infer that the happening was Paul's trial, resulting in his martyrdom.

But during these years he wrote *Philippians*, in which he expressed the hope—amounting almost to certainty—that he was about to be released (i. 19-26; ii. 23, 24); and in the note to Philemon he asks his friend to 'prepare a guest-room for him, because he hoped through their prayers to see them soon' (22). Were these hopes without foundation, and did Paul's trial issue in martyrdom in A.D. 63 in which year Luke's record ends?

If this were so it follows that Paul did not write the Pastoral Epistles. But such a supposition creates more problems than it solves.

Dr. Moffatt's view—and he speaks for many—is that these three Epistles 'are pseudonymous compositions of a Paulinist who wrote during the period of transition into the neo-catholic church of the second century, with the aim of safeguarding the common Christianity of the age in terms of the great Pauline tradition . . . The Pastorals, especially 2 Timothy, are composite, and they show further traces of subsequent accretion.'

(*Introduction to the Literature of the New Testament*, p. 398).

This view is opposed by many facts, and is supported by none that cannot be explained in another way.

It was the general tradition of the Church in the first centuries that Paul was released from his first imprisonment, and made further missionary journeys. And it was also the view from the age of the Apostolic Fathers, that the Pastoral Epistles were written by Paul. This is the witness of Clement of Rome, Polycarp, Irenaeus, Tertullian, Theophilus of Antioch, and many others.

Over against this witness are the subjective and speculative theories of critics such as Schmidt, Schleiermacher, Baur, and Renan; and these two points of view are irreconcilable.

If Paul was released from his first Roman imprisonment—and we may regard it as likely that he was—he could have taken a fourth missionary journey—and apparently he did—and have written the First Letter to Timothy and the Letter to Titus, and after his re-arrest and during his second imprisonment in Rome, his Second Letter to Timothy.

This course is confirmed by external and internal evidence.

The following would seem to have been the sequence of events:

A.D.

61-63	Paul in *libera custodia* at Rome. Epistles written to Colossae, Philemon, Ephesus, and Philippi.
63	Trial and Acquittal.
64	Great fire of Rome.
63-67	Fourth Missionary Journey: visiting—Ephesus, Colossae, Macedonia—Philippi, Spain, Corinth, Crete, Miletus, Troas, Nicopolis.
65	Murder of Seneca by Nero.
66	Outbreak of Jewish War against Rome.
67	First Epistle to Timothy. Epistle to Titus.
67	Paul re-arrested and taken to Rome. Re-tried: 'First answer.' Second Epistle to Timothy.
67-68	Paul condemned and executed.
68	Assassination of Nero.
70	Fall of Jerusalem.

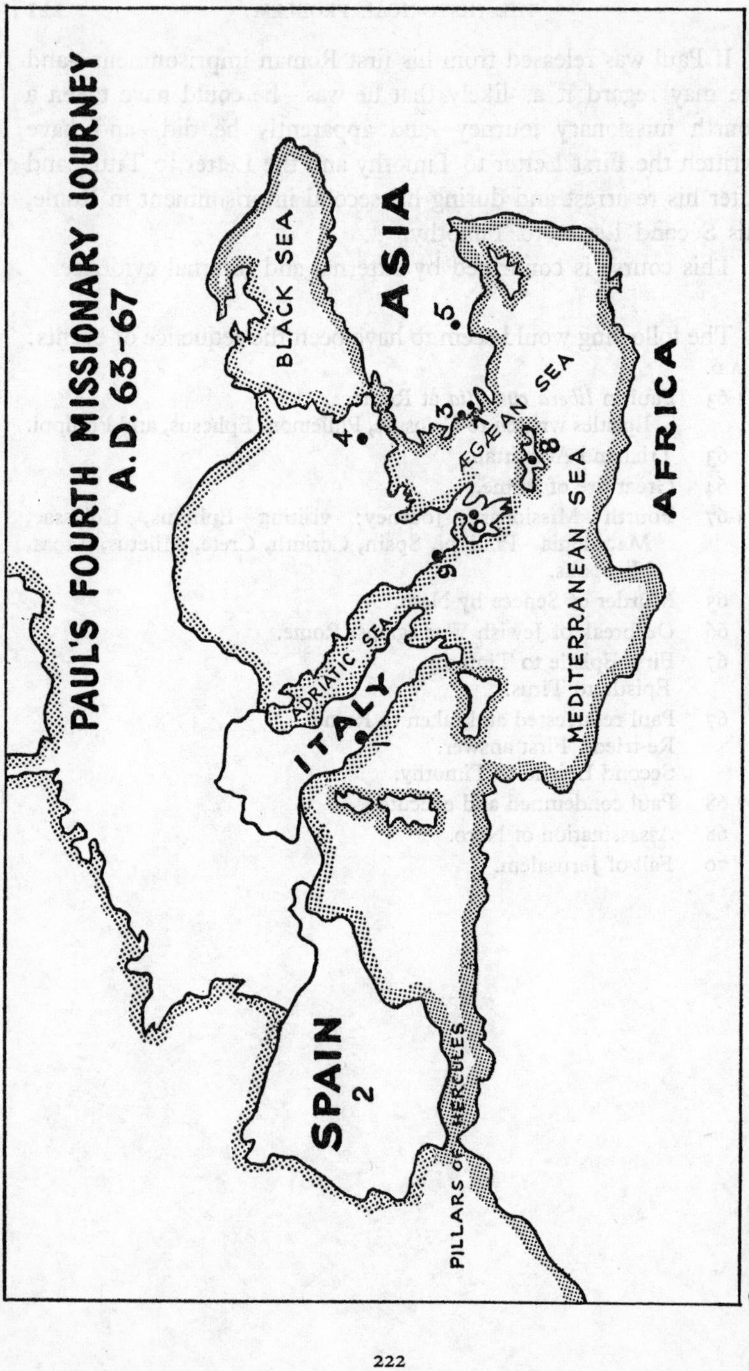

PAUL'S FOURTH MISSIONARY JOURNEY
A.D. 63-67

MAP 37

W.G.S.

Copyright

KEY TO MAP

When studying this map two things should be borne in mind:

(a) that it cannot be *proved* that Paul ever went to Spain;

(b) that the *order* in which the other places were visited cannot be determined. The numbers in the map indicate the *location* of the places, and not the order of the visits.

1. Rome.
2. Spain.   Rom. xv. 24, 28.
3. Ephesus.   1 Tim. i. 3.
4. Macedonia.   Philippi. 1 Tim. i. 3. Phil. ii. 24.
5. Colossae.   Phile. 22.
6. Corinth.   2 Tim. iv. 20.
7. Miletus.   2 Tim. iv. 20.
8. Crete.   Tit. i. 5.
9. Nicopolis.   Tit. iii. 12.

It is to the Pastoral Epistles that we turn for evidence of a Fourth Missionary Journey of which there is no trace in the Acts, for the simple reason that it lay beyond that record.

The places named in these Epistles are: *Ephesus* (1 Tim. i. 3; 2 Tim. i. 18; iv. 12); *Macedonia—Philippi* (1 Tim. i. 3; Phil. ii. 24); *Crete* (Tit. i. 5). *Nicopolis* (Tit. iii. 12); *Asia* (2 Tim. i. 15); *Rome* (2 Tim. I. 17; iv. 9); *Antioch, Iconium, Lystra* (2 Tim. iii. 11, referring to Acts xiii. 14-52; xiv. 1-20; xvi. 1-5); *Thessalonica, Galatia* (Gaul?), *Dalmatia* (2 Tim. iv. 10); *Troas* (2 Tim. iv. 13); *Corinth* (2 Tim. iv. 20); *Miletus* (2 Tim. iv. 20).

To these places which Paul visited after his release from Rome in A.D. 63 must be added *Colossae*, for he certainly would fulfil his promise to go there (Phile. 22). And being so near, it is not improbable that he visited *Laodicea* and *Hierapolis* also (Col. iv. 13).

Any attempt to determine in what order the Apostle visited these places is without value as there is no indication of it in the Epistles themselves.

The places we can be sure Paul visited are: *Philippi, Troas, Ephesus, Colossae, Miletus, Corinth*, and *Crete*; and the places he probably visited are: *Spain* and *Nicopolis* (see Map 37, p. 222).

Of the seven certain places, the Apostle was familiar with five of them, but he had not been to *Colossae* or *Crete* before, though he had touched on the latter island on his way from Caesarea to Rome (Acts xxvii. 13).

When writing to the Church at Rome, Paul expressed the desire and purpose to visit SPAIN (xv. 24), and there is some reason to believe that he did so.

Clement of Rome, writing to the Corinthians, says of Paul that he had 'reached the boundary of the West'. Of this expression, Lightfoot says its most natural interpretation is that it means 'the western extremity of Spain, the Pillars of Hercules' (see Map 28); and there is no tradition or evidence to the contrary of this view.

There were no fewer than eight places which bore the name of NICOPOLIS—'City of Victory'. Of these, *Nicopolis* in Epirus is most probably the one referred to in Titus iii. 12; and it may have been here (or at Troas) that the Apostle was re-arrested and taken to Rome.

Another evidence of the Pauline authorship of these Epistles is seen in the Apostle's references to himself, and to others of his circle.

Of references to *himself*, see 1 Tim. i. 1; i. 12-14; ii. 7; iii. 14, 15; iv. 13; Tit. i. 1-4, 5; iii. 12; 2 Tim. i. 1-8, 11, 12, 15, 16, 17; ii. 2, 9, 10; iii. 10, 11; iv.

Of references to *others*, the following were in the Apostle's circle: Timothy, Titus, Tychicus, Apollos, Lois, Eunice, Demas, Luke, Mark, Prisca, Aquila, Erastus, Trophimus (1 Tim. i. 2 *et al*; Tit. i. 4; iii. 12, 13; 2 Tim. i. 5; iv. 10, 11, 12, 19, 20). All these names would have been anachronisms in the second century.

2. THE LITERARY PROBLEM which the Pastoral Epistles present relates mainly to style and language, and it will be well briefly to consider this matter.

That the *style* of these Epistles differs from that of Paul's other Writings is acknowledged by all readers of them. Charged against them as un-Pauline have been 'want of logical connection, digression, imperfect transitions, and awkward beginnings of sentences' (Dr. S. Davidson).

Much to this effect that has been written leaves the impression that the critics would like to have told Paul how he should have said what he wanted to say; but he is spared this by the theory that these Epistles were written by an unknown imitator some time between A.D. 90-115. If this were so, the imitator was both clever and clumsy. If Paul did not write these Letters they are forgeries, and this idea is unproved and unprovable.

Those who fully believe that Paul wrote these Letters recognize that their style greatly differs from all else that the Apostle wrote, but they account for the fact in another way.

Bishop Lightfoot says that the syntax 'is stiffer and more regular than in the earlier Epistles, more jointed and less flowing . . .' that 'there is greater sententiousness, an abruptness, and positiveness of form'; but he does not use these facts to suggest that the Pastorals were not written by Paul (Biblical Essays).

It should not be overlooked that when these Epistles were written Paul was an old man (cf. Phile. 9, written about four years earlier), and there comes with old age a certain slowing down of mental action and vigour which God does not arrest but employs.

> 'The inspiration is as true, but it is not as strong; the heart and arteries and veins do their duty, but the blood does not course so quickly as in the days of youth.'   Dr. Newport White.

But remembering Philippians (A.D. 63) this explanation must be regarded with reservation.

Much has been made of the fact that the *language* of these Epistles differs from Paul's recognized vocabulary. But what is his recognized vocabulary?

Each of his groups of Letters has verbal peculiarities.

GROUP 1   1 Thess. 34; 2 Thess. 20. Total 54.
GROUP 2   1 Cor. 236; 2 Cor. 171; Gal. 78; Rom. 219. Total 704.
GROUP 3   Col. 55; Phile. 8; Eph. 42; Phil. 65. Total 170.

As, then, there are at least 928 verbal peculiarities in the first ten of Paul's Epistles, is it strange that in Group 4 there should be 239 such: 1 Tim. 118; Tit. 44; 2 Tim. 77?

There are various ways of reckoning the number of *hapax legomena* in the Epistles, so that different figures in the estimate of writers should not be regarded as errors or contradictions; but for our purpose the figures given here illustrate the point under consideration.

Dr. S. Davidson complains of this way of reckoning as 'mechanical', and Dean Wace replies: 'A mechanical objection is a valid answer to a mechanical argument'.

The language which Paul uses in the Pastoral Epistles is adapted to the subjects he is writing about. (See the author's *Know Your Bible*: Vol. 2, pp. 241, 242, 253, 260).

As to *style* differences are observable in Paul's other Epistles, so why not here? How different, for example, are Thessalonians and Galatians; Ephesians and Philippians. Change of time, circumstances, and address, may well affect a writer's style.

In the Pastorals the Apostle is writing to two comparatively young men about Church offices and organization, and he could not have done so in the style of Ephesians which was written to a group of Churches about their relation to Christ and to one another; or in the style of Romans which is a compendium of Paul's entire message.

When the Apostle wrote to the Thessalonians, the great controversies had not begun; when he wrote to the Galatians and the Romans the controversies were at their height; when he wrote the Colossian and Ephesian Letters they were beginning to decline; and when he wrote the Pastoral Epistles, though there was still a rumble of controversy, the Apostle's emphasis was on duty rather than on doctrine; on ethics rather than on theology.

3. THE DOCTRINAL PROBLEM is one which requires an examination which lies outside the scope of this book to give, but a few notes on the subject are necessary.

The idea that the teaching of these Epistles is not Pauline, or, if it is, that it is unsystematic and weak, is not confirmed by an examination of it.

Let it be granted that there is a change of emphasis in the Pastorals, and that aspects of truth which are prominent in former Epistles are not prominent here; but this will not be chargeable against them if we recognize that the object of these Epistles is practical rather than doctrinal.

There is nothing in the Epistles which is contrary to the former teaching of Paul; and, again be it said, having regard for the time, circumstances and occasion of the Pastorals, there was no need for the doctrinal emphasis of former years.

In these Epistles Paul is doctrinal when he combats false doctrine. The heresy which he assails is what has been called *Jewish Gnosticism*, and the nature of it at that time must be gathered from the way in which it is described.

The error was a syncretism of Jewish law and magical rites; of prohibitions and permissions. The heresy had appeared earlier, and the Apostle had attacked it, particularly in his Epistle to the Colossians.

It is described as: 'fables, endless genealogies, vain jangling' (1 Tim. i. 4, 6); 'profane and old wives' fables' (1 Tim. iv. 7); 'questions, strifes of words, railings, evil surmisings, disputings' (1 Tim. vi. 4, 5); 'profane and vain babblings, oppositions of science, falsely so-called' (1 Tim. vi. 20; 2 Tim. ii. 14, 16, 23); 'foolish questions, contentions, strivings about the law' (Tit. iii. 9).

From this it is evident that the error is more advanced and definite than it was when Paul wrote to the Colossians.

In combating this error, Timothy is not to teach anything new, but is to reiterate the doctrine of the Church which he had been taught.

Paul lays much emphasis on *teaching* or *doctrine*, for the word in one form or another occurs in these Epistles 24 times (*didaskalia, didaskalos, didaskō, didachē*); more often than in any of his other writings.

Another evidence of the doctrinal emphasis of these Epistles is in the recurrence (12 times) of the word *Truth*, or *The Truth*, meaning a recognized body of Truth—Truth which has been revealed. There was no need to say in detail at that time what the Truth included, for Timothy and Titus would know (1 Tim. ii. 4; iii. 15; iv. 3; vi. 5; Tit. i. 1, 14; 2 Tim. ii. 15, 18, 25; iii. 7, 8; iv. 4).

To like effect are the references in these Epistles to *The Faith*, not the faculty which apprehends the truth, but the truth which is apprehended. In places the word is used *objectively* to signify the *content* of the Gospel, the Christian Creed. Of the 33 occurrences of *pistis* in these Pastorals, nine seem to require this objective sense (1 Tim. i. 19; iv. 1, 6; v. 8; vi. 10, 21; Tit. i. 13; 2 Tim. iii. 8; iv. 7).

Some idea of the doctrinal content of these Epistles may be gathered from the six 'Faithful Sayings' (1 Tim. i. 15; iii. 1; iv. 8, 9; Tit. i. 9; iii. 4-8; 2 Tim. ii. 11-13); particularly the first, third, and fifth. These Sayings are peculiar to the Pastoral Epistles, and seem to indicate that there were current in the Church maxims, catechetical teaching, or portions of hymns.

'Faithful is the saying, and worthy of all acceptation, that CHRIST JESUS CAME INTO THE WORLD TO SAVE SINNERS' (1 Tim. i. 15).

'Bodily exercise is profitable for a little; but godliness is profitable for all things, having promise of *the life which now is*, and of *that which is to come*. Faithful is the saying, and worthy of all accepttation' (1 Tim. iv. 8, 9).

'When the kindness of God our Saviour, and His love toward man, appeared, not by works (done) in righteousness, which we did ourselves, but according to His mercy He saved us, through the washing (laver) of regeneration and renewing of the Holy Spirit, which He poured out upon us richly, through Jesus Christ our Saviour; that, being justified by His grace, we might be made heirs according to the hope of eternal life. Faithful is the saying' (Tit. iii. 4-8).

Of this, Dr. Bernard says: 'No nobler statement of doctrine is found anywhere in the Pauline Epistles than these verses present'.

'Faithful is the saying: if we died with Him, we shall also live with Him; if we endure, we shall also reign with Him: if we shall deny Him, He also will deny us: if we are faithless, He abideth faithful; for He cannot deny Himself' (2 Tim. ii. 11-13).

In addition to these great passages, so laden with Christian truth—truth which has its parallels in Paul's other Epistles—are other doctrinal statements of profoundest significance.

'There is one God, and one Mediator also between God and men, (Himself) man, Christ Jesus, who gave Himself a ransom for all; the testimony (to be borne) in its own times' (1 Tim. ii. 5, 6).

'Without controversy great is the mystery of godliness; He who was manifested in the flesh, justified in the spirit, seen of angels, preached among the nations, believed on in the world, received up in glory' (1 Tim. iii. 16).

'Our Lord Jesus Christ Who is the blessed and only Potentate, the King of kings, and Lord of lords; Who only hath immortality, dwelling in light unapproachable; Whom no man hath seen, nor can see; to Whom be honour and power eternal' (1 Tim. vi. 15, 16).

'For the grace of God hath appeared, bringing salvation to all men, instructing us, to the intent that, denying ungodliness and worldly lusts, we should live soberly and righteously and godly in this present world; looking for the blessed hope and appearing of the glory of our great God and Saviour Jesus Christ; Who gave Himself for us, that He might redeem us from all iniquity, and purify unto Himself a people for His own possession, zealous of good works' (Tit. ii. 11-14).

'Suffer hardship with the Gospel according to the power of God, Who saved us, and called us, with a holy calling, not according to our works, but according to His own purpose and grace, which was given us in Christ Jesus before times eternal, but hath now been manifested by the appearing of our Saviour Christ Jesus, Who abolished death, and brought life and incorruption to light through the Gospel' (2 Tim. i. 8-11).

That a forger could have written these words is a preposterous idea. That they are thoroughly Pauline is too obvious to need demonstration.

4. THE ECCLESIASTICAL PROBLEM is one of engaging interest, because it indicates on the part of the Apostle Paul a changed perspective relative to the Second Advent of our LORD.

It has been said that this subject faded out from the theology of the Apostle in the later years of his life, but this is simply not true.

The references in the Pastoral Epistles to the Second Advent, though few, are perfectly clear (1 Tim. iv. 1; vi. 14; Tit. ii. 13; 2 Tim. iv. 1, 8); but whereas in 1 Thessalonians the Advent is thought of as not distant, in the Pastoral Epistles it recedes as to time, and by Church organization preparation is made for an incalculable future.

The hope of the Advent was true from the beginning but the *perspective* of it was not (1 Thess. iv. 13, 14; 2 Thess. ii. 1-5. cf. Luke xix. 12, 13, 15).

The organization—if it can be called that—of the early Church was very simple.

'Day by day, continuing steadfastly with one accord in the temple, and breaking bread at home, they did take their food with gladness and singleness of heart, praising God, and having favour with all the people. And the Lord added to them day by day those that were being saved' (Acts ii. 46, 47).

'As many as were possessors of lands or houses sold them, and brought the prices of the things that were sold, and laid them at the apostles' feet; and distribution was made unto each, according as any one had need' (Acts iv. 34, 35).

'The Twelve called the multitude of the disciples unto them, and said: "It is not fit that we should forsake the word of God and serve tables. Look ye out therefore, brethren, from among you seven men of good report, full of the Spirit and of wisdom, whom we may appoint over this business"' (Acts vi. 1-6).

'God hath set some in the Church, first apostles, secondly prophets, thirdly teachers, then powers, then gifts of healings, helps, governments, (divers) kinds of tongues' (1 Cor. xii. 28).

'When He ascended on high, He led captivity captive, and gave gifts unto men. And He gave some (to be) apostles; and some, prophets; and some, evangelists; and some, pastors and teachers' (Eph. iv. 8-11).

'The bishops and deacons' (Phil. i. 1. 1 Tim. iii. 1-7; iii. 8-13 (11); v. 17-25. Tit. i. 5-9. 2 Tim. iv. 1-5.

The erection of special buildings for worship belongs to a later date. At first meetings were in the houses of Christians (Phile. 2).

From the beginning it was found necessary to appoint leaders where there was a Christian community; and so on his first missionary journey Paul appointed 'elders in every Church' (Acts xiv. 23).

These were called *Presbuteroi*, and *Episkopoi*, translated Elders, Bishops, and Overseers (Acts xx. 28; 1 Tim. iii. 1; v. 17; Tit. i. 5); and these designations refer to one office only (cf. Tit. i. 5, 7; Acts xx. 17, 28).

The other Church appointment was of *Deacons* (Phil. i. 1; 1 Tim. iii. 8-13; Acts vi. 1-6).

The Bishops attended to the spiritualities, and the Deacons to the temporalities; and the simplicity of Church organization at that time needed no other offices. These, however, must not be confused with the 'gifts' of the risen LORD (1 Cor. xii. 28; Eph. iv. 8-11).

It is worthy of notice that there is no reference whatever to *Priests*. Well has Lightfoot said—would that it had been believed:

'The only priests under the Gospel, designated as such in the New Testament, are the saints, the members of the Christian brotherhood (1 Pet. ii. 5, 9; Rev. i. 6; v. 10; xx. 6). As individuals, all Christians are priests alike.'

It is outside the scope of this book to say anything about when and how the present-day episcopacy and hierarchy arose, but neither can appeal to the New Testament for justification.

Sacerdotalism is not only not warranted by the New Testament, but is contrary to it.

It is worthy of notice that the Eucharist, the LORD's Supper, is never mentioned in the Pastorals, and that there is only one reference to baptism unless 'washing' is 'laver' (Tit. iii. 5).

Of all the letters which profess to have come from the Apostle Paul those to Timothy and Titus are the most disputed, but the affinities between these and Paul's other letters are more than sufficient to override the objections which have been raised to their Pauline authorship.

CHART 173

AFFINITIES BETWEEN PASTORALS AND OTHER PAULINE LETTERS					
1 TIMOTHY	ROMANS	2 TIMOTHY	ROMANS	TITUS	ROMANS
i. 8, 9	vii. 12	i. 7	viii. 15	i. 1-4	xvi. 25, 26
i. 17	xvi. 27	i. 8, 12	i. 16	ii. 13	v. 2
ii. 1, 2	xiii. 1	i. 9, 10	xvi. 26	iii. 10	xvi. 17, 18
	1 Corinthians		**1 Corinthians**		**1 Corinthians**
i. 20	v. 5	i. 2-6; ii. 1, 2	iv. 17	i. 7	iv. 1
ii. 11, 12	xi. 8, 9; xiv. 34	iii. 10, 11	xvi. 10, 11	ii. 13	i. 7
ii. 13, 14	xi. 3			iii. 3	vi. 11
	Ephesians		**Ephesians**		**Ephesians**
iii. 5, 15	ii. 19, 20	i. 9, 10	iii. 3, 5, 9, 10	i. 1-4	i. 9, 10
iii. 15, 16	iv. 21	ii. 8	i. 19, 20	ii. 14	i. 7, 14; v. 2, 25-27
iv. 1	ii. 2	ii. 9	iii. 1, 13	iii. 3	ii. 2; v. 8
	Philippians		**Philippians**		**Philippians**
i. 12	iv. 13	i. 3	iii. 5	ii. 13	iii. 20
i. 18	ii. 25	ii. 8-13 }	i. 29, 30	iii. 2	iv. 5
ii. 1	iv. 6	iii. 10-14 }	ii. 19-22	iii. 5, 7	iii. 9
			iii. 10, 11, 17		
			iv. 9		
	Colossians	i. 12	i. 20		
i. 1-4, 11, 12; iii. 15, 16	i. 23-27				

These references are selected from Dr. R. A. Falconer's article on the Pastoral Epistles in Hastings' Dictionary of the Apostolic Church, p. 591.

THE PASTORAL EPISTLES

I TIMOTHY

A.D. 63-65

In a letter from an old man to a young one it is not reasonable to expect systematic treatment of any subject, and any analysis which may be made of it must not be supposed to have existed in the mind of the Apostle. The letter is spontaneous and, in a sense, fragmentary; but the object Paul had in writing it he kept in mind throughout.

The following analysis of this First Epistle summarizes its contents.

CHART 174

I TIMOTHY	A.D. 63-65
Introduction i. 1, 2	

THE CHURCH OF GOD i. 3-iii. 13	THE MINISTRY OF TIMOTHY iii. 14-vi. 19
1. ITS DOCTRINE (i. 3-20)	**1. HIS WALK. PERSONAL (iii. 14-iv. 16)**
(i) The Character and Content of the Truth .. .. .. i. 3-11	(i) His Relation to Truth .. iii. 14-16
(ii) The Commission of Paul and Charge of Timothy .. .. i. 12-20	(ii) His Relation to Error .. iv. 1-11
	(iii) His Relation to All .. .. iv. 12-16
2. ITS WORSHIP (ii. 1-15)	**2. HIS WORK. OFFICIAL (v. 1-vi. 19)**
(i) The Matter of Prayer in Public Worship .. .. .. ii. 1-10	(i) His Duty toward the Flock v. 1-vi. 2
(ii) The Manner of Women in Public Worship .. ii. 11-15	(ii) His Duty toward the Evil ..vi. 3-16
3. ITS OVERSIGHT (iii. 1-13)	
(i) BISHOPS: their Qualifications and Functions iii. 1-7	(iii) His Duty toward the Rich vi. 17-19
(ii) DEACONS: their Qualifications and Functions iii. 8-13	Conclusion .. .. .. vi. 20, 21

It has been well said that 'Timothy was one of the magnificent compensations Paul enjoyed for the cruel treatment he received at Lystra' (Acts xiv. 8-21; xvi. 1, 2). This youth was the son of a

233

Grecian father and a Jewish mother, the former of whom died probably when Timothy was quite a child (2 Tim. i. 5). He was brought to Christ during Paul's first visit to Lystra, and later from that town accompanied the Apostle on his missionary journeys, and is very frequently referred to in his Letters, and always in the highest terms.

When Paul wrote his previous Letter—Philippians—he was a prisoner at Rome, but by this time evidently he was released, for he speaks of a visit he had paid to Ephesus, and of one he was paying to Macedonia (1 Tim. i. 3).

He had found that during the years of his confinement, heresies had entered the Church at Ephesus, as he had predicted they would (Acts xx. 28-30); and for that reason, instead of taking Timothy with him into Macedonia, he left him at the Asian city that he might 'charge some that they teach no other doctrine'. The object, then, of this and the companion Epistles is mainly two-fold—to caution and to confirm; to warn the Ephesian saints, and all saints, against false teaching in its many forms, and to warn these and all false teachers of the peril of their way (i. 20); and on the other hand, to encourage Timothy and the Ephesian Church, and every minister and every church, to continue in the truth and to live a holy life.

The features of this Letter, which is the second written to an individual, are many and striking. Special notice should be taken of (a) the errors present or threatened; fables, i. 4, iv. 7; speculations, vi. 20; legality, i. 5-11; asceticism, iv. 1-5. (b) the character of God as Saviour, and the references to salvation, i. 1; ii. 3; iv. 10; i. 15; ii. 4, 15; iv. 16, and in Titus and 2 Timothy. (c) the emphasis laid upon 'godliness', ii. 2; iii. 16; iv. 7, 8; v. 4; vi. 3, 5, 6, 11; 2 Timothy; Titus, and (d) the prominence given to 'doctrine,' i. 10; iv. 1, 6, 13, 16; v. 17; vi. 1, 3.

As we have already said (p. 229), notable also are the 'Faithful Sayings,' of which there are six—i. 15; iii. 1; iv. 9; Titus i. 9; iii. 8; 2 Tim. ii. 11. These, Angus says, 'may denote certain Logia current in the early churches, or, as some writers have suggested, the use of liturgical forms'. This suggestion is most interesting and seems to receive strong support from such a passage as I Tim. iii. 16, which appears to be the rudiment of a creed which may have been recited or chanted in the public assemblies. In it we find the first formal statement of Christian doctrine, and it may be compared line for line with I Pet. iii. 18-22.

It should be noticed that (a) 'Faithful is the saying,' *pistos ho logos*, stands first in all the five 'Sayings'; (b) in Nos. 1, 2, 4, the words 'faithful is the saying' precede the 'saying', and in Nos. 3 and 5 they follow it; (c) Nos. 1 and 3 of the 'sayings' are followed by the words 'and worthy of all acceptation.' The last word occurs only here and in iv. 9.

Further lines of important study in this Letter are: the place of women in the Christian Church; the advanced stage of Church organization; the predicted corruption of Christianity; the important teaching concerning stewardship; the authority of the Scriptures in the teaching and life of the Church. For those who are able to consult the Greek, many other lines of interest and profit are opened up. Some of the more notable passages of the Epistle, which are worthy of closer examination are: i. 5, 15, 17; ii. 4-6; iii. 16; vi. 9, 10, 11, 12, 13-16.

THE PASTORAL EPISTLES

TITUS

A.D. 64-67

It is evidence of the foresight and wisdom of the Apostle Paul that he selected two young men such as Timothy and Titus to assist him during the latter part of his strenuous ministry, and to carry on that work when he would no longer be able to do so. The life of each of these youths should be carefully studied.

TITUS

At the great Conference at Jerusalem in A.D. 50-51, when the freedom of the Gentiles from the bonds of Judaism was under discussion, Titus was made a test case (Acts xv; Gal. ii. 3). Later on, he was dispatched from Ephesus to Corinth to discover and report to Paul what was the effect upon the Achaian Church of the Letter he had written to them (2 Cor. ii. 12, 13; viii; ix). Titus met the Apostle in Macedonia, with comforting news (Acts xx. 2; 2 Cor. vii. 5-7). From the present Epistle we learn that this young bishop was left in Crete (i. 5) to attend to disorders which had arisen there, a work for which his experience at Corinth had eminently fitted him. From these few references to him 'we learn that he was a man of strong affection, of devout enthusiasm, of practical capacity, and of sound wisdom and discretion'.

The following is a brief outline of the Letter which Paul wrote to Titus—a Letter which falls between his First and his Second to Timothy.

The time and circumstances which gave rise to the writing of this Epistle are similar to those of 1 Timothy. In both, these

CHART 175

TITUS		A.D. 64-67
Introduction i. 1-4		
i. 5-16	ii. 1-15	iii. 1-11
THE RULE OF THE CHURCH	THE WALK OF THE CHURCH	THE STATE OF THE CHURCH
1. The Nature of it i. 5-9	1. The Guiding Precepts ii. 1-10	1. Her Outward Duty iii. 1-7
2. The Necessity for it i. 10-16	2. The Enabling Power ii. 11-15	2. Her Inward Discipline iii. 8-11
		Conclusion iii. 12-15

fellow-helpers were left behind to attend to disorders (1 Tim i. 3; Titus i. 5); to appoint bishops (iii. 1-7 and i. 5); to be examples (iv. 12 and ii. 7). In both, the evil was Jewish in character (i. 3-7 and i. 10); and the motive was greed for gain (vi.5 and i. 11); and in both the believers are exhorted to 'healthful words' and 'good works' (vi. 3, 18 and i. 9; iii. 8).

The Gospel of Jesus Christ has ever grappled with big problems, and forced its way into the most difficult places, such as Antioch, Corinth, Athens, Rome, and Crete; and in this it has ever gloried, as it has ever triumphed. The Church at Crete was not founded by the Apostle Paul, but probably by those who were blessed at that great Pentecostal Feast of Acts ii, see verse 11. Something of the character of the Cretans may be learnt from this short Letter, in which the witness of Epimenides, one of their own poets, is cited (i. 12), and the witness shows how difficult was the task of Titus on that island.

This Letter is notable for the fact that it was the last written by the great Apostle in days of liberty, for, shortly after writing it, he was re-arrested and taken again to Rome, this time to die. Some have thought lightly of this Epistle, considering it 'meagre, colourless, and monotonous'; but this estimate reflects rather upon the intelligence of those who make it.

Farrar has spoken of the Epistle as 'a priceless and unrivalled manual of pastoral advice'; and Luther said: 'This is a short Epistle, but yet such a quintessence of Christian doctrine, and composed in such a masterly manner, that it contains all that is needful for Christian knowledge and life'.

After a most pregnant introduction (i. 1-4), the Apostle instructs his younger brother concerning Government in the Church, showing, first of all, the nature of it (5-9), and then, the necessity for it (10-16).

The principal office in the Church is that of a bishop or elder, who, as to his private life, must be blameless, and as to his public life, must be loyal to the Word of God, able to teach, and faithful as the 'steward of God.' The need for one, or many, of such character and qualities is then shown, for at that time there was, and still in our time there is, alas, not infrequently in the Church, moral deflection, and doctrinal error, which need to be treated with firmness and discretion.

Following upon the Government of the Church, is a passage of singular beauty, concerning her Walk (ii). As in 1 Timothy, so here, various classes of persons are specified, and exhorted to good conduct; the aged men (2), aged women (3), young women (4, 5), young men (6-8), and servants (9-10), and the power by which alone they may fulfil this ideal of life is set forth in what is, no doubt, the profoundest paragraph of the Epistle (11-14).

Of these verses Farrar says: 'Which of all the Fathers of the first or second century was in the smallest degree capable of writing so masterly a formula of Christian doctrine and practice as these verses? Will any one produce from Clemens, or Hermas, or Justin Martyr, or Ignatius, or Polycarp, or Irenaeus—will anyone even produce from Tertullian, or Chrysostom, or Basil, or Gregory of Nyssa—any single passage comparable for terseness, insight, and mastery to either of these? Only the inspired wisdom of the greatest of the Apostles could have traced so divine a summary with so unfaltering a hand.

'Would it not be somewhat strange if all the great Christian Fathers of three centuries were so far surpassed in power and eloquence by the supposed *falsarii* who wrote the Epistles of the First and Second Captivity of St. Paul?'

In ii. 11, the first Advent is of *grace*, and in ii. 13, the second Advent is of *glory*. The grace of God brings salvation, and teaches us; and mark what it teaches—the two sides of our life, negative and positive (12a, 12b), and on the positive side, the threefold relation: Selfward, 'soberly', Manward, 'righteously', and Godward, 'godly'.

In the third chapter, the relation of the Church to the State is set forth; first of all, her outward Duty (1-7), and then, the inward Discipline, by which alone she may hope to discharge that Duty (8-11). The Duty is declared in verses 1 and 2 and the motive and impulse are furnished in 3-7.

THE PASTORAL EPISTLES

2 TIMOTHY

A.D. 67-68

The outstanding claim of this Epistle to our special attention consists in the fact that it is the last Letter written by the Apostle Paul, shortly before his execution. When he wrote his first to Timothy, and the one to Titus, he was travelling in Asia and Europe. It cannot be said with any degree of certainty what was the exact order of his movements at this time, but a probable journey can be constructed from scattered references in the Pastoral Epistles, judged in the light of what we know from the 'Acts' and the other Letters.

A draft outline of events from A.D. 61-70 is given in Vol. II, pp. 465-494. Here is a tentative plan of the Apostle's movements between his release from Rome in A.D. 63 to the time of his death in A.D. 67-68. See Map 37, p. 222.

Released in A.D. 63. Visited Philippi for the fourth time (Phil. ii. 24). Went to Colossae (Phile. 22); then, probably, to Spain (Rom. xv. 28. cf. Conybeare and Howson); back to Ephesus (1 Tim. i. 3); where he left Timothy in charge, and himself went on to Macedonia (1 Tim. i. 3); from Macedonia he wrote the first Letter to Timothy, and while there he probably visited Philippi and Corinth; went from there to Crete (Titus i. 5) where he left Titus in charge, when he himself went again into Asia, probably to Ephesus, and from whence he wrote the Letter to Titus.

He then went to Miletus, and left Trophimus there, sick (2 Tim. iv. 20), when he himself went on to Troas (2 Tim. iv. 13); then on to Corinth (2 Tim. iv. 20), on his way to Nicopolis to winter (Titus iii. 12); but he was arrested there or at Corinth, or Troas, and spent that winter at Rome (2 Tim. iv. 21), instead of at Nicopolis. And from Rome (i. 8; iv. 6) he wrote this last Letter to Timothy (cf. Lightfoot, Conybeare, and Farrar).

By this it is assumed (a) that these Letters are Paul's; and (b) that they were written after, and not before, his two years' imprisonment at Rome. The evidence for the late date of these Epistles is fully discussed by Lightfoot, Gloag, Zahn, and others, and need not be introduced here.

CHART 176

2 TIMOTHY	A.D. 67–68
INTRODUCTION (i. 1–5)	
i. 6–ii. 26	iii. 1–iv. 18
PERSONAL EQUIPMENT FOR THE MINISTRY	PUBLIC FULFILMENT OF THE MINISTRY
1. THE ESSENTIAL QUALITIES i. 6–18	1. THE COMING CHANGE iii. 1–17
(i) Zeal, and the Incentive to it i. 6, 7	(i) The Evil to be Faced iii. 1–9
(ii) Courage, and the Incentive to it i. 8–12	(ii) The Encouragement to Face it iii. 10–17
(iii) Steadfastness, and the Incentive to it i. 13–18	
2. THE NECESSARY DISCIPLINE ii. 1–26	2. THE CLOSING CHARGE · iv. 1–18
(i) The Minister's Duty to Himself ii. 1–7	(i) The Thing to be Done iv. 1, 2
(ii) The Minister's Duty to the Truth ii. 8–14	(ii) The Reason for Doing it iv. 3–8
(iii) The Minister's Duty to the Church ii. 15–26	(iii) Final Requests and Reflections iv. 9–18
	CONCLUSION (iv. 19–22)

This, Paul's last Letter, is of an intensely personal character, hardly permitting of analysis. His object in writing it was, firstly, to confirm and encourage Timothy in his ministry, who, perhaps upon hearing of his friend's re-arrest, had begun to fear and falter (i. 6-8); and secondly, to bid Timothy come to him to Rome with the utmost speed (i. 4; iv. 9, 13, 21). Whether he arrived in time to see Paul alive we do not know, but we may feel sure that Timothy would not hesitate to respond at once to this pathetic and affectionate Letter.

When Paul decided to communicate with Timothy, he knew that he was about to die a violent death (iv. 6). There he was, an old and infirm man, in a Roman dungeon; denied the privilege of his former imprisonment (cf. Acts xxviii. 30, 31; 2 Tim. i. 17, 18); forsaken by almost all his friends (i. 15; iv. 11, 14-16); having undergone a preliminary trial, probably towards the end of

A.D. 67; and was waiting for the next and last trial—how, we wonder, will such an one write? How would we write in such circumstances? Would we not be tempted to pour out the grief of our hearts, and the complaint of our spirits; or question the kindness and wisdom of God? Yet, there is nothing of that in this Letter; here we see how a true Christian faces death, firm in his faith, and proud of his sufferings (i. 8-12), knowing that to die is to reign with Christ (ii. 12), and looking with glistening eyes towards the crown laid up for him (iv. 8), to be given him by the LORD.

This greatest of saints and servants does not, in this dark hour, morbidly contemplate his coming decease, but is filled with love and desire for the welfare of Timothy, and the future of the Church. With his last breath, as it were, he exhorts all who are entrusted with the Gospel to zeal, courage, and steadfastness, and warns against cowardice, infidelity, and worldliness.

He presents us with a remarkable series of pictures of what the true Christian should be in the service of Christ: as a Soldier, devoted to the cause (ii. 3, 4); as a Wrestler, subject to discipline (5); as a Husbandman, labouring and waiting (6); as a Workman, rightly dividing (or cutting straight) the Word (15); as a Vessel, purged and separated from dishonourable vessels (20, 21); and as a Servant, serving in a worthy manner and spirit, the LORD JESUS (24-26).

Knowing that he may not write again, the Apostle foretells by the Spirit the future corruption of Christendom; of the coming of self-lovers, money-lovers, pleasure-lovers, and not God-lovers, men of corrupt minds and devoid of judgment concerning the faith. Surely we may say that the time which Paul predicted is even now come, and that we are not merely in the 'latter times' (1 Tim. iv. 1), but in the 'last days' (2 Tim. iii. 1).

And what is our security and hope in such a day? This Letter tells us—it is the Word of God. 'In the approaching corruption of Christianity, Paul directs Timothy to the true conservative principle of its purity, not new miracles, nor a fresh revelation, but the doctrine in which Timothy had been instructed, and those Scriptures which make the man of God perfect, thoroughly furnished unto all good works (iii. 14-17; 2 Thess. ii; 2 Pet. i. 15-21; iii. 1-4, 14-17). How instructive that in the last writings of both Peter and Paul, nor less in the writings of John (Rev. xxii), and in the prospect of the heresies that were to prevail in the Church, we should be directed to the study of the Scriptures, and that thus we are not led to expect additional disclosures of the Divine Will' (Angus).

Solemn, indeed, are these charges to Timothy and all ministers concerning the fulfilment of their ministry, seeing they are the last word of the Spirit through this 'chosen vessel', and uttered on the brink of a malefactor's grave (!) (ii. 9).

Chapter i relates to the past; chapter ii. to the present; and chapter iii to the future.

The Apostle says: 'I am already being offered, and the time of my departure is come' (iv. 6. R.V.); and yet, in iv. 21, he exhorts Timothy to come to him before winter. Surely between these two statements something must have happened, and, it would seem, the explanation is given in verse 16 where Paul speaks of his 'first answer'. This expression cannot refer to his trial just before his release from Rome in A.D. 63, but, apparently, to a preliminary trial after his re-arrest.

Evidently, Paul expected that trial to end in his death (ver. 6), but it ended in a remand which gave the Apostle an indefinite interval, and, in view of this, he sent for Timothy.

The order of events seems to have been:

trial, and Paul's expectation of death (iv. 6):
remand without a verdict (iv. 16):
letter to Timothy, in view of a possible winter in prison before the final trial (iv. 9, 13, 21).

If this be correct, there is a considerable break between verses 8, 9 of chapter iv; and in this light all that follows verse 8 is intelligible.

This Epistle is rich in personal allusions, some twenty-three persons being named—men and women, friends and foes.

Paul left Trophimus at Miletum sick (iv. 20). He tells us that Timothy had stomach trouble, and other infirmities (1 Tim. v. 23). Epaphroditus 'was sick nigh unto death' (Phil. ii. 27); and the Apostle himself had a 'thorn in the flesh' which the Lord refused to remove (2 Cor. xii. 7-9).

As Paul had the power to heal why did he not use it in these instances? In considering 'faith' or 'Divine' healing these must be taken into account.

2 Tim. iv. 5-18 is deathless literature. Here are heroic emotion, dauntless courage, and certain hope. Facing the executioner's block, Paul has no complaints nor murmurings on his own account, though he regrets the attitude of some whom he trusted (10, 16).

Not rarely have great men at the end of their life bent under depression; but Paul did not.

The Apostle was not now in a 'hired house' with much freedom (Acts xxviii), but in a deep, dark, damp dungeon, cold, and, no doubt, hungry. Yet he did not lose his interest in people, nor his love of reading and writing.

'The cloke that I left at Troas with Carpus, bring when thou comest, and the books, especially the parchments' (iv. 13). 'The cloke,' in all likelihood, was an old friend which had been a comfort to him on his many journeys by land and sea. Now he says: 'I want my old cloke, for I am cold'.

'The books' were papyrus rolls on which the Apostle may have been writing to some person or church. Or they may have been relics of his student days in Tarsus and Jerusalem.

'The parchments' were vellum rolls, of the Old Testament, perhaps; and among them may have been the diploma of his Roman franchise.

'Cloke, books, parchments'—these appear to have been all that Paul possessed, and, maybe, he wanted, after using them a little longer, to give them to Timothy or to Luke.

When William Tyndale, the translator of the English Bible, was in prison at Vilvorde in Belgium, in 1535, he addressed a letter to the Governor of the Castle, asking that his warm clothing and his Hebrew Bible, and Grammar, and Dictionary might be given to him.

The letter says:

> 'I believe, right worshipful, that you are not ignorant of what has been determined concerning me; therefore I entreat your lordship, and that by the Lord Jesus, that if I am to remain here during the winter, you will request the Procureur to be kind enough to send me, from my goods which he has in his possession, a warmer cap, for I suffer extremely from cold in the head, being afflicted with a perpetual catarrh, which is considerably increased in this cell. A warmer coat also, for that which I have is very thin; also a piece of cloth to patch my leggings; my overcoat is worn out; my shirts are also worn out . . . I wish also his permission to have a lamp in the evening, for it is wearisome to sit alone in the dark. But above all, I entreat and beseech your clemency to be urgent with the Procureur that he may kindly permit me to have my Hebrew Bible, Hebrew Grammar, and Hebrew Dictionary, that I may spend my time with that study. And in return, may you obtain your dearest wish, provided always it be consistent with the salvation of your soul. But if, before the end of the winter, a different decision be reached concerning me, I shall be patient, abiding the will of God to the glory of the grace of my Lord Jesus Christ, whose Spirit, I pray, may ever direct your heart. Amen.
>
> W. Tindale.'

We rightly attach importance to the last sayings of great souls: e.g., Nurse Cavell's, and Captain Scott's; but greater than all others is Paul's farewell word, in which he epitomises his whole life.

LIFE VIEWED FROM ITS END
2. Tim. iv. 6-8

6	7	8
'I am already being poured out, and the time of my release is come.'	'I have fought the good fight; I have finished the course: I have kept the faith.'	'Henceforth is laid up for me the crown of righteousness, which the Lord the righteous Judge will give me in that Day.'
PRESENT	PAST	FUTURE
Contemplation	Reflection	Anticipation
Looking Outward	Looking Backward	Looking Forward
Deepest Interest	Calmest Satisfaction	Sweetest Assurance
SPIRITUAL VIGOUR in the Face of Death	STRIKING VERDICT on his Christian life	SUBLIME VISION of the Coming Good

For Paul, death was an '*outpouring*' and an '*unmooring*'. The first metaphor refers to the libation which always formed the conclusion of the sacrifice; and the second likens his death to the loosening of the cable which holds the vessel to the land.

Paul viewed his life as a '*fight*'; not as war, but as the contests in the Olympic Arena.

Also, as a '*race*', which implies continuous progress in one direction (cf. Phil. iii. 13, 14).

Also, as a '*trust*'. He had been given a 'deposit' to guard, and he had guarded it (cf. 1 Tim. vi. 20; 2 Tim. i. 12, 14).

The 'fight' he had fought. The 'course' he had run. The 'faith' he had kept. And at the end of life he is peaceful, grateful, and hopeful.

His song was:

> I've wrestled on towards heaven,
> 'Gainst storm, and wind, and tide;
> Now, like a weary traveller that leaneth
>   on his Guide,
> Amid the shades of evening
> While sinks life's lingering sand,
> I hail the glory dawning
> In Immanuel's Land.

THE CURTAIN FALLS

We have contemplated the Pauline history and literature—the history in the book of the Acts, and the literature in the thirteen Epistles attributed to the Apostle.

Much of this man's life is seen in a blaze of light, but the end of it is in entire darkness.

Writing to Timothy, he spoke of his 'first answer' (2 Tim. iv. 16), by which he meant his first appearance in the Imperial Court after his re-arrest, probably in A.D. 67; but there is no record of his 'second answer', which sealed his doom.

Where was Luke during Paul's last trial? Did Timothy reach his old friend before the end, and if so, was he not at the trial? Had Paul no one to stand by him and speak for him when most he needed such? (2 Tim. iv. 16.)

The curtain fell, and only conjecture can supply probability. Farrar says: 'For nearly three miles the sad procession walked;

and doubtless the dregs of the populace, who always delight in a scene of horror, gathered round them.

'About three miles from Rome, not far from the Ostian Road, is a green and level spot, with low hills around it, known anciently as *Aquae Salviae*, and now as *Tre Fontane*. There, the word of command to halt was given; the prisoner knelt down; the sword flashed and the life of the greatest of the Apostles was shorn away.'

PAUL AND NERO

These were individuals, of course, but they were also symbols; they stood for totally different ideas and ends.

Dean Farrar, after detailing the course of Nero and of Paul, goes on to say:

'These two men were brought face to face—imperial power and abject weakness; youth cankered with guilt, and old age crowned with holiness; he whose whole life had consummated the degradation, and he whose whole life had achieved the enfranchisement of mankind.

'They stood face to face the representatives of two races—the Semitic in its richest glory, the Aryan in its extremest degradation: the representatives of two trainings—the life of utter self-sacrifice, and the life of unfathomable self-indulgence: the representatives of two religions—Christianity in its dawning brightness, Paganism in its effete despair: the representatives of two theories of life—the simplicity of self-denying endurance ready to give up life itself for the good of others, the luxury of shameless Hedonism which valued no consideration divine or human in comparison with a new sensation: the representatives of two spiritual powers—the slave of Christ and the incarnation of Antichrist.'

'Hopes have precarious life;
They are oft blighted, withered, snapped sheer off
In vigorous youth, and turned to rottenness;
But faithfulness can feed on suffering,
And knows no disappointment.'   SPANISH GYPSY.

There they were face to face; the one about thirty years old and the other about sixty-six. The one went to hell, and the other to heaven. Each looked on the other for the last time—the one eternally to die, the other eternally to live. The memory of the one is loathsome and execrable, and of the other, challenging and inspiring.

There are only two choices, only two ways, only two masters, and only two destinies. 'Whatsoever a man soweth that shall he also reap.'

THE EPISTLE TO

THE HEBREWS

A.D. 64-67

THE EPISTLE TO THE HEBREWS

A.D. 64-67

Notes

Of the epistolary writings in the New Testament, the one to
The Hebrews stands by itself; that is, it cannot be placed in any
Group, either Pauline or Catholic. In subject and style there is
nothing with which to compare it.

A library has been written on: who wrote it, where it was
written, and where was its destination, and no answer can be
given to any of these inquiries.

Relative to *authorship*, Paul, Barnabas, Luke, Clement of
Rome, Silas, Philip, Priscilla and Apollos have been advocated.

As to *destination* of the Epistle, claims have been made for
Palestine, Egypt, Italy, Greece, Syria; and more particularly,
for Antioch, Jerusalem, Alexandria, and Rome.

These guesses show how unprofitable and hopeless it is to
search for what cannot be found.

The value of no New Testament Writing depends on who
wrote it. If it could be proved that the Apostle John did not
write the Fourth Gospel, the Writing itself would lose none of its
value as Scripture; and could it be proved that Paul wrote
'Hebrews', the Epistle itself would have no more value than it
now has as Scripture.

Here are two thoughts for what they are worth: (*a*) On the way
to Emmaus, the LORD, 'beginning at Moses and all the Prophets,
expounded in all the Scriptures the things concerning Himself'.
That is what is done in 'Hebrews'. Did one of the two who heard
Him write down what He said?

The second thought is (*b*) in 'Hebrews' only is the LORD called
an *Apostle* (iii. 1). Could we expect to see any human star when
the Divine Sun was at the meridian?

What God has been pleased to hide from us, we should be
content not to know.

The writer of the Epistle calls it a '*word of exhortation*' (xiii. 22).
This shows that it is not a theological treatise but a letter, though

not having the epistolary opening that Paul's letters have. There is, however, an epistolary conclusion (xiii. 23-25).

How truly the Epistle is a unity can be seen by bringing together i. 1, 2 and xii. 25.

'God who *spake* in time past . . . hath in these last days *spoken* . . . See that ye refuse not Him that *speaketh*.'

This shows in what sense the whole Epistle is an 'exhortation' (xiii. 22).

It may be said that the subject of the Epistle is *The Finality of Christianity*, and this subject is summarized in chapter i. 1-4.

The title 'To Hebrews', which is in the oldest MSS., settles the question as to who the readers were intended to be, but, by itself, it does not indicate whether the Epistle was for Hebrews in general, or for a special company of Hebrews.

That it was for the latter is made clear in the Epistle itself (ii. 3; v. 11-13; vi. 9-12; x. 32-35; xii. 3-5), though the locality cannot be named.

Tradition is silent as to the *place* from which the Epistle was written. The statement in xiii. 24 may mean one or other of two things: (*a*) Italian Christians in Italy, or (*b*) Italian Christians abroad; and so, as Bishop Westcott says: 'The place of writing must be left in complete uncertainty. Plausible conjectures unsupported by evidence cannot remove our ignorance even if they satisfy our curiosity.'

The Style of the Epistle differs from that of any other New Testament Writing. Westcott says it is 'purer and more vigorous'. Though this is a matter that will appeal specially to grammarians and rhetoricians, it is not without interest to those who are unversed in the art of style.

Even in a translation it can be seen that the writer has constructed his sentences with much care.

Prof. A. B. Davidson has spoken of 'the stately march of the oratory' of this Epistle; 'the rhythmical balance of the sentence; the straight course pursued by the exposition, which never allows itself to be diverted into side paths by the starting of incidental points; the skilful planning and clear laying out of the whole, illustrated in the habit of throwing in a catchword in preparation for a new development, and showing that the Author saw along the whole line and the end before he spoke his first word'; all this, and much more is characteristic of this Writing.

A good example of the Author's method of construction is seen in chapter i. 1, 2.

'GOD—

'at sundry times and in divers manners	1	(at one time and in one manner)
'spake	2	'hath spoken
'in time past	3	'in these last days
'unto the fathers	4	'unto us
'by the prophets	5	'by His Son'

There are at least 153 words which occur in 'Hebrews' only, and 167 which occur here and elsewhere but not in Paul.

There is no allusion in the Epistle to Gentile believers but the Hebrews to whom it is written are described in some detail.

They had received the Gospel from men who knew the LORD (ii. 3), and who now were dead (xiii. 7).

They had been Christians for a considerable time (v. 12).

They had suffered much persecution (x. 32, 33), and had faced it bravely (x. 34).

They were not a poor community, and had been generous to their poorer brethren (vi. 10).

Their early promise was not fulfilled, for their spiritual progress was slow (v. 11-14).

Disappointment had affected their diligence and had dimmed their hope (vi. 11, 12).

Spiritual fellowship with one another was deteriorating, and meeting together for mutual edification was less frequent (x. 24, 25).

They were in danger of being 'carried away by divers and strange teachings' (xiii. 9); of 'departing from the living God' (iii. 12); and of 'falling from the grace of God' (xii. 15), instead of 'going on unto perfection' (vi. 1).

The danger of these Hebrews and, of course, of all professing Christians, is spoken of in two very solemn passages (vi. 4-8; x. 26-31).

The cases here described must not be confused with a falling into sin, as in Gal. vi. 1; or with backsliding, as we commonly understand this word (cf. 2 Cor. vii. 9-11).

In chapter vi, presumably, and in chapter x, certainly, it is clearly a case of *apostasy*. The sin described is the same as 'the blasphemy of the Holy Spirit', of which the LORD spoke (Luke xii. 10).

Mark what is said about the people the Writer has in view.

CHAPTER vi. 4, 5	CHAPTER x. 26, 29
1. They were once enlightened	6. They received the knowledge of the truth
2. They tasted of the heavenly gift,	
3. They were made partakers of the Holy Spirit	7. They were sanctified with the blood of the covenant.
4. They tasted the good word of God	
5. And the powers of the age to come	

These were their blessings. What did they do with them?

CHAPTER vi. 6	CHAPTER x. 26, 29
1. They fell-aside (the *act*)	4. They sinned wilfully;
2. Crucifying unto themselves the Son of God afresh;	5. They trod under foot the Son of God;
3. Putting Him to an open shame (the *way* cf. Matt. i. 19)	6. They counted the blood of the covenant an unholy thing;
	7. They did despite unto the Spirit of Grace

These are the sins. What are the results?

CHAPTER vi. 6	CHAPTER x. 26, 27
It is impossible to renew them again unto repentance	There is no other sacrifice for sins Fearful expectation of judgment Fierceness of fire which shall devour the adversaries

Two questions arise here: (*a*) Were the people thus spoken of ever truly converted? (*b*) If so, must we believe that a converted person may perish at last? (vi. 4-8; x. 27, 28, 39).

We must guard as much against making the apostolic warning a rack of despair, as against making it a pillow of carnal security (Delitzsch).

'*It is impossible,*' *adunatos*, in vi. 4, is a terrible word in its setting. For the finality of it see the other occurrences of it in this Epistle.

'It is *impossible* for God to lie' (vi. 18).
'It is *impossible* that the blood of bulls and goats should take away sins' (x. 4).
'Without faith it is *impossible* to be well-pleasing unto God' (xi. 6).

In both these awesome passages (vi. 4-8; x. 26-31) it appears that the Hebrews were warned of the sin and doom of apostates, which they had *not* already become.

'But, beloved (only occurrence of in Hebrews), we are persuaded better things of you' (vi. 9).

'Cast not away therefore your boldness' (x. 35).

From what has been said it will have been gathered that the danger of which the writer is warning his readers is that of willingly and knowingly denying the Christ whom they had confessed, and turning again to make common cause with the antichristian synagogue. This would be a deliberate turning from light to darkness, from freedom to bondage, and from life to death (cf. Gal. iv. 1-11; v. 1).

Be it said again, this is not backsliding, but apostasy.

This warning is presented in a systematic and comprehensive way. The argument of the writer is close-knit and conclusive.

At that time it concerned a body of Christian Jews; to-day it concerns all—Jews and Gentiles—who profess the name of Christ.

CHART 177

THE EPISTLE TO THE HEBREWS

A.D. 64-67   ANONYMOUS

SUBJECT: THE FINALITY OF CHRISTIANITY

PROLOGUE: I. 1-4

The Doctrinal Dissertation	The Central Exhortation	The Practical Application
i. 1-x. 18	x. 19-39	xi. 1-xiii. 21
A. THE PERSONALITIES .. i. 4-vii. 28 1. ANGELS and CHRIST .. i. 4-ii. 18 2. MOSES and CHRIST .. iii. 1-6 3. JOSHUA and CHRIST .. iv. 1-10 4. AARON and CHRIST .. iv. 14-v. 10 5. MELCHISEDEC and CHRIST .. vi. 20-vii. 28	1. Exhortation to FREEDOM and FELLOWSHIP x. 19-25	1. The 'WORK OF FAITH' xi. 1-40
B. THE WARNINGS First .. ii. 1-4 Second iii. 7-19 Third .. iv. 11-13 Fourth v. 11-vi. 20	Fifth Warning .. x. 26-31	2. The 'PATIENCE OF HOPE' xii. 1-24
C. THE INSTITUTIONS .. viii. 1-x. 18 1. The SANCTUARY and CHRIST .. viii. 1-6 2. The COVENANT and CHRIST .. viii. 7-13 3. The TABERNACLE and CHRIST .. ix. 1-10 4. The DAY of ATONEMENT and CHRIST .. ix. 11-28 5. The OFFERINGS and CHRIST .. x. 1-18	2. Exhortation to PATIENCE and PERSEVERANCE x. 32-39	Sixth Warning .. xii. 25-29 3. The 'LABOUR OF LOVE' xiii. 1-21

EPILOGUE: xiii. 22-25

Stated briefly, what this great Epistle declares is that *Christianity is Christ, and Christ is Final*. Christ is God's last word (i. 1, 2). The chart analysis shows this, especially the first division—i. 1-x. 13.

Christianity does not supplement Judaism—it displaces it.

When the Temple of Christianity was built the scaffolding of Judaism was no longer needed.

The Old Dispensation prepared for the New, and when the latter came the former no longer availed. This is what non-Christian Jews have not yet learned; and this is what a multitude of Christians have not yet learned—such as are the devotees of ritual.

The New Covenant has made the first old, so that when the former appeared the latter, in the purpose of God, vanished (viii. 13).

If the Old Testament is not read in the light of this Epistle it is misread.

The Prologue of the Epistle (i. 1-4) is altogether sublime, and there is nothing comparable except perhaps John i. 1-14. It is presented in 72 words in the Greek, and in 106 words in the R.V.

The whole Bible is here in view: the Old Testament (verse 1), and the New Testament (verse 2).

Both are divinely inspired because in both God has spoken. He did so 'in time past', and He has done so 'in these last days' (1, 2).

These two revelations are intimately related. The same God has spoken in both, and what He has said is progressive and complete (1, 2).

God's first utterance—the Old Testament—prepared for the the second—the New Testament.

The first utterance was fragmentary and multiform. It was 'by divers portions', and 'in divers manners' (1).

The second utterance is single, perfect, and final (2).

The first revelation was communicated by 'the Prophets' (i. 1); the second, by 'the Apostle and High Priest' (iii. 1).

The saints of the Old Covenant are called 'the fathers', and of the New Covenant, 'us'. Compare 'they' and 'us' in xi. 40. And compare both together in Rev. iv. 4.

The Father dominates i. 1, 2, and the Son, i. 2b-4. With the mention of the Son revelation bursts forth in blinding glory, and He is seen in relation to God; in relation to the Universe; and in relation to the Church (i. 2, 3).

Christ is Prophet, for God has spoken by Him.

Christ is Priest, for He has made purification of sins.

Christ is King, for He is on the right hand of the Majesty on high.

Christ is the Creator, Sustainer, and Possessor of all things. By Him God 'made the *matter* and *time* worlds' (2). He 'upholds all things by the word of His power' (3). He has 'inherited' all things (4).

Christ is 'the effulgence of God's glory', and 'the express image of His substance' (3). The first refers to what Christ was before the incarnation; to the Source of the Son's Being. The second refers to the true representation in the Son of the divine essence. These are fathomless utterances; a complete Christology.

> 'To our fathers in days gone by God spake in
>   the ministry of their prophets—a revelation of
>   Himself given in many instalments and by many
>   different methods.
> To us in the last hour of this era He has spoken
>   in the ministry of a Son.
> Him He made His sole heir. Age after age,
>   plan after plan, He has dealt with man through Him.
> In Him, as in a ray of light that comes from God to man,
>   His glory is expressed.
> In Him, as in a word engraved, men read,
>   shorn of all accidents, the basic fact of all—
>   God's deity.
> He, by His word, endued with God's own power,
>   upholds the universe, and now He sits, Himself
>   the Cleanser of our sin's foul guilt, at the right
>   hand of God's own majesty, in highest heaven.'
>
> (Isaacs).

> Eternal Light! Eternal Light!
> How pure the soul must be
> That stands within Thy searching sight,
> And shrinks not, but with calm delight
> Can live and look on Thee.
>
> (Thomas Binney).

This Prologue (i. 1-4) summarizes the theme of the Epistle—

the Finality of Christianity; and, as the Chart shows (p. 256), the truth is unfolded, urged, and applied.

In the doctrinal division (i. 4-x. 18), Christ is shown to be greater than the great Personalities and Institutions of the former dispensation.

COMPARISON OF CHRIST WITH THE PERSONALITIES
(Chapters i. 4-vii. 28)

1. The Angels and Christ (i. 4-ii. 18)

In chapter i, the true Deity of the Son is proved, in which view He is higher than the Angels; and in chapter ii, His true humanity is proved, in which view He is lower than the Angels. The Angels are introduced here because, the Law having been given by means of them, they were regarded as 'the highest theocratic authority next to God Himself; and the writer would show the inferiority even of the angelic hierarchy to Jesus'. Perhaps it is not too much to say that these two chapters furnish us with the greatest statement in the Bible on the subject of the God-Man (cf. John i. 1-18).

2. Moses and Christ (iii. 1-6)

Christ is shown to be greater than Moses inasmuch as the builder is greater than the house he builds. 'Here the force of the argument lies in the fact that Moses is identified with the system which was entrusted to him. He was himself a part of it; he did not originate it; he received it and administered it with absolute loyalty. But its Author was God, and Christ is the Son of God. Hence the relation of Moses to Christ is that of a system to its author' (Westcott).

3. Joshua and Christ (iv. 1-10)

True it is that Joshua led Israel over Jordan into the promised land, but the history plainly shows that that experience was not the realization of God's promised rest; had it been so, He would not have spoken of another rest. There remaineth therefore to the people of God the keeping of a Sabbath, and into this rest Christ does actually lead all who place their faith in Him.

4. *Aaron and Christ* (iv. 14-v. 10)

First of all, the fact and character of Christ as our High Priest is stated (iv. 14-16), and then, as such, His qualifications and work (v. 1-10). It is in this section that the priesthoods of Aaron and of Christ are compared and contrasted, as to their office, fitness, and appointment, and Christ's is shown to be greater, inasmuch as it is 'after the order of Melchisedec'.

Christ having been shown to be greater than Moses, Joshua, and Aaron, another Old Testament character is introduced, with whom He is not contrasted, but compared.

5. *Melchisedec and Christ* (vii. 1-28)

In chapter v. 6, 10; vi. 20, we read of Melchisedec, but it is in chapter vii alone that the significance of this man and his office is explained. We hear of him but thrice in Scripture—in Gen. xiv, Psalm cx, and here—and between each of these references a thousand years elapse. He was 'made like unto the Son of God' in this, that with Melchisedec of his beginning and end there is *no record*, with Christ of His beginning and end there is *no existence*, for He has neither. Melchisedec received tithes from Abram, and as Levi, the priestly tribe of whom came Aaron, was potentially in the loins of its father Abram when this was done, Mlechisedec is shown to be greater than Aaron; therefore Christ is greater than Aaron (vii. 1-10).

Christ's Priesthood is now set forth as *new*, that He was of another tribe and order, acting according to another law and in another sphere (11-14); as *true*, by reason of its potency and perpetuity, in contrast to the Law (15-19); as *sure*, because His office and work are sealed with an oath, and the former priesthood was not (20-22); as *one*, for, unlike all others, 'He ever liveth', and so none can succeed Him, for He never vacates His office (23-25); and as *final*, by reason of what He Himself is, and of the completeness of His work (26-28).

It will be seen from iv. 14-v. 10; vii. 1-28, that the ruling thought of this Epistle is *priesthood*, and chiefly Christ's priesthood.

It is an impressive fact that the words 'priest' and 'high-priest' occur in none of the 21 Epistles except 'Hebrews'; and in

'Hebrews' *priest* occurs 15 times, and *high-priest*, 17 times—8 of these latter, of Christ; and *priest's office*, once. These facts are of great doctrinal significance.

Here are the occurrences of the *words*, but, of course, the *subject* is much more extensive (cf. chapter vii). The words themselves make a total of 33.

PRIEST (*hiereus*):
      v. 6. vii. 1, 3, 11, 14, 15, 17, 21, 21, 23. viii. 4, 4.
      ix. 6. x. 11, 21.
HIGH-PRIEST (*archiereus*):
      iv. 15. v. 1, 5. vii. 27, 28. viii. 3. ix. 7, 25.
      xiii. 11.
    Of Christ: ii. 17. iii. 1. iv. 14. v. 10. vi. 20.
      vii. 26. viii. 1. ix. 11.
PRIEST'S OFFICE (*hierateia*): vii. 5.

To these must be added chapter i. 3, where 'purification of sins' implies priesthood. In other passages also the office is implied (e.g., xiii. 15).

Christ fulfils two Priesthoods, one typified by *Aaron*, and the other by *Melchisedec*. The first is *Levitical*, and the second is *Royal*. The first was fulfilled on *earth*, and the second is being fulfilled in *heaven*. The first is a Priesthood of *intercession*, and the second is a Priesthood of *benediction*. The first is represented with hands palms upward, and the second, by hands with palms downward.

The Aaronic priesthood was hereditary; the Melchisedecan, was not. The former came to an end; the latter does not. The former was a single office—that of Priest; the latter is a double office—that of Priest and King (see Psalm cx).

In the Monarchy of Israel the two offices were not combined, but in Christ they are. Aaron was an Israelite, but Melchisedec was not. Aaron represented priesthood for a nation; Melchisedec did not.

With few exceptions, e.g. iv. 15, Christ's present Priesthood is seen to be Royal (i. 3; viii. 1; x. 12; xii. 2).

> Where high the Heavenly Temple stands,
> The House of God not made with hands,
> A great High Priest our nature wears,
> The Guardian of mankind appears.

He who for men their surety stood,
And poured on earth His precious blood,
Pursues in Heaven His mighty plan,
The Saviour and the Friend of man.

Though now ascended up on High,
He bends on earth a brother's eye;
Partaker of the human name,
He knows the frailty of our frame.

Our Fellow-Sufferer yet retains
A fellow-feeling of our pains,
And still remembers in the skies
His tears, His agonies and cries.

In every pang that rends the heart
The Man of Sorrows had a part;
He sympathizes with our grief,
And to the sufferer sends relief.

With boldness, therefore, at the Throne,
Let us make all our sorrows known;
And ask the aids of heavenly power
To help us in the evil hour.

'We have a mighty High-Priest Who has passed through all the heavens and beyond them—Jesus, the Son of God. Then let us be strong in the faith which we confess—strong in spite of weakness, for our High-Priest is not such an one as cannot feel our frailties with us.

'To no temptation did He ever yield; yet were His temptations as real as ours. Having, then, such a friend at Court, let us come with outspoken petitions to Grace enthroned, that we may get pardon for past offences, and find grace to help in time of need.'

For valuable exposition of this subject see Westcott's *The Epistle to the Hebrews*, and especially pp. 70, 137, 199, 210, 227, 229.

Following the section in which Christ is compared with the Old Testament *Personalities* (i. 4-vii. 28), follows one in which He is compared—or rather His work is—with the Old Testament *Institutions* (viii. 1-x. 18).

Chapter viii treats of *The Old Sphere and the New*; chapter ix. 1-12, of *The Old Service and the New*; and chapter ix. 13-x. 18, of *The Old Sacrifices and the New*.

Under the first (viii), we learn about the New Sanctuary, of heaven, not of earth (1-6); and of the New Covenant, of grace, not of works (7-13).

Under the second (ix. 1-12), the *Old Sanctuary and Service* are shown to be faulty, to be but figures of the true, for the way into the Divine Presence was not open to all.

And under the third (ix. 13-x. 18) Christ is presented as *Minister of the Sanctuary* (13-22), and then as *Mediator of the Covenant* (23-28).

In chapter x. 1-18, where the *Sacrifices* are more specifically treated, their provisional character under the old dispensation is shown (1-4); then, the perfect efficacy of Christ's Self-Sacrifice (5-14), and finally it is seen that the *New Covenant* is fulfilled in Him (15-18).

Looking over the Doctrinal division of this Epistle (i. 4-x. 18), two ideas press themselves upon our attention, namely, that in Christ all things are *new*, and are *better*.

There are two words for *new*: *neos*, which means new as to time; and *kainos*, which means new as to quality. Both words occur in Hebrews: the former in xii. 24, and the latter in viii. 8, 13; ix. 15.

Kainos is used much by the Apostle John.

'*Better*' (kreissōn) is one of the words which dominate this Epistle, occurring 13 times.

Christ is *better* than the angels (i. 4). It is *better* to go forward than to go back (vi. 9). Melchisedec is *better* than Abraham (vii. 7). The hope of the Gospel is *better* than the commandment of the Law (vii. 19). Jesus is the sure pledge of a *better* covenant (vii. 22). The New Covenant and the promises that it makes are *better* than the Old (viii. 6). The blood of Christ is *better*, because more efficacious, than the blood of all the Old Covenant Sacrifices (ix. 21-24). The believer's substance in heaven is *better* than anything he can possess on earth (x. 34). The heavenly country is *better* than Israel's inheritance of old (xi. 16). The resurrection of the martyrs was *better* than the restoration to any earthly good (xi. 35). The Christian's portion is *better* than the Israelites' (xi. 40). The voice of Jesus' blood is *better* than that of Abel's, because the latter called for vengeance, but the former calls for forgiveness (xii. 24).

Though the Outlines of the Epistle do not generally make chapter x. 19-39 a division, yet it seems to be such; and here a twofold exhortation unites the Doctrinal Dissertation and the Practical Application.

The first exhortation is to *freedom and fellowship* (19-25), and the second is to *patience and perseverance*; and the two are separated by *a most solemn warning*—the fifth in the Epistle (26-31).

Like all the Epistles, this one also has a practical end in view. Abstract and academic truth may entertain the mind but it does not help the life; but Christ came that 'we might have life, and have it abundantly'.

Writing to the Thessalonians Paul spoke of their 'work of faith, and labour of love, and patience of hope' (I. i. 3. cf. Rev. ii. 2), and these are the three notes on which the Epistle to the Hebrews concludes:

Faith in chapter xi: *Hope* in chapter xii; and *Love* in chapter xiii.

> 'Faith is the giving substance to things hoped for, the test of things not seen' (xi. 1).
>
> 'Let us run with patience the race that is set before us, looking unto Jesus' (xii. 1, 2).
>
> 'Let love of the brethren continue' (xiii. 1).

Paul lays emphasis on Faith; Peter on Hope; and John on Love. But they all have them all, as we should.

The eleventh chapter of Hebrews is one of the greatest in the Bible—and surely also in all literature! This chapter was written because it is more important to exhibit faith than to define it.

The spiritual history of the world is the history of the triumphs of faith.

The treatment here of *faith's triumphs* is systematic. After a statement on the nature and work of faith (xi. 1-3), it is illustrated in action from age to age.

The period before the Flood: Abel, Enoch, Noah (xi. 4-7). The period of the patriarchs: Abraham, Sarah, Isaac, Jacob,

Joseph (xi. 8-22). The period of Moses: Moses and the Israelites (xi. 23-29). The period from Joshua onwards: (xi. 30-40).

One of the most eloquent and moving passages ever written is xi. 32-38; and the verdict is beyond controversy: 'Of whom the world was not worthy' (38).

Why is it that the world has persistently persecuted—very often unto death—the best people that have ever lived? Why? (Psalm lxxiii).

The figure of the Christian life as a race (chapter xii. 1, 2)—which implies start, track, and goal—calls attention to the believer's outlook, that is, his *hope*.

It is then shown that if the goal is to be reached discipline must be endured (xii. 3-13); peace and holiness must be pursued (xii. 14-17); and encouragement is given in a magnificent passage contrasting Sinai and Zion, the Christian belonging to the latter (xii. 18-29).

The two contrasted pictures are introduced by: '*Ye are not come*' (xii. 18), and '*Ye are come*' (xii. 22).

These pictures represent two covenants and two dispensations, and are really the subject of the whole Epistle.

It is well that this great Epistle ends on the note of *love* (xiii. 1-6) —'Let love of the brethren abide' (ver. 1). The word is *philadelphia*, not *agapē*, so that it is not love for God that is in view, but the love of His people for one another. But, of course, a true relation horizontally is dependent on a true relation vertically.

A Christian's duties are both *social* (xiii. 1-6), and *religious* (xiii. 7-17), so that our life moves, not in a circle, but in an ellipse.

The exhortations in xiii. 1-17 touch upon many subjects, and should receive our close and obedient attention.

Mark what is said about hospitality (2), sympathy (3), purity (4), covetousness (5), contentment (5), which belong to our *social obligations*.

Our *religious obligations* include keeping green the memory of those who have helped us spiritually, but who no longer are here. (7). It is to be feared that too often not only the deceased are forgotten, but the living whose spiritual care we are.

The exhortations in xiii. 9-15 are based upon the Tabernacle of old, its sacrifices and service.

Separation from all compromises and contaminations which would imperil or injure the life of a Christian is insisted on in xiii. 9-15. Note: 'Without the camp' (11, 13). 'Without the gate' (12).

The Epistle concludes with intercession and exhortation (xiii. 18-25). Supplicate (18); Suffer (22); Salute (24).

> Father of peace, and God of love
> We own Thy power to save,
> That power by which our Shepherd rose
> Victorious o'er the grave.
>
> Him from the dead Thou brought'st again,
> When, by His sacred blood,
> Confirmed and sealed for evermore
> Th' eternal Cov'nant stood.
>
> O may Thy Spirit seal our souls,
> And mould them to Thy will,
> That our weak hearts no more may stray,
> But keep Thy precepts still;
>
> That to perfection's sacred height
> We nearer still may rise,
> And all we think, and all we do,
> Be pleasing in Thine eyes.
>
> (xiii. 20, 21).

A subject of profoundest interest and importance is *the use of the Old Testament in this Epistle*. To deal with this in detail is beyond the scope of this book, but all who can should study Bishop Westcott's treatment of the subject in his *The Epistle to the Hebrews*, pages 67-70, 469-495; a treatment characterized by clarity, fulness, and precision, as is all that the Bishop does.

In the Epistle there are 29 *quotations* from and 53 allusions to the Old Testament. Westcott shows that 12 of these are from the Pentateuch, 11 are from the Psalms, 1 is from the Historical Books, 4 are from the Prophets, and 1 is from Proverbs.

Of *allusions*, 39 are from the Pentateuch; 11 are from the Prophets; 2 are from the Psalms; and 1 is from Proverbs.

In these 13 chapters, there are, therefore, not fewer than 82 references to the Old Testament. This, of itself, indicates the scope and purpose of the Epistle, for, in this way, it is shown that both Dispensations constitute one Revelation, and that this Revelation is progressive.

It shows also that the whole Revelation is consummated in the Person and Work of Christ.

Of the 29 quotations, 21 are peculiar to this Epistle.

The quotations are from the Septuagint Version of the Old Testament. There are no quotations from the Apocryphal Books, though possibly some allusions (e.g., xi. 35).

In Dr. Weymouth's *New Testament in Modern Speech* all these Old Testament references are printed in capitals, and the passages are located, so that they can be recognized as one reads.

A feature of these Old Testament references which is peculiar to this Epistle is that they are made anonymously. Study the way in which they are introduced.

In chapter i they are attributed to God. In chapter ii. 6, 'One hath somewhere testified'. In ii. 11, 12; x. 5, 9; xiii. 5; attributed to Christ; and in iii. 7; x. 15, to the Holy Spirit; and in iv. 3, 4, to God (also v. 5; vi. 13, 14; viii. 5, 8; xii. 25, 26). Indefinite (x. 37, 38; xii. 5).

Nowhere in this Epistle are found such expressions as 'it is written', or 'the Scripture says,' which are very frequent in other books.

Without interfering with the historical truth of Old Testament passages, the writer of this Epistle assumes and proves that they have also a spiritual meaning. An outstanding example of this is the use that is made of the historical Melchizedec (chapter vii).

The delineation of Christ in this Epistle is a vital revelation, and is more complete than in any other Book of the New Testament.

Each of the following designations is laden with meaning for all who will put themselves at the disposal of this LORD Jesus Christ.

1. Apostle (iii. 1).
2. Captain (ii. 10; xii. 2).
3. Christ (iii. 6, *et al*).
4. Finisher (xii. 2).
5. Firstborn (i. 6).
6. Forerunner (vi. 20).
7. God (i. 8).
8. Heir (i. 2).
9. High Priest (ii. 17, *et al*).
10. Jesus (ii. 9, *et al*).
11. Jesus Christ (x. 10).
12. Lord (ii. 3, *et al*).
13. Lord Jesus (xiii. 20).
14. Mediator (viii. 6, *et al*).

15. Priest (v. 6, *et al*).
16. The Same (i. 12; xiii. 8).
17. Shepherd (xiii. 20).
18. Son (i. 2, *et al*).

19. Son of God (iv. 14, *et al*).
20. Son of Man (ii. 6).
21. Surety (vii. 22).

It is not difficult to trace an outline of our LORD's life in the Epistle. The seven great events are in the texture of the Writing.

The Incarnation	-	i. 2; ii. 16, 17.
The Ministration	-	v. 7-9.
The Crucifixion	-	vi. 6; vii. 27; ix. 12, 14, 28; x. 10, 12, 14, 19, 29; xiii. 12, 20.
The Resurrection	-	xiii. 20. (*The only reference*).
The Ascension	-	iv. 14; vi. 20.
The Present Session	-	ii. 9; vii. 25; viii. 1; ix. 12, 24; x. 12, 13.
The Second Advent	-	ix. 28.

Repetition means emphasis, and so, words which occur often in any New Testament Book are of special importance. The following in Hebrews call for attention.

Better, 13 times (see p. 263). *Perfect*, 14 times. *Eternal, For Ever*, 15 times. *Partakers*, 9 times, and in the translation of five Greek words. *Heaven, Heavenly*, 17 times, *Take-heed*, 8 times. *Lest*, 5 times. (See the writer's *Know Your Bible*, Vol. 2, p. 281.)

THE SIX WARNINGS

1. Against not heeding the word of Salvation (ii. 1-4).
2. Against coming short of the promised rest (iii. 7-19).
3. Against the fatal consequences of disobedience (iv. 11-13).
4. Against sloth and apostasy (v. 11-vi. 20).
5. Against sinning wilfully and incurring judgment (x. 26-31).
6. Against not listening to God (xii. 25-29).

Innumerable topics call for attention in this Epistle. Progressive revelation (i. 1). The Deity of Christ (i. 2-14). Angels (i. 4-14). Drifting (ii. 1).

Great Salvation (ii. 3). The humanity of Christ (ii. 5-18). The Church (ii. 12). The Devil (ii. 14). Fear of death (ii. 15). Suffering and sympathy (ii. 18).

Hardening the heart (iii. 8). Unbelief (iii. 12, 18, 19). The living God (iii. 12). To-day (iii. 13, 15). Grieved for forty years (iii. 17).

Coming short (iv. 1). United by faith (iv. 2). The seventh day (iv. 4). God's rest and the Christian's (iv. 4-11). The Word of God (iv. 12, 13). Our confession (iv. 14). The temptations of Christ (iv. 15). The throne of grace (iv. 16).

The priesthood of Christ (v. 5). Aaron and Melchizedec (v. 4-6). Christ's prayers (v. 7). Dullness of hearing (v. 11). Spiritual immaturity (v. 11-14). Milk and meat (v. 12-14).

First principles (vi. 1). Pressing on (vi. 1; xii. 1). Dead works (vi. 1; ix. 14). Perfection (vi. 1). Apostasy (vi. 4-6; x. 26-31). Crucifying the Son of God (vi. 6). Fruitful and unfruitful soil (vi. 7, 8).

Labour of love (vi. 10). Faith and patience (vi. 12). The heirs of promise (vi. 17). The immutability of God's counsel (vi. 17). Two immutable things (vi. 18). Impossible for God to lie (vi. 18). Fleeing for refuge (vi. 18). Laying hold of the hope (vi. 18). The soul's anchor (vi. 19). Within the veil (vi. 19). The Forerunner (vi. 20).

By interpretation (vii. 2). Righteousness and peace (vii. 2). Tithes (vii. 4-9). The Altar (vii. 13; xiii. 10). The inadequacy of the Law (vii. 19). Saving wholly and for ever (vii. 25).

The chief point (viii. 1). The throne of the Majesty in the heavens (viii. 1). The true Tabernacle (viii. 2). Finding fault (viii. 8). Led by the hand (viii. 9). Decaying and departing (viii. 13).

A parable (ix. 9). The conscience (ix. 9, 14; x. 2, 22; xiii. 18). Good things to come (ix. 11). Eternal redemption (ix. 12). The blood of Christ (ix. 14). Eternal inheritance (ix. 15). Type and Antitype (chapter ix). The Second Advent (ix. 28; x. 37).

The Incarnation (x. 5-7). The Offerings (x. 1-18). Christ sitting down (i. 3; x. 12). Christ expecting (x. 13). Hearts and minds (x. 16). Holding fast (x. 23). Provoking (x. 24). Sinning wilfully (x. 26-31). Judgment (x. 27, 30). A fearful thing (x. 31). Forgetting and remembering (x. 17, 32). Living by faith (x. 38). Perdition (x. 39).

The ages (i. 2; xi. 3). The Old Testament heroes (chapter xi). Looking for a city (xi. 10, 16; xiii. 14). God an architect (xi. 10).

As good as dead (xi. 12). Stars and sand (xi. 12). Seeing things
afar off (xi. 13). Seeking a country (xi. 14-16). Choosing
affliction (xi. 24-26). Seeing the invisible (xi. 27). Shortage of
time (xi. 32). An unworthy world (xi. 38).

The Christian race (xii. 1, 2). Looking unto Jesus (xii. 2).
The Beginner and the Finisher (xii. 2). The joy that carries one
through (xii. 2). The Cross (xii. 2). The example of Christ
(xii. 3). Short of the worst (xii. 4). Discipline (xii. 5-11).
Endurance (xii. 3, 7, 20). Afterward (xii. 11). Hanging hands
and feeble knees (xii. 12). Roots of bitterness (xii. 15). Selling
one's birthright (xii. 16). Sinai and Sion (xii. 18-24). A terrible
sight (xii. 21). Refusing (xii. 25). Godly fear (xii. 28).

Brotherly love (xiii. 1). Hospitality (xiii. 2). Sympathy
(xiii. 3). Purity (xiii. 4). Covetousness and contentment (xiii. 5).
Two great sayings (xiii. 5, 6). The unchanging Christ (xiii. 8).
Outside (xiii. 11-13). Lip fruit (xiii. 15). Don't forget (xiii. 16).
Watching for souls (xiii. 17). Live honestly (xiii. 18). The God
of Peace (xiii. 20). The Great Shepherd (xiii. 20).

> Not all the blood of beasts
>   On Jewish altars slain
> Could give the guilty conscience peace
>   Or wash away the stain.
>
> But Christ, the heavenly Lamb,
>   Takes all our sins away;
> A sacrifice of nobler name
>   And richer blood than they.
>
> My faith would lay her hand
>   On that dear head of Thine,
> While like a penitent I stand,
>   And there confess my sin.
>
> My soul looks back to see
>   The burden Thou did'st bear
> When hanging on th' accursed tree,
>   And knows her guilt was there.
>
> Believing, we rejoice
>   To see the curse remove:
> And bless the Lamb with cheerful voice
>   And sing redeeming Love.
>   Isaac Watts.

NOTABLE FEATURES

'The people'

This word occurs 13 times in the Epistle, and always refers to God's people Israel. Nowhere does the writer refer to Gentiles, unbelieving, or Christian. This indicates the essentially Hebrew character of the Epistle. (ii. 17; iv. 9; v. 3; vii. 5, 11, 27; viii. 10; ix. 7, 18, 19; x. 30; xi. 25; xiii. 12.)

'Perfect'

The aspects of perfection which are expressed in the five words teleios, teleiotes, teleioō, teleiōsis, and teleiōtēs, are all in this Epistle. Summarily, they refer to (a) the perfection of Christ, and (b) of His people. References to the former are in ii. 10ff; v. 7ff; vii. 28; and to the latter, in v. 14; vi. 1; vii. 11, 19; ix. 9; x. 1; xi. 40; xii. 2, 23; xiii. 21 (katartizō).

So far as Christians are concerned the word does not signify sinless perfection, but 'that which has reached the highest perfection in the sphere which is contemplated, as contrasted with that which is partial, imperfect, provisional, or incomplete' (Westcott). Chs. v. 11-vi. 1 show that perfection means maturity in contrast to immaturity, to full growth in contrast to stunted growth.

The passages which speak of Christ being made perfect emphasise the reality of His human life, and the discipline which as man He accepted. His not being perfect from the beginning does not imply that at any time His human life was faulty.

What Christ learned by suffering is the ground and pledge of His sympathy with us, and of our progressive realization of perfection.

'Lest'

This word (translating μή ποτε; ἵνα μή, etc.) runs throughout Hebrews, occurring many times. 'Lest haply we drift'.

'*Lest* haply there shall be in any of you an evil heart of unbelief, in falling away from the living God'. '*Lest* any of you be hardened by the deceitfulness of sin'. '*Lest* haply, a promise being left of entering into his rest, any of you should seem to have come short of it'. '*Lest* anyone fall after the same example of disobedience'. '*Lest* the destroyer of the firstborn might touch them'. '*Lest* ye wax weary, fainting in your souls'. '*Lest* that which is lame be turned aside'. '*Lest* any lack the grace of God'. '*Lest* any root of bitterness springing up should trouble you, and by this many be defiled'. '*Lest* (there be) any fornicator, or profane person, as Esau'.

This is a solemn word of warning. It implies that we always have alternatives, and must choose. (ii. 1; iii. 12, 13; iv. 1, 11; xi. 28; xii. 3, 13, 15, 16).

'*Eternal*'

Eternity is stamped on this Epistle. From the beginning its outlook is vast, and the temporal is viewed in the light of the eternal. Christ is 'the author of *eternal* salvation'. Redemption is '*eternal*'. The believer's inheritance is '*eternal*'. Judgment is '*eternal*'; and the Holy Spirit is '*eternal*'. (v. 9; ix. 12, 15; vi. 2; ix. 14.)

THE STERN PASSAGES

Of these there are three, which have been variously interpreted (vi. 4-6; x. 26-31; xii. 16, 17).

Chapter vi. 4-6

'In the case of those who were once for all enlightened, having both tasted of the heavenly gift, and been made partakers of the Holy Spirit, and who tasted the good word of God and the powers of the world to come, and fell away, it is impossible again to renew them to repentance, seeing they crucify to themselves the Son of God afresh, and put Him to an open shame.'

We must not bring our prejudices to this solemn passage, but frankly accept what it says. The following points seem clear:

1. That the people addressed are converted, are really Christians. Five things are said of them:

they were 'once for all enlightened';
they had 'tasted of the heavenly gift';
they had 'been made partakers of the Holy Spirit';
they had 'tasted the good word of God';
they had tasted 'the powers of a world to come';

None of these things is true of an unregenerate person.

2. Moreover, no unsaved person could be exhorted to 'press on unto perfection', because such a person has not started.

3. Again, the passage does not refer to backsliders, for the Bible teaches that where there has been a back move, there can be a move back (1 Pet. ii. 25). The Apostle Peter is sufficient illustration of this fact.

4. Obviously the reference is to apostates; to those who deliberately abandon their profession of Christ, and turn again to their former life.

5. It does not say that the readers of the Letter had done this, but that they were in danger of doing it. Mark the third person, 'those', 'them', 'they'.

6. The people referred to 'fell-away', they deliberately turned aside from the right path, and a time is implied (2 aor. part.).

7. What such are doing is 'crucifying for themselves the Son of God, and exposing (Him) publicly'. The participle of both verbs is in the present tense, which indicates continuous and persistent action.

8. The passage affirms that it is 'impossible again to renew to repentance' those who so act. This is absolute. The apostate crucifies again the Crucified.

Chapter x. 26-31

'If we wilfully sin after that we have received the knowledge of the truth, there is no longer left a sacrifice for sins, but a certain fearful expectation of judgment, and a jealousy of fire ready to devour the adversaries'.

'Of much sorer punishment . . . shall he be judged worthy who trampleth under foot the Son of God, and counteth the blood of the covenant a common thing, the blood wherein he was sanctified, and doeth outrage to the Spirit of Grace'.

Here again is the case of a Christian turning apostate. He is a *Christian*, because he 'received the knowledge (epignōsis) of the truth' (26); and because he 'was sanctified' (29).

And he is an *apostate*, because he 'is sinning wilfully' (pres. part.); and because 'he trampled under foot the Son of God, and insulted the Spirit of Grace'. The tenses indicate what he deliberately did and continues to do.

There is no hope for such an one because the crucified and saving Christ has been abandoned. What lies before the apostate is 'judgment', punishment, and a 'jealousy of fire' (R.V.).

Chapter xii. 16, 17

'Esau for one mess of meat sold his own birthright. . . . For ye know that even afterward, when he wished to inherit the blessing, he was rejected—for he found no place for repentance—though he sought it diligently with tears'.

The words 'for he found no place for repentance' may be parenthetic; so that what Esau was refused was not repentance, but the blessing which he had forfeited. Another interpretation of the passage would mean that Esau '*found no way of changing his father's mind*', though he sought *the blessing* with tears. In this view 'repentance' does not refer to Esau, but to Isaac (cf. Gen. xxvii. 30-40). Neither interpretation can by any means favour the exclusion of any sinner from repentance.

THE TABERNACLE AND THE TEMPLE

It is very impressive that, whereas the Temple was not once mentioned in this Epistle, the Tabernacle is referred to nine times (viii. 2, 5; ix. 2, 3, 6, 8, 11, 21; xiii. 10).

From this fact we must not conclude that the Temple was not in existence, and so that the Epistle was written after A.D. 70 (Zahn), but the significance of the fact should not be overlooked. Bishop Westcott regards the Temple as a sign of retrogression; '. . . an endeavour to give fixity to that which was essentially provisional'. At any rate, the writer of Hebrews goes behind the Temple to that which gave it rise, to the Tabernacle, the original type of God's presence with men (John i. 14. 'The Word became flesh, and *tabernacled* among us'). 'The ritual of the Tabernacle was the divine type of which the ritual of the Temple was the authoritative representation' (Westcott).

What is said in Hebrews of the Tabernacle should be carefully noted. As Christ is the fulfilment of the ancient archetype (viii. 2; ix. 11), it was essential that the structure be made exactly 'according to the pattern that was shewed in the mount' (viii. 5); some of the features of which are referred to in chapter ix. 2-10. Because Christ was the Tabernacle, His people can be the Temple (1 Cor. iii. 16; vi. 19).

TYPICAL INTERPRETATION

If there is no such thing as type and antitype in Scripture the Epistle to the Hebrews may well be left alone. Dr. Samuel Davidson says of it: 'The circle of ideas in which the writer moves is too Judaic to commend itself to the acceptance of Christian readers'. But rightly or wrongly, the writer of this Epistle regards persons, institutions, and events of the Old Testament to be typical, and the whole plan of the Writing assumes this (see Analysis, pp. 256, 259-263).

Two outstanding illustrations of this view are Melchizedec, and the *Tabernacle*. Both are presented as types of Christ. The former, by what is not said, as well as by what is recorded (vii. 3); and the latter, in its structure and furniture (ix. 1-14).

Of course, regard must be had for the first and historical meaning of the Old Testament, but that never exhausts its meaning. The Apostle Paul, speaking of Israel's history in the wilderness, says: 'These things became *types* for us'; and 'All these things happened to them as *types*, and were written for our admonition' (1 Cor. x. 6, 11). If this does not harmonize with the ideas of certain people, so much the worse for their ideas. Moses typified Christ as Prophet (Deut. xviii. 18); Melchizedec and Aaron represented Him as Priest (Heb. v-vii); and David represented Him as King (Ps. xlv. 6, 7; Heb. i. 8, 9). Because man is blind he needs a revealer; because he is sinful, he needs a representative; and because he is wilful, he needs a ruler. Christ meets all these needs. In the Gospels He is the Prophet; in the Acts and Epistles He is the Priest; and in the Revelation He is the King, and in each capacity He was typified.

The Epistle to the Hebrews shows also that the *sacrifices* and *covenants* of old were typical, and are fulfilled in Christ (chs.

viii, ix). 'A type', says Bishop Westcott, 'presupposes a purpose in history wrought out from age to age'.

THE AUTHORISED VERSION AND OTHER RENDERINGS

Dr. Nairne has said: 'In Hebrews A.V. is particularly good, not merely as a piece of English, but as an equivalent of the uncommon Greek style. . . . But the satisfaction of R.V. is presently discovered'.

A comparison of the two Versions cannot but be fruitful. The following instances should stimulate further study.

i. 1. 'At sundry times and in divers manners'. Better, 'in many parts and in many modes'; 'in successive portions and in varying fashions'. The one refers to the *periods* of Israel's history (see the writer's *Unfolding Drama*, Vol. I); and the other, to the *form* of the records—types, prophecies, visions, and symbolic actions.

i. 2; vi. 5; ix. 26; xi. 3. 'The worlds'. Greek *aiōnas*, 'the ages', the sum of the periods of time; the universe as an order which exists through time developed in successive stages.

i. 3. 'The express image of His Person'. The Son is not the image of the Person of God, but of His essence; so read; 'the exact expression of His substance'.

i. 4. 'Being made'. R.V. 'having become'; of our Lord's human nature, not of His divine personality.

ii. 1. 'Therefore we ought to give the more earnest heed to the things which we have heard, lest at any time we should let them slip'. For this read: 'Therefore we must give the more earnest heed to the things that were heard lest haply we drift away from them'.

'The idea is not simply that of forgetfulness, but of being swept along past the sure anchorage which is within reach. The image is singularly expressive. We are all continuously exposed to the action of currents of opinion, habit, action, which tend to carry us away insensibly from the position which we ought to maintain'.

iii. 1. 'Consider the Apostle and High Priest of our profession

Christ Jesus'. R.V. 'Consider the Apostle and High Priest of our confession, (even) Jesus'.

Note 'confession' instead of 'profession'. 'Apostle', of Christ, occurs here only. 'Apostle and High Priest' combine the functions of Moses and Aaron. 'Jesus', not 'Christ Jesus'. The name which points to His human nature is distinctive of the Epistle, occurring 7 times (ii. 9; vi. 20; vii. 22; x. 19; xii. 2; xii. 24; xiii. 12).

iv. 6, 11. For 'unbelief' read 'disobedience'. *Unbelief* is a want of faith (*apistia*); *disobedience* is a want of will (*apeitheia*), the active expression of unbelief. The genealogy of this sin is, *unbelief, disbelief, disobedience* (cf. John iii. 36 R.V. Mark xvi. 14 R.V.; Acts xxviii. 24 R.V.). *Unbelief* is negative, but *disbelief* is positive, and *disobedience* is the issue of the latter (cf. xi. 31 R.V.).

iv. 8. 'Jesus', read 'Joshua'.

iv. 10. 'He that is entered into his rest, he also has ceased from his own works, as God did from His'.

'Ceased' should be 'rested'. Why translate the same word in two ways in a single verse?

iv. 14. 'That is passed into the heavens'. Rather, 'Who hath passed through the heavens'. The one signifies *into space*; the other, *beyond space*.

iv. 15. 'Was in all points tempted' points to a past fact, but 'that hath been tempted' refers to a present effectual reality following that fact.

v. 11. 'Ye are dull of hearing'. This might be a fault of nature, but 'Ye are become dull of hearing' is a fault of neglect.

vi. 1. 'Let us go on unto perfection'. The verb *pherō*, used here, is translated in other passages 'to bear', 'to uphold', 'to carry', and in one place 'to rush' (Acts ii. 2). Westcott translates it in this passage, 'let us be borne on to perfection', and says: 'The thought is not primarily of personal effort, but of personal surrender to an active influence—an influence and surrender which are continuous, and not concentrated in one momentary crisis'.

'Perfection' means 'full maturity' (cf. v. 12-14).

vi. 20. 'Whither the forerunner is for us entered; (even) Jesus, *made* an High Priest for ever after the order of Melchisedec'. R.V. 'Whither as a forerunner Jesus entered for us, *having become* a high priest for ever after the order of Melchizedek'.

The difference between 'made' and 'become' is seen again in i. 4; vii. 22.

ix. 6. 'The priests *went* always *into* the first Tabernacle'. The R.V. has, 'The priests *go in* continually'. This would seem to have some bearing on the date of the Epistle.

ix. 28. 'So Christ was once offered to bear the sins of many, and unto them that look for Him shall He appear the second time without sin, unto salvation'.

R.V. 'So Christ also, having been once offered to bear the sins of many, shall appear a second time, apart from sin, to them that wait for Him, unto salvation'. The meaning is not 'to them that wait for Him unto salvation', but 'shall appear a second time unto salvation'. That is, when Christ comes again it will be to consummate salvation.

x. 1. 'Good things to come', should be 'the good things to come', that is, from the standpoint of the law, the blessings of the coming age (cf. vi. 5; ix. 11 R.V.).

x. 10, 14. What in the A.V. is obscure is made clear by the R.V. that *sanctification* is both complete and progressive. In verse 10 it is: 'By the which will we *have been sanctified* (perf. pass.) cf. 1 Cor. vi. 11; and in verse 14 it is, 'He hath perfected for ever them that *are being sanctified* (pres. part. pass.). What we *are*, we are to *become*. Compare 'being saved' (1 Cor. i. 18), and 'have been saved' (Eph. ii. 8).

x. 23. For 'profession of our faith', read 'confession of our hope'. This does not mean that we should confess that we have a hope, but confession of the things hoped for. 'Faith' relates rather to the past and present, but 'hope', to the future (cf. iii. 6; vi. 11; vi. 18; vii. 19). Significantly, 'hope' is not found in the Gospels.

x. 34. 'Ye had compassion of me in my bonds'. The R.V. has:

'Ye both had compassion on them that were in the bonds'. 'My bonds' is used in the Epistles only by Paul of himself, and so the A.V. rendering is used as an argument for Pauline Authorship of Hebrews. In the R.V. 'the' bonds points to some familiar fact.

xi. 17. The tenses in the R.V. are graphic and impressive. 'By faith Abraham, being tried (pres. part. pass.), hath offered up (perf. ind.) Isaac; yea, he that had gladly received (aor. part.) the promises was offering up (imperf. ind.) his only begotten son'.

Abraham is regarded as having sacrificed Isaac, though the slaying of him was not carried out.

xii. 2. The R.V. here should be closely contemplated. 'Looking unto Jesus the captain and perfecter of faith'. The word *archēgos* is 'leader' rather than 'author'. It occurs only here and in ii. 10; Acts iii. 15; v. 31. The word 'perfecter (*teleiōtes*) does not occur again in the N.T. The 'our' of the A.V. should be omitted. Christ is the beginning and end of the ruling principle of true life.

xii. 7. Read 'It is for chastening that ye endure; God dealeth with you as with sons'.

xii. 11. In this verse the R.V. makes clear the idea that 'peaceable fruit' as the result of 'chastening' is the portion only of them who were 'exercised' by the chastening while they were experiencing it.

'Yet afterward it yieldeth peaceable fruit unto them that *have been exercised* thereby, (even the fruit) of righteousness'.

xiii. 2. For 'Be not forgetful to entertain strangers', read, 'Forget not to shew love unto strangers'.

xiii. 5. For 'Let your conversation be without covetousness', read, 'Be ye free from the love of money'.

These various renderings should show how important is as exact a translation as is available.

THE CATHOLIC EPISTLES

GROUP 5

JAMES

1 PETER

2 PETER

JUDE

1-3 JOHN

THE CATHOLIC EPISTLES

JAMES 1 PETER 2 PETER JUDE 1-3 JOHN

Notes

It must be obvious to the reader of the New Testament Epistles that they fall into three categories—the *Pauline Epistles* (13); the *Catholic Epistles* (7); and distinct from both of these is the *Epistle to the Hebrews*.

As we contemplate these 21 Epistles we should be impressed by the fact that the three categories are so different.

If, of the groups, we had only the Pauline, or only the Catholic, Epistles, our apprehension of Christianity would be partial only. To communicate the revelation of the New Covenant God chose men whose mental and spiritual equipment served His purpose, and we see that for this end six men were chosen—Paul, Peter, John, James, Jude, and the author of 'Hebrews'.

The Writings of these men represent phases of Christianity, and these several phases constitute the revelation. No description of these phases can avoid criticism, but it may be said that *Paul* represents *Gentile Christianity*; *James* and *Jude*, *Judaic Christianity*; *Peter*, *Mediating Christianity*; *John*, *Mystical Christianity*; and the author of *'Hebrews'*, *Alexandrian Christianity*.

These descriptions are not exclusive, and inevitably they overlap, yet they do represent distinctions, and stand for phases of truth.

Paul is pre-eminently the Apostle to the Gentiles; *James* and *Jude* present truth in a Jewish mould; *Peter* represents a position mediating the Paulinists and the Judaists; in *John's* Writings there is a mystical element which, while not exclusive, is distinctive; and the writer to the Hebrews—perhaps Apollos—shows the influence of the School of Philo, and of Alexandrian theology.

It will never be easy to synthesize these various aspects of truth, but only in the attempt to do so shall we discover the necessity for doing so, and the reward.

The gem of Epistolary truth has six facets. Each facet is a

surface, but the gem is one; and as it is handled now one and now another of its beauties will flash out.

We associate *faith* with Paul; *hope* with Peter; *love* with John; *works* with James; *zeal* with Jude; and *steadfastness* with 'Hebrews'.

What Paul begins Peter continues and John finishes.

James, Jude, and 'Hebrews' we may relate to Matthew's Gospel; 1-2 Peter, to Mark's; Paul's Epistles, to Luke's Gospel and the Acts; and John's Epistles and the Revelation to his Gospel.

Paul is *theological*; Peter is *experimental*; John is *expository*; James is *ethical*; Jude is *remonstrative*; and 'Hebrews' is *interpretative*.

Paul is the *scholar*; Peter, the *enthusiast*; John, the *mystic*; James, the *moralist*; Jude, the *loyalist*; and 'Hebrews' the *dispensationalist*.

In these writers of Holy Scripture is varying emphasis on the *Law*, the *Covenant*, the *Priesthood*, the *Theocracy*, *Symbolism*, and the *Gospel*. Together they present the full orb of Revealed Truth.

These seven Epistles have been called *Catholic* from an early date. The term occurs from the time of Clement of Alexandria (A.D. 200).

In the MSS. they always stand together.

Various meanings have been given to the term *Catholic* as applied to these Epistles. It has been taken to refer to their *canonicity*, by which is meant their authority as Scripture: to their *orthodoxy*, claiming for them doctrinal harmony with the teaching of the Universal Church: to their *apostolicity*, that is, apostolical writings in addition to Paul's: and to their *universality*, that is, Epistles to the Church in general; not written, as Paul's Epistles, to particular Churches and individuals. Almost certainly this last meaning is the one the term was intended to convey.

The openings of these Epistles show their unlikeness to the openings of Paul's.

JAMES - 'To the Twelve Tribes which are of the Dispersion.'
1 PETER - 'To the elect who are sojourners of the Dispersion in Pontus, Galatia, Cappadocia, Asia, and Bithynia.'

2 PETER	-	'To them that have obtained a like precious faith with us in the righteousness of our God and Saviour Jesus Christ.'
1 JOHN	-	No introduction.
2 JOHN	-	'The elder unto the elect lady and her children.'
3 JOHN	-	'The elder unto Gaius the beloved.'
JUDE	-	'To them that are called, beloved in God the Father, and kept for Jesus Christ.'

Of these introductions only 2 Peter, 1 John, and Jude are strictly universal. James is addressed to Jewish converts, or, perhaps, to Jews generally; 1 Peter, to believers in certain areas in Asia Minor; 2 John, to an individual, or a Church; and 3 John to an individual.

Nevertheless, five of the seven were for a wide circle of readers; and, perhaps, 2-3 John were regarded as appendices to 1 John. The difference between these introductions and Paul's is obvious.

The two great events of the first century A.D., were the Crucifixion of Christ and the Fall of Jerusalem. The first took place in A.D. 30, and the second, forty years later, in A.D. 70.

By the latter date Paul had been dead for at least two years, so that all his Epistles were written before the Fall.

Not so, however, all the Catholic Epistles. The following Chart envisages the probabilities.

CHART 178

THE FALL OF JERUSALEM—A.D. 70					
BEFORE			AFTER		
BOOK	DATE	PLACE OF WRITING	BOOK	DATE	PLACE OF WRITING
JAMES	45–49?	Jerusalem	1 JOHN	90–96	Ephesus
1 PETER	64–67	Babylon?	2 JOHN	90–96	Ephesus
2 PETER	66–68	Rome?	3 JOHN	90–96	Ephesus
JUDE	64–67	Jerusalem?			

THE CATHOLIC EPISTLES

JAMES

A.D. 45-49

Notes

The authorship of this *epistle*, as it is called, is a matter of considerable controversy. All that the author says about himself is:

'James, a bondslave of God and of the Lord Jesus Christ' (i. 1):

and Jude says:

'Judas, a bondslave of Jesus Christ, and brother of James' (1).

But the New Testament refers to six persons of this name: the son of Zebedee (Matt. iv. 21); the son of Alphaeus (Matt. x. 3); one of four brothers (Matt. xiii. 55); 'the little' (Mark xv. 40); 'the Lord's brother' (Gal. i. 19); and the brother of Jude (1).

In all likelihood the son of Alphaeus and James 'the less' are the same person.

James, 'the Lord's brother' and the brother of Jude are also the same person.

It seems clear also that these two and James, the son of Zebedee were first cousins; so that the six men of this name are reduced to three.

Apparently one of these three wrote this Epistle, but which of them?

Three answers have been given to this question:

(a) that the author was James the son of Alphaeus and of the Virgin's sister, and, therefore, a cousin of the Lord:
(b) that the author was James a son of Joseph by a former wife, and, therefore, a foster-brother of the Lord; and
(c) that the author was James, a son of Joseph and Mary after the Virgin had given birth to Jesus, and, therefore, a half-brother of the Lord.

An exhaustive examination of these theories will be found in Mayor's *Epistle of James*, pp. i-lxv.

If the first view be correct (a), the author of the Epistle was one of the Twelve, James the son of Zebedee.

Relative to this theory, observe: (1) that this James was martyred in A.D. 44 (Acts xii. 1); (2) that no ancient authority ever thought of attributing the Epistle to him; and (3) that 'the Lord's brother' is always distinguished from the Apostle of this name (cf. Acts i. 13, 14; Gal. i. 19 R.V. marg. Acts xv. 13).

The second view (b) is based on Jerome's doctrine of the Perpetual Virginity of Mary. Of this it will suffice to say two things: first, there is no historical evidence that Joseph had a wife, and a family by her, before he married Mary, the mother of Jesus; and secondly, Scripture does not warrant the view that, after the birth of Jesus, Joseph had no children by Mary (Matt. i. 18-25, especially 25).

The evidence goes to show (c) that the author of this Epistle was James the eldest son of Joseph and Mary, the brother of Joses, Jude, Simon, and some unnamed sisters (Mark vi. 3).

With this our thoughts turn to Nazareth and the typically Jewish home there. Seven children, at least, grew up in that godly home, where they were thoroughly versed in the Mosaic Law and Levitical worship.

Jesus was the eldest of the family, though how much older than James we do not know. It may be assumed that of the mystery of the eldest Son's origin none of the family knew except Joseph and Mary, but the influence of Jesus on His brothers and sisters must have been profound.

Together, for long years, they grew up in happy harmony, and it was only when Jesus left the home, and, going South was baptized of John in the Jordan; began to attach to Himself a group of youthful disciples—one of whom was His cousin John, a son of Zebedee; claimed great authority for Himself, even to being the Messiah; and acted in disregard of the 'traditions of the fathers', of the Oral Law, and of Levitic rules—only in these circumstances and events became evident the alienation of His brethren, which led them later to attempt to restrain Him (Mark iii. 21, 31; Matt. xii. 46).

How complete the alienation was is seen in the contrasted pronouns in John vii. 6-8: 'my,' 'yours,' 'you,' 'me,' 'ye,' 'I'. But when we read: 'For neither did His brethren believe in Him' (John vii. 5), we must understand it to mean that whereas He had broken with Judaism they had not; and that they could not accept His claims to be the Messiah.

The brethren were profoundly religious and reverent, but, as yet, they were in total darkness as to the significance of their Brother.

After the event at Capernaum (Matt. xii. 46-50) we do not read again of the 'brothers' in the Gospels. They were not at the Trial; they were not at the Cross; and they did not go to the grave. In death Jesus committed His mother to her nephew, John—not to any other sons. Where the 'brothers' were, and what they were thinking about what was going on we do not know.

But the next time we read of them they are Christians and have joined the company of the Apostles for prayer in 'an upper room'. Mary their mother and other women were there also (Acts i. 12-14).

What has happened? The answer is given in 1 Cor. xv. 7: 'He—the risen Christ—was seen of James'. We have no information of Joses, or Simon, or the sisters, but definite information of James and Jude.

To three individuals only did the risen LORD appear—to Peter, Mary Magdalene, and James (1 Cor. xv. 5, 7; John xx. 1, 11-18).

The LORD's appearance to His own brother was to the latter a revelation which for ever dispelled all hesitancy and doubt as to the Messiahship and Divinity of Jesus.

He knew that Jesus had died on Calvary, and now that he saw Him risen light was flashed back on those thirty years at Nazareth, and all that James had then seen and heard glowed with a heavenly splendour.

James did not step out of Judaism into Pauline Christianity, but, to the day of his martyrdom, he represented Christianity within Judaism.

References to him after his conversion are of great interest and importance. He became the head of the Church in Jerusalem. Paul, three years after his own conversion, saw James in Jerusalem, and again many years later. He presided at the first Church Council, and drafted the Letter which excluded Gentile Christians from subjection to the Mosaic ritual. Paul, on his last visit to Jerusalem, reported to James and the Elders, and yielded to their advice—wrongly, it would seem—to take a vow (Acts xii. 17; Gal. i. 19; ii. 9; Acts xv. 13-21; xxi. 18-25).

After this he disappears from Scripture history, but Josephus tells us that he was martyred about A.D. 63.

The date of this Epistle is necessarily connected with the authorship of it. If it was written by a brother of the LORD martyred about A.D. 63, the date is fixed at that end. The question is, how long before A.D. 63 was the Epistle written? The absence of any reference to the events, controversies and circumstances of the Pauline period suggests an early date.

If, as seems certain, the Epistle is referred to by Paul in Romans and Galatians, and, perhaps, in Corinthians and Thessalonians, it must have been written before the earliest of these Writings. If it had been written after the decision of the Council of Jerusalem in A.D. 50-51 (Acts xv) it surely would have made some reference to this momentous event. It will be felt also that the Epistle must have been written before the Church controversies had begun, or after they had died down, and it is certain that they had not died down, but were at their height, when James was martyred.

It is practically certain, then, that this Epistle is the earliest portion of the New Testament, written in the fifth decade of the Christian era, and that it presents a picture of pre-Pauline Christianity.

This conclusion is of both historical and theological importance.

There is no evidence that James ever left Jerusalem after the Ascension, so that he must have written his Epistle at the Jewish Capital. This fact gives interest to such references as i. 6; i. 11; iii. 4; iii. 11, 12; v. 7.

The writer addresses himself to 'the twelve tribes which are of the dispersion' (i. 1).

This has been taken to refer to Christian believers widely scattered; to Jewish believers settled in Babylon and Mesopotamia; to Jewish Christians outside Palestine who gathered in synagogue worship (ii. 2); and to Jews generally (ii. 6, 7; v. 1-6).

The most natural meaning would seem to be that he wrote to Jewish Christians of the 'Dispersion' scattered throughout the world (cf. Acts ii. 9-12).

This Writing is called an *Epistle*, but judged by the other Writings—of Paul, for instance—there is nothing epistolary about it. The address is impersonal (i. 1), and there are no salutations. The writer's references to his 'brethren' (19 times) is to the Christian Jews of the Dispersion, and nothing more intimate than this is in the Writing.

It must be evident also that the Writing has no one subject as have most of the Epistles, more than a dozen themes being treated almost disconnectedly. This fact makes analysis difficult, but the following subjects are dealt with.

> Trials and Temptations (i. 2-18).
> Hearing and Doing the Word (i. 19-27).
> Respect of Persons (ii. 1-13).
> Faith and Works (ii. 14-26).
> Control of the Tongue (iii. 1-12).
> True and False Wisdom (iii. 13-18).
> The World and God (iv. 1-10).
> Censoriousness (iv. 11, 12).
> The Uncertainty of Life (iv. 13-17).
> The Doom of Oppressors (v. 1-6).
> Patience in Suffering (v. 7-11).
> Profanity (v. 12).
> Praise and Prayer (v. 13-18).
> The Blessedness of Soul-Saving (v. 19, 20).

The nature and variety of these subjects suggest that they are abstracts of sermons which James had preached at Jerusalem; or, answers to inquiries which had reached him from Jews at a distance who desired the guidance of the LORD's brother relative to matters which were being discussed in their synagogues.

Above it is said that these subjects are almost disconnected, but a closer examination will show that though they are distinct, and in a sense complete, in quite a remarkable way they are connected by the repetition of leading words (paronomasia). The following are a few illustrations of this.

CHAPTER i.   Patience (3); patience (4).
Nothing lacking (4); if any of you lack (5).
Let him ask (5); but let him ask (6).
Nothing doubting (6); he that doubteth (6).
Temptation (12, 13, 14); tempted (13, 14).
Lust (14); lust (15).
Wrath (19); wrath (20).
Word (21); word (22, 23).
Doers (22); doer (23, 25).
Religious (26); religion (27).

CHAPTER iii.   Stumble (2); stumbleth (2).
                 Whole body (2); whole body (3, 6).
                 Turn about (3), turned about (4).
                 Fire (5); fire (6, 6).
                 Tamed (7); tame (8).

CHAPTER iv.   Wars (1, 1); war (2).
                 Fightings (1); fight (2).
                 Pleasures (1); pleasures (3).
                 Ask (2); ask (3).

The subjects which constitute this Writing show that its complexion is not theological, but ethical. It does not treat of the doctrines of the Christian religion but of the expressions of it in the conduct of Christians.

When Luther said that this Writing is 'a downright strawy Epistle, which lacks all Evangelical character', he did not lessen the value of what James has given us, but only displayed a deplorable want of insight and understanding. There are numberless people who will fight for a creed, who, however, have little or no interest in the application of it.

The Ethic of James is the Ethic of the Sermon on the Mount. No Writing of the New Testament is more deeply pervaded with the moral teaching of Christ than in this 'Epistle', which, one might almost say, is modelled on the Sermon.

This is not to say that James was acquainted with Matthew's Gospel. Of course he could not have been if his was the first of the New Testament Writings. But the teaching of Christ was widely diffused before it was committed to writing, and it is evident that James was intimately acquainted with it.

In both the Sermon and the 'Epistle' there is an absence of doctrinal statement and a strong emphasis on the ethical element.

In this brief 'Epistle' there may be as many as twenty-six references, more or less direct, to the Sermon.

The following parallels are worth studying:

JAMES	MATTHEW	JAMES	MATTHEW
i. 2	v. 10–12	iii. 17, 18	v. 9
i. 4	v. 48	iv. 3	vii. 8
i. 5; iv. 3	vii. 7–11	iv. 4	vi. 24
i. 9; ii. 5	v. 3	iv. 8	v. 8
i. 19, 20	v. 22	iv. 9	v. 4
i. 21; iii. 13	v. 4	iv. 11, 12	vii. 1–3
i. 22	vii. 24, 26	iv. 13, 14	vi. 34
i. 26	v. 22	iv. 13–16	vi. 25
ii. 5	v. 3	v. 2, 3	vi. 19, 20
ii. 8	vii. 12	v. 6	v. 39–42
ii. 13	v. 7, 9, 13; vi. 14, 15; vii. 2	v. 7–9	vii. 21–23
ii. 14–26	vii. 21–23	v. 10, 11	v. 12
iii. 12	vii. 16	v. 12	v. 33-37

None of these parallels is an actual quotation, but the references are distinctly recognizable.

It is claimed by some that in this 'Epistle' there are references to some of Paul's Epistles, and to Peter's. If this is so the early date of 'James' must be abandoned. But if the early date is correct the idea that in chapter ii. 14-26 the writer is opposing Paul's view of justification by faith must be abandoned.

Parallel passages in 'James' and I Peter must be due to Peter's acquaintance with 'James', and not *vice versa*. That there are such parallels is clear.

JAMES	I PETER	JAMES	I PETER
i. 1	i. 1	iv. 1	ii. 11
i. 2	i. 6	iv. 6	iv. 8
i. 10	i. 24	iv. 7	v. 5
i. 21	ii. 1, 2	iv. 10	v. 8, 9
		v. 20	v. 6

Though this 'Epistle' is pervaded with the spirit of the Old Testament yet there are few quotations from it, and these few are not exact. The writer applies passages to his own immediate purpose without any scrupulous reference to its original context (cf. iv. 4-6).

But the following should be noted. Chapter ii. 8: Lev. xix. 18. Chapter ii. 11: Exod. xx. 13, 14; Deut. v. 17, 18. Chapter ii. 23: Gen. xv. 6. Chapter ii. 23: 2 Chron. xx. 7; Isa. xli. 8. Chapter

iv. 6: Prov. iii. 34. Chapter v. 20: Prov. x. 12. Chapter ii. 14-26: Gen. xxii. 9-12; Josh. ii. 1ff.

No one can read this 'Epistle' with care without seeing that on many subjects of evangelical importance it is silent. There is no reference to the Atoning Sacrifice of Christ (but cf. v. 6); nor to the Incarnation, the Resurrection nor the Ascension; nor to the Sacraments; nor to the Messiahship of Christ; nor to Circumcision; nor to the Sabbath; nor to the Gospel; nor to the influence of the Holy Spirit.

There is no reference to Gentiles, not even to proselytes. Specific Christian doctrine and motive are largely wanting.

Yet it would not be correct to say that here there is no Christology. Christ is called 'LORD', and is bracketed with the name of God, and James says that he is this LORD's 'Bondslave' (i. 1). Christ is spoken of as 'the LORD of Glory' (ii. 1. cf. 1 Cor. ii. 8; John i. 14; Exod. xl. 35). 'The good name' in ch. ii. 7 refers to Christ rather than to the designation 'Christian'. Christ is referred to as the Coming One (v. 7, 8), and is spoken of as the final Judge (v. 9).

In this 'Epistle' there is not that development of doctrine which we see in the Pauline Epistles; nor before A.D. 50 could there be. 'James' must be read in the light of its date and purpose.

In the early Church there were three types of Christians— Jewish, Alexandrian, and Pauline. The Pauline were universally catholic; the Alexandrian were those who were influenced by Greek culture; and the Jewish were those who, though Christians, were still Judaic in outlook. The outstanding example of the last of these three was James, the Lord's brother, the bishop of Jerusalem. He embraced the New without forsaking the Old. He believed in the Gospel, but he does not refer to it in his Epistle, and he never alludes to the Gentiles. His tone is much more like that of John the Baptist than that of Paul, or Peter, or John.

His and Paul's references to the Law are different, and both are true. He gave his verdict at the Jerusalem Conference in favour of the Gentiles (Acts xv), but his sympathies were with the Jews and with the Judaic outlook.

No one can fail to recognize the severity of this Epistle, notwithstanding that James addresses his readers as 'brethren', and 'beloved brethren'. He is more frank than tender, and more caustic than conciliatory, and more the moralist than the evangelist. He was known as 'the Just' because of the stern sanctity of his character.

His Epistle stands alone among the N.T. Writings, the nearest approach to it being the Note of his brother Jude. It is truly impressive that of the family at Nazareth that did not understand Jesus, and did not accept His Messiahship, two of His brothers became writers of Holy Scripture, and that each speaks of himself as 'a bondslave of . . . Jesus Christ', and James adds 'Lord' (i. 1).

The style of this Writing is something to be contemplated. The grammar of this writer need not concern us in this survey but his manner and modes of expression are of engaging interest and importance.

Dr. Mayor says: his 'sentences are short, simple, direct, conveying the impression of a strong and serious individuality as well as of a poetic imagination'.

Dean Farrar says: this writer 'presents the singular combination of pure, eloquent, and even rhythmical Greek, with the prophetic vehemence and fiery sternness of the Hebrew prophet'.

And again: 'The sententious form is the expression of a practical energy which will tolerate no opposition.

'The changes—often apparently abrupt—from one topic to another; the short sentences, which seem to quiver in the mind of the hearer from the swiftness with which they have been launched forth; the sweeping reproofs, sometimes unconnected by conjunctions, sometimes emphasised by many conjunctions; the manner in which the phrases seem to catch fire as the writer proceeds; the vivid freshness and picturesque energy of the expressions—all make us fancy that we are listening to some great harangue which has for its theme the rebuke of sin and the exhortation to righteousness, in order to avert the awfulness of some imminent crisis. The power of his style consists in the impression which it leaves of the burning sincerity and lofty character of the author'.

Dr. Gloag says: 'The style of the Epistle is peculiar; it bears no resemblance to any other writing in the New Testament; it might be described as the Christian book of Proverbs.

'It is strikingly fresh and vivid; the writer is rich in illustrations which are always appropriate and impressive. A vein of poetry pervades it, so that it may almost be considered as a prose poem. There is a remarkable vividness in his address; the persons whom James addresses are brought forward and spoken to as if present.'

Dr. S. Davidson says: 'Our author was familiar with the Hebrew prophets; and his manner, which is bold, aspiring and vigorous, resembles theirs. His denunciations are powerful, his strokes nervous and weighty, so that he even becomes sublime at times.'

These opinions will suffice to indicate the attractiveness of this writer's style.

When we recollect that the mother of James and Jude was a poetess (Luke i. 46-55) we need not be surprised that they inherited her gift; and it is providential that the practical and stern character of James did not quench this living flame.

The man who cannot make up his mind is like a wave of the sea driven and tossed by the wind (i. 6).

The transitoriness of riches is like the flower that so soon withers under the burning sun (i. 10, 11).

The development of sin is likened to conception, birth, growth, and death (i. 15).

Renewal of man's nature by the Word of Truth is likened to birth (i. 18).

God, the source of light, is compared to a sun which never suffers obscuration or change (i. 17).

A careless listener is compared to one who takes a hasty look at himself in a mirror (i. 23, 24).

Putting a check on one's tongue is likened to guiding and controlling a horse by a bridle, and a ship by a rudder (iii. 3, 4).

A careless word is like the spark which sets a forest on fire (iii. 5).

The tongue is like the deaf adder which refuses to hear the voice of the charmer (iii. 8).

The impossibility of a fountain sending forth both sweet and bitter water is a rebuke to the mouth that both blesses and curses (iii. 10, 11).

Worldly pleasures are like a hostile army encamped in our body (iv. 1).

Unfaithfulness to God is likened to adultery (iv. 4). Man's life is like a shifting mist (iv. 14).

The disease of the unjust and covetous soul is likened to the rust and decay to which stored up wealth is liable (v. 2, 3).

Patience under persecution is likened to a husbandman waiting for the rains which shall bring the crops to perfection (v. 7, 8).

Here are some of the character studies of this 'Epistle': the double-minded man (i. 6-8); the man who appreciates good sermons, but has no further use for them (i. 22-25); the man who is theoretically religious, but practically irreligious (i. 26, 27); the man who relates himself to people according to the clothes they wear—the wordly church steward (ii. 1-9); the insincere and useless philanthropist (ii. 14-17); the man who has an indolently inoperative creed, whose belief and practice are on different levels (ii. 14-26); the person who talks out of his turn, and even then, says the wrong thing (iii. 1-12); the Christian who is characterized by greed and pride (iv. 1-12); the person who leaves God out of account in his daily life (iv. 13-17); the rich who brow-beat and push about those who are poor (v. 1-6); the man who patiently endures (v. 7-11).

The freshness of the thought of this writer is nowhere more in evidence than in the fact that in these five chapters over sixty words occur which are not to be found anywhere else in the New Testament; and many of them are word-pictures.

i. 5, Liberally.   i. 6, 23, Is-Like.   i. 6, Driven-by-the-wind.   i. 6, Tossed.   i. 8; iv. 8, Double-minded.   i. 8, Unstable.   i. 11, The grace (goodly appearance).   i. 13, Cannot-be-tempted.   i. 15, 18, Bringeth-forth.   i. 17, Variation.   i. 17, Turning.   i. 21, Filthiness.   i. 21, Implanted (ingrown, inborn).   i. 25, Forgetteth (cf ver. 24).   i. 25, Doing (the act).   i. 26, Religious.   i. 26; iii. 2, Bridleth.

ii. 1. 9, Respect-of-persons (to lift up the face on a person).   ii. 2, Gold-fingered.   ii. 13, Without-mercy.   ii. 15, Lack of daily food.   ii. 16, Needful.   ii. 19, Shudder.

iii. 3, 4.   Turn-about (to guide).   iii. 5, Boasteth.   iii. 5, Wood.   iii. 6, Setteth-on-fire.   iii. 6, Wheel.   iii. 7, Things in the sea.   iii. 8, Restless (cf. i. 8).   iii. 9, Likeness.   iii. 10, Ought (not).   iii. 11, Send-forth (bubble-up, gush-forth).   iii. 11, 14, Bitter.   iii. 12, Salt water.   iii. 13, Understanding.   iii. 15, Devilish.   iii. 17, Easy to be intreated   iii. 17, Without variance (cf. i. 6).

iv. 4, Friendship. iv. 5, In vain. iv. 5, Made-to-dwell. iv. 9, Be-afflicted. iv. 9, Laughter. iv. 9, Be-turned. iv. 9, Heaviness. iv. 12, Lawgiver. iv. 13; v. 1, Go-to.

v. 1, Weep. v. 2, Corrupted. v. 3, Rusted. v. 4, Flowed. v. 4, Kept-back-by-fraud. v. 4, Crieth-out. v. 5, Lived-delicately. v. 7, Early. v. 7, Latter. v. 10, Suffering. v. 11, Full of pity.

If half the time that has been spent in discussing Christianity had been used in practising it, it would have been for the good of both the Church and the world.

The need to-day for the teaching of James is deep and urgent. If the alternatives are theologians or Christians, let us have Christians.

James, as well as Paul, had a faith, but his mission was not to expound the Christian's creed, but to examine the Christian's conduct.

Christians still lack wisdom and should pursue it: still are tried, and should endure: still are more interested in reading the Bible than in living it (ch. i): still are rudely partial and dis-respectful: still are more ready to hunt heresy than to live soundly (ch. ii): still a multitude who do not know how to discipline their tongue, who speak more than they think, who generate more heat than light: still people who are queering the pitch for many by envy and strife (ch. iii): still Christians who are trying to make the best of both worlds: still people who do not believe that God should plan one's life (ch. iv); still those who are money-conscious, who get rich at the expense of other people, who don't pay what they owe: still those who suffer in body, and are much in need of sympathy and help: still brethren who err from the truth (ch. v).

As long as all these kinds of people are to be found this Epistle will be needed, and should be resorted to.

USE OF THE OLD TESTAMENT

The use which James makes of the O.T. is both interesting and important. There are in his Epistle only four quotations (ii. 8; ii. 11; ii. 23; iv. 6), but in addition to these there are at least 53 references to the O.T., one for every two verses; and to these must be added references to the Law.

The mind of James was immersed in the Jewish Scriptures,

and so completely, that his belief and utterances are rooted in them. His references are traceable to Genesis, Exodus, Leviticus, Deuteronomy, Joshua, 1 Kings, 1 Chronicles, 2 Chronicles, Job, Psalms, Proverbs, Ecclesiastes, Isaiah, Jeremiah, Ezekiel, Joel, Amos, Zechariah; and there may be references to other O.T. books.

This familiarity with the Scriptures (ii. 8) was due, in the first place, to his education in the school at Nazareth, but it is attributable also to his personal interest and industry in the sacred records, a habit which accounts for his deep piety.

There are 15 references in ch. i; 12 in ch. ii; 9 in ch. iii; 7 in ch. iv; and 14 in ch. v.

The following will mean little or nothing to the reader unless the O.T. passages are turned up and read.

JAMES	O.T.	JAMES	O.T.
i. 5	1 Kings iii. 9-12	i. 15	Ps. vii. 14
i. 5	Prov. ii. 6	i. 18	Deut. xxxii. 18
i. 8	Ps. xii. 2	i. 19	Eccles. vii. 9
i. 9, 10	Jer. ix. 23, 24	i. 22, 23	Ezek. xxxiii. 31, 32
i. 10	Isa. xl. 7	i. 25	Ps. cxix. 45
i. 10, 11	Job xxiv. 24	i. 26	Isa. i. 11-17
i. 12	Job v. 17	i. 27	Exod. xxii. 22
i. 13, 14	Prov. xix. 3		
ii. 1, 9	Lev. xix. 15	ii. 11	Exod. xx. 13, 14
ii. 5	Deut. xiv. 2	ii. 19	Deut. vi. 4
ii. 6; v. 4	Deut. xxiv. 15	ii. 23	Gen. xv. 6
ii. 6	Prov. xiv. 21	ii. 23	2 Chron. xx. 7
ii. 7	Deut. xxviii. 58	ii. 23	Isa. xli. 8
ii. 8	Lev. xix. 18	ii. 25	Josh. ii. 5, 11, 12, 15, 16
iii. 2	Prov. x. 19	iii. 8	Ps. cxl. 3
iii. 5	Ps. lxxxiii. 13, 14	iii. 9	1 Chron. xxix. 10
iii. 5	Isa. ix. 18; x. 17, 18	iii. 9	Gen. i. 26
iii. 6	Prov. xvi. 27	iii. 18	Isa. xxxii. 17
iii. 7	Gen. i. 26; ix. 2	iii. 18	Prov. xi. 30
iv. 6	Prov. iii. 34	iv. 11	Ps. l. 20
iv. 8	Deut. iv. 7	iv.13,14,16	Prov. xxvii. 1
iv. 8	Ps. xxiv. 4	iv. 14	Job vii. 9
iv. 8	Zech. i. 3		
v. 1	Isa. xiii. 6	v. 7	Deut. xi. 14
v. 1	Jer. xxv. 34	v. 7	Zech. x. 1
v. 1-4	Isa. v. 7-9	v. 8	Joel ii. 1
v. 2	Job xiii. 28	v. 11	Job, book of
v. 2	Isa. l. 9	v. 11	Ps. ciii. 8
v. 3, 4	Amos iii. 10	v. 17, 18	1 Kings xvii. 1
v. 5-6	Jer. xii. 3	v. 20	Prov. x. 12; xi. 30

It is claimed that James was very familiar with the O.T. Apocrypha, and that he frequently refers to it. Dr. Mayor traces 32 references to Ecclesiasticus, and 12 to the Wisdom of Solomon.

A striking resemblance is the passage on the tongue (iii. 1-12 and Ecclesiasticus xxviii. 13-26. Verses in this passage are:

'Curse the whisperer and double-tongued, for such have destroyed many that were at peace' (13).

'Many have fallen by the edge of the sword, but not so many as have fallen by the tongue' (18).

'Weigh thy words in a balance, and make a door and bar for thy mouth. Beware thou slide not by it, lest thou fall before him that lieth in wait' (25, 26).

Other passages in Ecclesiasticus on the tongue are xix. 6-12; and xx. 5-8, 18-20.

A.V. and R.V.

In this Epistle the differences between the Authorized and Revised Versions are neither many nor of major importance; yet some of them are worth noting.

	A.V.	R.V.
i. 17	Every good gift and every perfect gift is from above, and cometh down from the Father of lights, with whom is no variableness, neither shadow of turning.	Every good gift and every perfect *boon* is from above *coming down* from the Father of lights, with whom *can be no variation,* neither shadow *that is cast by turning.*
i. 21	Wherefore lay apart all filthiness and superfluity of naughtiness, and receive with meekness the engrafted word . . .	Wherefore *putting away* all filthiness and *overflowing of wickedness,* receive with meekness the *implanted* word . . .
i. 25	Being not a forgetful hearer, but a doer of the work . . . blessed is his deed.	Being not a hearer that forgetteth, but *a doer that worketh* . . . blessed is his *doing.*
ii. 2	If there come unto your assembly . . . in goodly apparel...in vile raiment...	If there come into your *synagogue* . . . in fine *clothing* . . . in vile *clothing* . . .

		A.V.	R.V.
ii.	4	Are ye not then partial in yourselves, and are become judges of evil thoughts?	Are ye not *divided in your own mind,* and become judges *with* evil thoughts?
ii.	5	Hath not God chosen the poor of this world?	Did not God choose them that are poor as to the world?
ii.	6	Do not rich men oppress you, and draw you before the judgment seats?	Do not the rich oppress you, and *themselves drag you* before the judgment seats?
ii.	10	Offend . . . is guilty of all.	*Stumble* . . . is *become* guilty of all.
ii.	17	Faith if it hath not works, is dead being alone.	Faith, if it have not works, is dead *in itself.*
ii.	19	Thou believest that there is one God . . . tremble.	Thou believest that *God is one* . . . *shudder.*
iii.	4	Turned about with a very small helm, whithersoever the governor listeth.	Turned about by a very small *rudder,* whither the *impulse of the steersman willeth.*
iii.	5	How great a matter a little fire kindleth!	How much wood is kindled by how small a fire!
iii.	9	God even the Father.	The Lord and Father.
iii.	13	Who is a wise man and endued with knowledge among you?	Who is wise and *understanding* among you?
		Out of a good conversation.	By his good *life.*
iv.	4	Is the enemy of God.	*Maketh himself* an enemy of God.
iv.	5	The spirit that dwelleth in us lusteth to envy.	Doth the spirit which he made to dwell in us long unto envying? or, The Spirit which He made to dwell in us jealously yearns for the entire devotion of the heart.
v.	3	Your gold and silver is cankered, and the rust . . .	Your gold and your silver are *rusted,* and *their* rust . . .
v.	5	Lived in pleasure . . .	Lived delicately, or in indulgence. The word does not occur anywhere else.
v.	11	We count them happy which endure . . .	We *call* them *blessed* which *endured* . . .
v.	16	Your faults . . .	Your sins . . .
		Effectual fervent prayer . . .	Supplication . . .

THE CATHOLIC EPISTLES

I **PETER**

A.D. 64-67

Notes

Peter and *John* were the two outstanding Apostles of the Lord in the circle of the Twelve, and they were more intimately associated with Him than were any of the others.

The Apostles were sent out 'two and two,' and it is most likely that Peter and John went together (Mark iii. 14). They had previously been partners (Mark i. 16-20; Luke v. 7, 10). They were together at the raising of a dead girl (Mark v. 37), at the Transfiguration (Mark ix. 2), and in Gethsemane (Mark xiv. 33). Together they made ready the Passover (Luke xxii. 8). Peter made signs to John at the Last Supper (John xiii. 24). At the Trial of Jesus they entered the palace of the High Priest together (John xviii. 15). They alone visited the Sepulchre (John xx. 2-10). It was of John's future that Peter asked the risen Lord (John xxi. 20). Together they healed a cripple (Acts iii. 1-10). Together they were arrested by the Sanhedrin (Acts iv. 3). Together they visited Samaria (Acts viii. 14). They, with James, were regarded as 'pillars' of the Church, and supported Paul's work among the Gentiles (Gal. ii. 9).

Peter figures largely in the New Testament—in the Gospels, the Acts, his two Epistles, and several times in Paul's Epistles.

He had three Calls—to friendship with Jesus (John i. 41, 42); to discipleship (Mark i. 16-18); and to Apostleship (Mark iii. 14).

Pentecost divided Peter's story into two parts: before, he was the learner; after, the teacher: before, he was the man of promise; after, the man of fulfilment.

Most Christians get stuck between Calvary and Pentecost, and so they are imprisoned 'for fear' (John xx. 19).

That Peter the Apostle wrote this First Epistle is not open to question. It bears many recollections of his intercourse with

Christ; there are undesigned coincidences between it and Peter's speeches in the Acts; and throughout it bears the impress of the Apostle's strongly marked individuality.

The date of the Epistle can be fixed within narrow limits. If, as seems certain, Peter had read James and Romans and Ephesians he must have written after the latter, the date of which was about A.D. 62. And if, as also is almost certain, he was martyred about A.D. 67, his Epistle must have been written during the Neronian persecution, between the fire of Rome in A.D. 64 and the Emperor's death in A.D. 68.

This short period fits the situation envisaged in the Letter.

The Epistle is addressed 'To the elect who are sojourners of the Dispersion in Pontus, Galatia, Cappadocia, Asia, and Bithynia' (i. 1). Three words here are important: *'elect,' 'sojourners'*, and *'Dispersion'*. By the first word is meant that believers —constituting the Church of God—are chosen by God (cf. ii. 9, 10). By the second word is meant that this world is not the home of believers. We are 'sojourners and pilgrims,' and pilgrims because sojourners (ii. 11). The third word (*diaspora*) occurs three times in the New Testament (in Jas. i. 1; John vii. 35; and here: cf. Acts viii. 1, 4; xi. 19), and refers to Christians as a scattered body of sojourners in the world, as the Jews of the Old Testament period had been. This scattering, we learn from the Acts was divinely designed in the interests of world evangelization.

The Greek Fathers held that the persons addressed were Jews by birth; and the Latin Fathers held that they were Gentiles. The fact is that they were both, with Gentiles predominating (cf. i. 14, 18; ii. 9; iv. 2-4). It must be evident that the Churches in Asia Minor would be composed mostly of converts from heathenism, largely the result of Paul's missionary labours in these areas.

Map 18, Vol. 2, p. 314 shows that the letter was designed to reach the five Roman provinces mentioned above, known commonly as Asia Minor. Perhaps the order in which these are named indicates the order in which Silvanus was expected to visit them (v. 12).

In the countries named is a remarkable proof of the rapid diffusion of Christianity before A.D. 70. This is borne witness to by Pliny in a letter he wrote to Trajan in A.D. 108. (See Paley's *Evidences of Christianity*, chapter ix).

There is no historical evidence that Peter had visited these provinces; nor is there any evidence that he had not.

The design of Peter in writing this Epistle was not controversial but exhortatory (v. 12); it is not theological but experimental, but the experience is, of course, based on theology. The Epistle is intended to comfort and strengthen believers in the sufferings to which they were exposed, and to assure them of final triumph. It is pre-eminently the Epistle of Hope.

The place of writing was 'Babylon' (v. 13). This must mean either Babylon on the Euphrates, or Rome, metaphorically so named. Each view is influentially supported, but almost certainly Rome is meant, as in the Apocalypse. This was the generally accepted view until the Reformation.

The following charts present the contents of this Epistle.

CHART 179

I PETER	PART I	i. 1–ii. 10

INTRODUCTION: i. 1, 2

The Writer, i. 1a.   *The Readers*, i. 1b–2a.   *The Benediction*, i. 2

The Vocation of the Christian . . . Salvation. i. 3–ii. 10

THE DOCTRINE EXPOUNDED i. 3–12	THE DUTY ENJOINED i. 13–25	THE DESIGN EXHIBITED ii. 1–10
	THE PERSONAL DUTY i. 13-21	THE INDIVIDUAL DESIGN GROWTH As of a Body ii. 1–3
SALVATION THE HOPE OF THE FUTURE i. 3–5	The Nature of it HOLINESS i. 13–17	The Preparation ii. 1
	The Ground of it REDEMPTION i. 18–21	The Prescription ii. 2
		The Presupposition ii. 3
SALVATION THE JOY OF THE PRESENT i. 6–9	THE RELATIVE DUTY i. 22–25	THE CORPORATE DESIGN STRUCTURE As of a Building ii. 4–10
	The Nature of it LOVE i. 22	An Exposition: Setting Forth the Plan ii. 4–5
	The Ground of it LIFE i. 23–25	A Confirmation: Presenting the Proof ii. 6
SALVATION THE THEME OF THE PAST i. 10–12		An Application: Displaying the Privilege ii. 7–10

CHART 180

I PETER	PART II	ii. 11–iii. 12

The Behaviour of the Christian . . . Submission

THE FOREWORD—PERSONAL: ii. 11, 12

Negative, ii. 11
Positive, ii. 12

SUBMISSION IN CIVIL RELATIONS	SUBMISSION IN SOCIAL RELATIONS	SUBMISSION IN DOMESTIC RELATIONS
ii. 13–17. FREEDMEN	ii. 18–25. BONDMEN	iii. 1–7. ALL MEN
The Duty: ii. 13, 14	The Servants: ii. 18-20	Wives: iii. 1–6
The Motive: ii. 15-17	The Saviour: ii. 21–25	Husbands: iii. 7

THE FINAL WORD—RELATIVE: iii. 8–12

Negative: iii. 9, 10, 11, 12
Positive: iii. 8, 9, 11, 12

CHART 181

I PETER	PART III	iii. 13–v. 14

The Discipline of the Christian . . . Suffering

DISCIPLINE IN THE WORLD iii. 13–iv. 6	DISCIPLINE IN THE CHURCH iv. 7–v. 7	DISCIPLINE IN THE HEAVENLIES v. 8–11
The Attitude: iii. 13-17	Christian Fellowship: iv. 7–11	The Enemy: v. 8
The Example: iii. 18–22	Christian Fortitude: iv. 12–19	The Conflict: v. 9
The Object: iv. 1–6	Christian Faithfulness: v. 1–7	The Victory: v. 10, 11

CONCLUSION: v. 12–14

The Amanuensis	v. 12–b
The Exhortation: ..	v. 12–b
The Salutation:	v. 13, 14–a
The Benediction:	v. 14–b

That Peter was deeply influenced by the Old Testament this Epistle shows. His presentation of Christianity is in a Jewish frame, and his references are taken from the LXX version. The following should be studied: i. 7; i. 10-12; i. 16; i. 17-19; i. 24; i. 25; ii. 3; ii. 4-8; ii. 9; ii. 10; ii. 11; ii. 22-25; iii. 4; iii. 6; iii. 11; iii. 13; iii. 14; iii. 20; iii. 22; iv. 17, 18; iv. 18; v. 5; v. 7. The most of these are not direct references, but they are echoes in Peter's memory of passages with which he was familiar.

The evidence in the Epistle of Peter's personal acquaintance with the Lord and His teaching is most impressive.

In i. 8 he says, 'ye,' because 'having seen' the Lord he could not have said 'we.' In ii. 23 he speaks of what he saw in the High Priest's vestibule; and in v. 1, he says that he witnessed Christ's sufferings. Chapter v. 5 arises from the scene recorded in John xiii. 4 ff.

Christ had called Peter a rock, and he speaks of 'living stones' (ii. 5), and of Christ as the 'chief corner Stone' (ii. 6). Christ had warned Peter against Satan, and of this enemy the Apostle warns his readers (v. 8). Peter had denied Christ, and he constantly exhorts his readers to steadfastness (i. 13). Christ had said that Peter was an 'offence', and the Apostle uses this word (ii. 8). Christ had taught that State obligations must be discharged, and Peter enjoins this on his readers (ii. 13, 14, cf. Matt. xvii. 24-27). Christ had enjoined generous forgiveness, and Peter does the same (i. 5; v. 4, cf. Matt. xviii. 22). These are but few of the reminiscences in this Epistle of incidents recorded in the Gospels.

The Apostle's familiarity with our Lord's teaching is not something that can be shown from specific verses in his Epistle but it is in the very texture of his Letter, inseparable from the substance of his thought.

An illustration of this is in the echoes throughout of what is commonly called The Lord's Prayer.

Our, i. 4. Father, i. 3, 17. In Heaven, i. 4, 12. Hallowed be Thy Name, i. 15, 16. Thy Kingdom come, ii. 9. Thy will be done, ii. 15; iii. 17; iv. 2, 19. Daily bread, v. 7. Forgive, iv. 8. Temptation, iv. 12. Deliver, iv. 13. Kingdom, v. 11. [Power,

i. 5. iv. 11. Glory, i. 11, 21; iv. 11. 14; v. 1, 10. For ever and ever, iv. 11, v. 11. Amen, iv. 11; v. 11.

The resemblances between Peter's speeches in the *Acts* and this Epistle, are, to say the least, striking.

The following are illustrations of this.

EPISTLE	ACTS	EPISTLE	ACTS
i. 3, 4, 21;	ii. 32–36; iii. 15;	i. 10	iii. 18; x. 43
i. 17	x. 28, 34	ii. 7	iv. 11
ii. 24	v. 30; x. 39	iv. 5	x. 42
iii. 21	iv. 10; x. 40	i. 12	v. 32
v. 1	ii. 32; iii. 15; x. 41		

It cannot be doubted that there are some close resemblances between this Epistle and that of *James*. These relate to the Dispersion (1 Pet. i. 1; Jas. i. 1); to temptation or trial (1 Pet. i. 6, 7; Jas. i. 2-4); to being born again by the Word of God (1 Pet. i. 23; Jas. i. 18, 21); to the frailty of man (1 Pet. i. 24; Jas. i. 10); to covering a multitude of sins (1 Pet. iv. 8; Jas. v. 20); to humility and submission (1 Pet. v. 5, 9; Jas. iv. 6, 7, 10); to warring lusts (1 Pet. ii. 11; Jas. iv. 1).

The following resemblances show how familiar Peter was with the Epistle to the *Romans*.

PETER	ROMANS	PETER	ROMANS
i. 14	xii. 2	i. 17	ii. 6, 11
i. 20 f.	xvi. 25 f.	i. 21	iv. 24
i. 22	xii. 9, 10	ii. 5	xii. 1
ii. 6 ff.	ix. 33	ii. 10	ix. 25
ii. 13-17	xiii. 1, 3, 4, 7	ii. 24	vi. 11
iii. 8 f.	xii. 14-19	iii. 18	vi. 10
iii. 21	vi. 4	iv. 1	vi. 7
iv. 3	xiii. 13	iv. 9-11	xii. 3-15
iv. 13	viii. 17	v. 1	viii. 18

These resemblances indicate Peter's indebtedness to Paul, and not Paul's to Peter. Romans, A.D. 51. 1 Peter A.D. 64-67.

It seems evident also that Peter was familiar with the Epistle to the Ephesians; and this is the more interesting when we remember that Ephesus was the capital of the Asia to which Peter's Letter went (i. 1).

PETER	EPHESIANS	PETER	EPHESIANS
i. 3–5	i. 18–20	i. 7	i. 6, 12, 14
i. 10–12	iii. 5	i. 12	iii. 10
i. 18; i. 14	iv. 17, 18	ii. 9	v. 8
i. 20	i. 4, 8, 11;	i. 14, 15	ii. 1–3
	ii. 10		
ii. 5 f.	ii. 20	iii. 1–6	v. 22, 23
iii. 8–10	iv. 31, 32	iii. 18	ii. 18
iii. 21, 22	i. 20		

Dr. Hort says: 'The truth is that in the First Epistle of St. Peter many thoughts are derived from the Epistle to the Ephesians, as others are from that to the Romans, but St. Peter makes them fully his own by the form into which he casts them, a form for the most part unlike what we find in any Epistle of St. Paul's.'

In the Cambridge Greek Testament on 1 Peter, Mr. Blenkin has shown that implicitly, where not explicitly, the teaching of the Apostles' Creed is traceable in 1 Peter.

'I believe in God the Father (i. 2, 3, 17)
'Almighty (iv. 11; v. 6)
'Maker of heaven and earth (iv. 19)
'And in Jesus Christ His only Son our Lord (iii. 15: R.V.)
'Incarnate (i. 19; ii. 24; iii. 18; iv. 1)
'Who suffered (i. 11; ii. 21, 23; iv. 1, 13; v. 1)
'Was crucified (i. 2; ii. 24)
'Dead (iii. 18)
'He descended into hell (iii. 19)
'He rose again (i. 3, 21; iii. 21)
'He ascended into heaven (iii. 22)
'He sitteth at the right hand of God (i. 21; iii. 22)
'He shall come again with glory (i. 7, 13; iv. 13; v. 4)
'To judge both the quick and the dead (iv. 5; v. 4)
'I believe in the Holy Ghost (i. 2, 12; iv. 14)
'The holy catholic Church (i. 1; ii. 5, 9, 10)
'The Resurrection of the body (i. 3)
'The life everlasting' (i. 4; v. 4, 10).

This does not include the whole of the Creed, but indicates that it is rooted in the teaching of the New Testament.

About sixty words occur in this Epistle which do not occur again in the New Testament, and they are worthy of careful study.

i. 3, 23: To-beget-again. i. 4: Fadeth-not-away; that does not dry up, or wither; cf. amaranth. i. 8: Unspeakable. i. 10:

Searched-diligently. i. 11: To-testify-beforehand. i. 13: To-gird-up. 'Vivid metaphor for habit of the Orientals, who quickly gathered up their loose robes with a girdle when in a hurry, or starting on a journey' (Robertson). i. 13: Perfectly. i. 17: Without-respect-of-persons. i. 18. Handed-down-from-your-fathers. i. 23: Seed.

ii. 2: New-born. ii. 2: Sincere, i.e., without guile. ii. 5, 9: Priesthood. ii. 12; iii. 2: Behold; i.e., to be an overseer, to view carefully. ii. 14: A well-doer. ii. 16: Cloke. ii. 17; v. 9: Brotherhood. ii. 20: Glory. ii. 21: Leaving. ii. 21: Example— from a word that means to write under, a writing-copy for one to imitate. ii. 23: To-revile-again. ii. 24: Having-died. ii. 24: Stripes.

iii. 3: Plaiting. iii. 3: Putting-on. iii. 6: Terror. iii. 6: Dwell-with. iii. 7: To assign, to impart. iii. 7: Wife, female. iii. 8: Like-minded. iii. 8: Loving-as-a-brother. iii. 8: Humble-minded. iii. 21: Putting-away (cf. 2 Pet. i. 14). iii. 21: Inquiry, appeal.

iv. 1: Arm yourself. iv. 2: Live. iv. 2: Remaining. iv. 3: Wine-bibbings; from *wine*, and to *bubble up*; drunkenness. iv. 3: Carousing. iv. 4: Excess; To pour forth. iv. 8: Fervent, intense. iv. 14: The name of Christ. iv. 15: A busy-body in other men's matters. 'One who spies out the affairs of other men.' iv. 19: Creator. iv. 19: Well-doing (cf. ii. 14).

v. 1: Fellow-elder. v. 2: By constraint v. 2: Filthy lucre. v. 2: Willingly; a ready mind. v. 4: Chief Shepherd. v. 5: Gird. The reference is to the apron of a slave, and, perhaps, Peter was thinking of what Jesus did (John xiii. 4 ff.). v. 6: Mighty. v. 8: Roar. v. 10: Strengthen. v. 12: Testify. v. 13: Elected-together.

On one passage in this Epistle (iii. 18-22) a library has been written, and, no doubt, it will be a subject of controversy to the end of time.

1. Does 'spirit' (18) refer to the Holy Spirit, or to Christ's human spirit?

2. What is meant by 'quickened'? (18).

3. In the expressions 'in the flesh,' and 'in the spirit' (R.V.), both datives must be regarded as of the *sphere*, 'in'; not the first of the *sphere*, and the second of the *instrument*, 'by' (A.V.).

4. 'In which' (19), that is 'in the spirit,' Christ's holy human spirit.

5. 'He went' must mean a local transference, as in verse 22, and so cannot mean that Christ preached through Noah, or through the Apostles.

6. 'And preached.' There are two principal words for 'to preach': *kērussō*, which means *to proclaim as a herald*; and *euaggelizō*, which means *to proclaim glad tidings*. The former word is used in verse 19, and while it might refer to preaching the Gospel, it need not necessarily have that meaning, but only that a proclamation was made, without revealing the nature of it.

7. Does verse 22 throw light on the nature of the preaching?

8. Who are meant by 'the spirits' (19)? Are they the spirits of angels, or of men?

9. What is meant by 'in prison' (19)? Is it Hades, called Hell?

10. Were the spirits in prison when they were preached to, or afterwards?

11. Are only the 'disobedient' in Noah's time referred to? Why should a proclamation be made to a limited number and not to all 'disobedient' spirits?

12. What was the issue of the proclamation? Did these 'disobedient' spirits have a chance to repent? Did any of them repent?

13. Does this passage teach that sinners will have a chance of salvation after death?

14. What light, if any, is thrown on this passage by chapter iv. 6?

It will be seen from these inquiries that the passage is by no means easy of interpretation. Luther admits that he does not know what Peter means.

Dr. A. T. Robertson says: 'It is a slim hope for those who neglect Christ in this life to gamble with a possible second chance after death which rests on very precarious exegesis of a most difficult passage.'

The eschatology of Peter (iii. 18-22; iv. 6) raises the whole question of human destiny. It may be said that there are five main views.

1. Purgatory

This is the Roman Catholic doctrine that 'there is a purgatorial fire where the souls of the righteous are purified by punishment of some fixed period, that entrance may be given them into their eternal home, where nothing that is defiled can have a place' (Council of Trent).

2. HEAVENLY BLESSEDNESS

This is the truth, which Scripture clearly teaches, that the believer at death goes to be with Christ (Phil. i. 23; 2 Cor. v. 6-8).

3. CONDITIONAL IMMORTALITY

This is not, as is often said, *annihilationism*, but affirms that man is not immortal except in Christ, and will in due course, after death and judgment, cease to be. The age-long belief in man's immortality is a Greek and not a Hebrew or a Christian dogma.

4. UNIVERSALISM

This view is that, ultimately, no one can say when, the Cross will be triumphant in the restoration of all things redemptively; that none will finally perish. The view is that expressed by Tennyson in his poem *In Memoriam*:

> Oh, yet we trust that somehow good
>   Will be the final goal of ill,
> To pangs of nature, sins of will,
> Defects of doubt, and taints of blood;
> That nothing walks with aimless feet;
>   That not one life shall be destroyed,
>   Or cast as rubbish to the void,
> When God hath made the pile complete.

5. ETERNAL PUNISHMENT

The orthodox view is that the doom of everlasting damnation is incurred by the majority of mankind: that this doom is passed irreversibly at death on all who die in a state of sin: and that the duration of torment is necessarily endless for all who incur it.

'All that God is in Himself, all that He is known to be to me through this revelation of Himself in Christ Jesus, give us an infinite satisfaction in leaving the matter with Him.'

All that Scripture has to say on any given subject is the truth about that subject.

Peter's First Epistle is full of comfort, and in this regard it differs, as a whole, from all other New Testament Epistles. It assures the believer that in spite of inevitable suffering, the horizon is bright (i. 3, 4, 13, 21; iii. 5, 15). He insists on well-doing (ii. 12, 14, 15, 20; iii. 6, 11, 17; iv. 19); and enjoins submissive resignation (ii. 13-25; iii. 1, 5; iii. 18-iv. 1).

Dr. Chase has pointed out that Peter's imagery is drawn from the associations of *birth, childhood,* and *family life* (i. 3, 14, 17, 22 f; ii. 2); *nomadic life* (i. 1, 17; ii. 11); *temple and worship* (ii. 5; iii. 15); *building* (ii. 4); *the fields and pastoral life* (i. 4 (24); v. 2, 8); *military life* (i. 5; ii. 11; iv. 1); *painting* (ii. 21); *working of metals* (i. 7; iv. 12).

This imagery is derived almost entirely from the Old Testament, and finds parallels in the Lord's sayings.

The Epistle is full of subjects which provoke thought, strengthen faith, and inspire confidence:

The Dynamics of the Regenerate Life (i. 3-5). The Compatibility of Sorrow and Joy (i. 6, 7). Loving One who has not been seen (i. 8, 9). The Momentum of a Beautiful Life (ii. 11-17). The Sufferings of Christ (ii. 21-25). Husbands and Wives (iii. 1-8). Christ Sanctified as Lord (iii. 8-15 R.V.). The Mystery of Hades (iii. 18-22; iv. 6). Fiery Trial (iv. 12-19). The Shepherd and the Flock (v. 1-7). The Lion and the Sheep (v. 8-10).

The Heavenly Inheritance (i. 3-5). The Theology of Suffering (i. 6, 7). Salvation the Central Subject of Study (i. 10-12). Holiness (i. 14-16). Redemption (i. 18-21). The Word of God (i. 24, 25). Spiritual Milk (ii. 1-3). The Stone and the Stones (ii. 4-8). The True Israel (ii. 9, 10). The Plea for a Blameless Life (ii. 11, 12). The Reason for Submission (ii. 13-16). The Virtue of Patience (ii. 20). Following the Example (ii. 21-25). Guidance for Christian Married Women (iii. 1-7). Christian Behaviour (iii. 8-12). How to Suffer (iii. 13-17). The Just and the Unjust (iii. 18). Christian Love (iv. 8, R.V.). Solemn Questions (iv. 17, 18). Humility (v. 5, 6). Care and the Carer (v. 7). Called to Eternal Glory (v. 10).

The Trinity (i. 2). Deathless Joy (i. 6-9). The Foundations of Faith and Hope (i. 20, 21). Strangers and Pilgrims (ii. 11, 12). The Cement of Sympathy (iii. 8). A Good Conscience (iii. 9-17). Spirits in Prison (iii. 18-22). Wilfulness and the Will of God (iv. 1-6). The Shadow of the End (iv. 7-11). Old and Young (v. 1-5).

THE CATHOLIC EPISTLES

2 PETER

A.D. 64-67

Notes

Most critics are agreed that the Apostle Peter did not write this Epistle. Prof. James Moffatt states this view when he says: 'The author reveals himself as the composer of a pseudepigraphon under the honoured name of Peter. If the writer felt himself a true disciple of the apostles he probably chose this literary artifice, with its self-effacing spirit, for the purpose of conveying a message which he believed to be timely and inspired. The prestige of Peter, owing to the circulation of the first epistle and the tradition of the Churches, would naturally suggest the use of his name for this encyclical.' (*Introduction to the Literature of the New Testament*, p. 366).

That apocryphal writings were fathered upon Jewish patriarchs and prophets does not warrant or justify the application of this literary device to a Writing of the New Testament. Either Peter wrote this Epistle, or he did not. If he did not, it is a forgery, for it claims to be Peter's. The motive of the forger is irrelevant, for we must regard *fact* and not *intention*.

That 2 Peter presents difficult problems no one will deny, but the attempt to solve these by denying to the Epistle Apostolic Authorship is no way out of the difficulties.

Those who deny Peter's authorship of the Epistle place the date of the Writing between A.D. 130-170.

Those who hold to the apostolic authorship place it between A.D. 64-67; and probably the place of writing was Rome.

The Author calls himself 'Simon Peter' (i. 1, R.V.), and claims to be one of Christ's apostles (i. 1). He says that this is the 'second epistle' which he has written (iii. 1). He speaks as an old man nearing the end of his journey, and, on account of what the Lord had said to him (John xxi. 18) he is not anticipating a natural death (i. 14). We know that he was martyred.

There are references in the Epistle which connect with the Gospels, especially Mark's, whose Gospel is due to Peter, as very early and widespread tradition affirms.

The most important of such connections is the reference to the Transfiguration (i. 17, 18). It was Peter who, on the Mount, used the word 'tabernacles' (Matt. xvii. 4), and he used the word again in this Epistle in speaking of his body (i. 13, 14).

Again, Luke records that on the Mount Jesus spoke of the 'decease' which He would accomplish at Jerusalem (ix. 31). The word He used was not *death*, but *exodus*, for His sacrifice was 'a way out'. Now, in this Epistle, speaking of his approaching death, Peter uses the same word (i. 15): 'That ye may be able after my *exodus* to call these things to remembrance.'

But there are other contacts between this Epistle and the Gospels. Remembering Peter's connection with the Second Gospel it is impressive that the word *dōreō, to give*, occurs only in Mark xv. 45, and 2 Pet. i. 3, 4.

The word *basanizō* is a word which means to test *metals*, and it is variously rendered; but both Peter and Mark use it in the sense of vexation: Mark vi. 48, '*distressed* in rowing'; and in 2 Pet. ii. 8, 'Lot *vexed* his righteous soul.'

Tremō, to *tremble*, is found in Mark v. 33, and 2 Peter ii. 10.

Lailaps, meaning *storm* occurs in Mark iv. 37, and 2 Peter ii. 17.

The last three words occur elsewhere than in Mark and 2 Peter, but the influence of Peter upon Mark makes them of special interest.

Prof. Lumby points out that Peter speaks of '*dog*, and *sow*' (ii. 22), as does his Lord in Matt. vii. 6.

Peter, following the Lord, likens the secrecy of the Advent to the coming of a '*thief in the night*' (Matt. xxiv. 43; 2 Pet. iii. 10).

With Peter's reference to the *Flood*, and *Sodom*, and *Gomorrah* (ii. 5, 6) should be compared Luke xvii. 26-30.

Surely Peter's reference to the 'latter end' and the 'beginning' (ii. 20) is an echo of Matt. xii. 45!

We are not surprised at these connections, assuming Peter to be the author of this Epistle, but it would be very surprising to find them in a writing of the mid-second century.

The connections between this Epistle and Peter's speeches

recorded in the Acts must not be overlooked. Examples of this are:

'Obtained', langchanō (i. 1, and Acts i. 17). *'Piety'*, eusebeia (i. 7, and Acts iii. 12). *'Unlawful'*, anomos (ii. 8, and Acts ii. 23). *'Godly'*, devout, eusebes (ii. 9, and Acts x. 2, 7). *'Speak'*, phtheg-gomai (ii. 16, 18, and Acts iv. 18). *'The day of the Lord'*, hēmera Kuriou (iii. 10; Acts ii. 20; and 1 Thess. v. 2). *'Reward of un-righteousness'*, misthos adikias. Of Balaam (ii. 13, 15); of Judas (Acts i. 18).

'Punish', kolazō (ii. 9 (cf. ii. 4), and Acts iv. 21). *'Denying'*, arneomai (ii. 1, and Acts iii. 14). *'Lord'*,Despotēs (ii. 1, and Acts iv. 24).

The language of First and Second Peter should be compared. In both Peter is an Apostle (1. i. 1; 2. i. 1). In both is the same salutation (1. i. 2; 2. i. 2). In both *'conversation'*, anastrophē (1. i. 15, 18; *et al*; 2. ii. 7, iii. 11) meaning moral conduct is used. In both *'virtue'*, aretē is applied to God (1. ii. 9; 2. i. 3). In both *'putting-off'*, apothesis occurs, and nowhere else in the New Testament (1. iii. 21; 2. i. 14). *'Without blemish (amōmos) and without spot (aspilos)'* (1. i. 19; 2. iii. 14; cf. 2. ii. 13). The word *'eye-witness'*, epoptēs, occurs only in 2. i. 16; and the cognate verb epopteuō only in 1. ii. 12; iii. 2.

Other occurrences in both Epistles relate to prophecy (1. 10, 11; 2. i. 20, 21); to Noah and the Flood (1. iii. 20 ; 2. ii. 5): and to the Second Advent (1. i. 5, 7; 2. iii. 12: cf. apokalupsis and parousia).

These correspondences surely prove common authorship!

In conclusion, and referring again to the Authenticity of this Epistle, in spite of difficulties which must not be overlooked, the internal evidence of Peter's authorship is very strong, both by reason of what it says, and of what it does not say.

There is no hint that Jerusalem had been destroyed (A.D. 70), an event which would have served the author's purpose had it already taken place; and there is no reference to the heresy of Gnosticism, which was vigorous at the time of the alleged date suggested by some critics.

And a fact of considerable importance is that no uncanonical writing of the second and third centuries can be compared with

2 Peter for richness of spiritual quality; and there never lived a forger who was clever enough to deceive the Councils of Laodicea (A.D. 366), Hippo (A.D. 393), and Carthage (A.D. 397).

We may assume, then, that the Apostle Peter wrote this Letter, and would have readers beware of error and grow in grace (iii. 17, 18).

Peter's reference to Paul and his Epistles is of great importance (iii. 15, 16).

> 'Account that the longsuffering of our Lord is salvation; even as our beloved brother Paul also, according to the wisdom given to him, wrote unto you; as also in all (his) epistles, speaking in them of these things; wherein are some things hard to be understood, which the ignorant and unsteadfast wrest as (they do) also the other Scriptures, unto their own destruction.'

The following points should be noted:

1. Peter calls Paul a *'beloved brother'*; which shows that he cherished no ill feeling about Paul's rebuke of him years before (Gal. ii. 11-21).

2. *'Wrote* unto you' (aorist). We do not know which of Paul's writings Peter is referring to.

3. *'Unto you.'* This means that Paul and Peter wrote to the same Churches in Asia Minor (1 Peter i. 1).

4. *'All his epistles.'* This does not imply a canon of Paul's Epistles, but that Peter was familiar with many of them—it cannot be said how many.

5. *'Things hard to be understood'*. *Dusnoētos* occurs here only in the New Testament. Peter does not say what things it was difficult to understand; but this statement is as true now as it was then.

6. *'Ignorant'*, *amathēs* unlearned; occurs here only.

7. *'Unstable'*, *asteriktos* in 2 Peter only (ii. 14; iii. 16).

8. *'Wrest'*, *strebloō*. Here only in the New Testament. The word means, to put on the rack, to subject to torture, to hoist with a windlass or screw, to twist or dislocate the limbs on a rack.

9. *'The other Scriptures.'* Peter puts Paul's Epistles on the same level with the Old Testament Writings.

We have noted comparisons between First and Second Peter, but there are also differences.

In the First the keynote is *hope, elpis, elpizō* (i. 3, 13, 21; iii. 5, 15); but in the Second the keynote is *knowledge, epignōskō* (ii. 21, 22); *epignōsis* (i. 3, 8; ii. 20); *gnōrizō* (i. 16); *gnōsis* (i. 5, 6; iii. 18); *proginōskō* (iii. 17).

In the First there are about thirty references to the Old Testament, but in the Second, not more than five.

In the First there are frequent references to Christ's sufferings (i. 11, 19; ii. 21-25; iii. 18; iv. 1, 13; v. 1); but in the Second, there are none.

In the First the example of Christ is set before believers (ii. 21-25; iii. 18; iv. 1), but not in the Second.

In the First there are references to the persecution of Christians, but not to false teachers; but in the Second, the references are to false teachers, but not to persecutions.

The intention of the *First* is to *comfort*, but of the *Second*, to *warn*.

The two Epistles appear to have been addressed to the same readers (1. i. 1; 2. iii. 1, 15).

The omissions in 2 Peter are noticeable.

These relate to the LORD's teaching, and to the great events of His life (but cf. i. 16-18). There is no mention of the Crucifixion, (but cf. ii. 1), nor of the Resurrection . The only reference to the Holy Spirit is in i. 21. Prayer is not alluded to. This is in contrast to 1 Peter.

If the evidence of the apostolicity of an epistle were the amount of Christian doctrine in it, 'Philemon,' 'James,' and 'Jude' would fare badly.

As Peter was writing a second letter to the readers of his first there was no need for him to repeat what he had already said and regarded as assumed.

Every Writing must be judged by the intention of the writer— not by the subjective ideas of the critic—and in his Second Epistle Peter's purpose was to warn, not to teach.

The similarity of 2 Peter chapter ii and Jude's Epistle has often been pointed out. Some hold that *Peter* uses *Jude*: some that

Jude was Peter: and some, that they both use another source. This is a problem that has not been solved; and if it could be, what the better would we be?

What Peter regards as in the future, Jude regards as present.

The following parallels should be studied.

2 PETER	JUDE	2 PETER	JUDE
ii. 1	4	ii. 13	12
ii. 4	6	ii. 15	11
ii. 6	7	ii. 17	12, 13
ii. 10	8	ii. 18	16
ii. 11	9	iii. 2	17
ii. 12	10	iii. 3	18

The vocabulary of 2 Peter should be studied. Prof. A. T. Robertson says: 'There are some 361 words in 1 Peter not in 2 Peter, 231 in 2 Peter not in 1 Peter. There are 686 *hapax legomena* in the New Testament, 54 in 2 Peter instead of the average 62, a large number when the brevity of the Epistle is considered.'

The words peculiar to 2 Peter are:

'Like-precious' (i. 1). 'Exceeding great' (i. 4). 'Promises' (i. 4; iii. 13). 'Having escaped' (i. 4; ii. 18, 20). 'Adding-on-your-part' (i. 5). 'Seeing-only-what-is-near'; to close the eyes in order to see; shortsighted (i. 9). 'Having-forgotten' (i. 9). 'Swift' (i. 14; ii. 1). 'Always' (i. 15). 'Remembrance' (i. 15). 'Follow-out' (i. 16; ii. 2, 15). 'Eye-witness' (i. 16). 'Such' (i. 17). 'Excellent' (i. 17). 'Dark,' murky, squalid (i. 19). 'Dawn,' to shine through (i. 19). 'Day-star' (i. 19); from *phōs*, light, and *pherō*, to bring; i.e., light-bringing; hence our word *phosphorus*. 'Interpretation' (i. 20).

'False-teachers' (ii. 1). 'Bring-in-privily' (ii. 1). 'Feigned' (ii. 3). 'From-of-old' (ii. 3; iii. 5). 'Linger' (ii. 3), meaning *not working*. 'Pit' (ii. 4). 'Cast-down-to-hell' (ii. 4). 'Turn-to-ashes' (ii. 6). 'Wicked' (ii. 7; iii. 17). 'Dwell-among' (ii. 8). 'Seeing' (ii. 8). 'Uncleanness' (ii. 10). 'Defilement' (ii. 20); hence *miasma*. 'Daring' (ii. 10). 'To-be-taken' (ii. 12). 'Blemish' (ii. 13). 'That-cannot-cease' (ii. 14); unable to stop. 'Unsteadfast' (ii. 14; iii. 16). 'Rebuked' (ii. 16). 'Transgression' (ii. 16). 'Madness' (ii. 16). 'Mist' fog (ii. 17). 'But-a-little' (ii. 18); slightly, just. 'Vomit' (ii. 22). 'Sow' (ii. 22). 'Mire,' dung (ii. 22). 'Wallowing' (ii. 22).

'Mockery' (iii. 3). 'Being-overflowed' (iii. 6). 'Slackness' (iii. 9). 'With-a-great-noise' (iii. 10); 'A whizzing sound of rapid motion through the air like the flight of a bird, thunder, fierce flame'. 'With fervent heat' (iii. 10. 12); always employed for fever temperature. 'Melt' (iii. 12). 'Blameless' (iii. 14). 'Hard-to-be-understood' (iii. 16). 'Unlearned' (iii. 16). 'Wrest' (iii. 16). 'Steadfastness' (iii. 17).

CHART 182

2 PETER		
The Knowledge of God and The Christian's Growth	The Knowledge of God and The Christian's Peril	The Knowledge of God and The Christian's Hope
THE TRUE TESTIMONY	FALSE TEACHERS	THE ADVENT TRUTH
1. Our Ample Provision i. 2-4	1. Their Doctrine Defined ii. 1-3a	1. Assailed: iii. 1-4
2. Our Actual Progress i. 5-11	2. Their Destruction Declared ii. 3b-9	2. Attested: iii. 5-10
3. Our Abiding Pledge i. 12-21	3. Their Doings Described ii. 10-22	3. Applied: iii. 11-18

The Keynote of 2 Peter is *Full Knowledge,* and *Knowledge,* words which occur twelve times; and on this our outline is based.

The chapters of this Epistle treating of the Christian's Growth (i) and the Christian's Hope (iii) are of very great importance.

Chapter i. 5-11 is a passage which should long be lingered over, because it presents a picture of perfection of Christian character. Here is an octave of graces beginning with *faith,* and ending with *love.* The one is the foundation, and the other, the consummation of Christian character.

In verse 5 the A.V. is at fault in several respects. *'Besides this',* should be *'for this very cause '* (vv. 2-4). *'Add'* should be *'supply.'* The idea is not of adding one thing to another, as of a brick to a brick, for the subject is growth, and that is not how one grows. The verb *epichorēgēsate* is derived from *choros,* a chorus, such as was employed in the representation of the Greek tragedies. It means *to bear the expense of a chorus*, which was done by a person selected by the State, who was obliged to defray all the expenses of training and maintenance. '*To*' should be '*in*,' because what is signified is the development of one virtue in the exercise of another, and not increase by accumulation. These graces are not like so many beads on a string, but they are organic, one producing the other by development. In this way Christian character is a closely compact whole; the virtue is *in* the faith, and the knowledge is *in* the virtue—and so on.

'*Virtue*,' i.e., moral energy. '*Knowledge*,' i.e., understanding, insight; not intellectual furniture. '*Temperance*', not abstinence from alcoholic liquor, but *self-control*, in the sense of *holding oneself in* (1 Cor. ix. 25). '*Patience*', meaning *to remain behind, to wait* (cf. 1 Pet. ii. 23; Heb. xii. 3). '*Godliness*,' meaning reverence paid to worth. Never ascribed to God. '*Love of the brethren*'; *philadelphia*. '*Love*.' This is another word; not *philia*, but *agapē*, not the love of feeling, but the love of principle (cf. John xxi. 15-17, Gr.; 1 Cor. xiii).

The consequence of having or not having these graces is seen in verses 8-11. The words here are notable: '*not idle nor unfruitful*'; '*for*,' not '*but*'; '*lacketh*,' i.e., not present; '*blind*'; '*seeing only what is near*,' i.e., short-sighted, suffering from *myopia*; '*having-forgotten*,' failure of memory; '*the cleansing*'; '*richly supplied*'; '*entrance into the eternal Kingdom*.'

May these few observations show how rich a passage this is. If possible read Dr. Alexander Maclaren's *A Rosary of Christian Graces*.

Peter's testimony in i. 12-21 urges the need of spiritual earnestness. He is anxious that his testimony shall be perpetuated, and made permanent; thus, in view of the nearness of his violent death, predicted by Jesus (John xxi. 18, 19), he writes these two Epistles (12-14), and proposes to leave a record of the life of Jesus also (15), which thing he has done in Mark's Gospel.*

*Mark acted as Peter's interpreter during his missionary journeys and wrote his Gospel by reproducing without alteration Peter's account which he translated from Aramaic into Greek (Papias, quoted by Eusebius, Ecclesiastical History III. 29. 15).

The substance of his testimony is 'the power and coming of the Lord Jesus Christ', facts revealed on the Transfiguration Mount, and witnessed by Peter himself. This is the New Testament pledge, and leads the Apostle back to the Old Testament, to the testimony of *Hebrew Prophecy* (19-21). By the happenings on the Mount, together with all the facts of the earthly life and ministry of Jesus, 'the word of O.T. prophecy, concerning the Messiah, is made more sure,' and to that word we should take heed in our hearts, knowing that such is not the 'invention' of men, but the work of the Holy Spirit through chosen writers.

'No prophecy of Scripture comes out of private disclosure.' No prophet starts a prophecy himself. Prophecy is of divine origin. The prophets are 'moved' by the Holy Spirit (i. 21). 'Moved' means *borne along*, and is a favourite word with Peter. He uses it six times (1 Pet. i. 13; 2 Pet. i. 17, 18, 21; ii. 11).

The mention of 'prophets' leads the Apostle to say that there were false among the true prophets, that in these days the false would abound, and that these constituted a real danger, threatening the Christian's progress. Thus, chapter ii treats of the Knowledge of God and *the Christian's Peril*. The false teachers are the subject throughout, and first of all:—

Their Doctrine is defined (1-3a). They deny the Atonement, and perhaps the Deity of the Lord Jesus (1); with the result that they have a large following of religious persons, who bring the truth into disrepute (2); and the motive of these false teachers is shown to be covetousness (3a).

Their Destruction is declared (3b-9). It is first asserted that judgment would overtake all such (3b), and then, that destruction is argued from analogies in the past: (a) the doom of the Angels; (b) the Flood; (c) the overthrow of Sodom and Gomorrha (4-8); and finally, the foregoing is affirmed in its aspects both of deliverance to, and from (9). The Apostle lastly, sets forth the character of these teachers, as exhibited in their conduct.

Their Doings are described (10-12). The points to be marked here are, their presumption (10-13a), their sensuality (13b-16), their enticements (17-19), and their apostasy (20-22).

Nor have we done with the false prophets yet. Not only did they attack the foundation of the Christian's faith, but the reality of his hope. Hence the next chapter.

We have already called attention to the similarity of this chapter and Jude's Epistle.

The subject of chapter iii is the Second Advent, a doctrine firmly held by all the Apostles. It is noticeable that in his First Epistle Peter speaks of it as an *apokalupsis*, a revelation or unveiling, but not as a *parousia*, a presence (i. 5, 7, 13; iv. 13; v. 1); but in the Second Epistle it is a *parousia*, and not an *apokalupsis* (i. 16; iii. 4, 12). In neither Epistle is the Advent spoken of as an *epiphaneia*, a forth-shining (cf. 2 Pet. i. 19).

First of all, *The Advent Truth is Assailed* (1-4). Scoffers would rise who would ridicule the idea that Christ was to return to this world, and they would appear to have the uniformity of history on their side. But the Apostle shows that this is not the case.

So in the next place, *The Advent Truth is Attested* (5-10). Peter begins by refuting what the false teachers were saying (5-7). He shows that the former world *did* perish, and that these scoffers were 'willingly ignorant' of that fact. They were not lacking in capacity, neither was there a scarcity of evidence. And as surely as that world was destroyed by water, this world would be destroyed by fire.

After the refutation comes an explanation of the delay of which the scoffers had made so much (8-10). Firstly, the Lord's relation to Time is set forth (8); He does not reckon as we do. Secondly, His relation to Men (9). The delay is not an evidence of indifference on the Lord's part, but of his tender long-suffering, not willing that any should perish. Thirdly, His relation to Evil (10). The Lord, being what He is, must visit all the works of the world with judgment, and as predicted throughout the Scriptures, that 'day of the Lord' would come suddenly. The Apostle, finally, brings these truths home to the hearts of his readers.

The Advent Truth is Applied (11-18a). Our conduct must take shape in the light of these facts; we must both 'look for' and 'hasten' the day of God, and give diligence to be found, when He comes, spotless and blameless; for, in the new earth and heaven beyond the judgment, only righteousness dwells. On this subject there is perfect harmony between the teachings of the Apostles. Therefore, knowing these things, we must 'beware' and 'grow', beware of the Evil, and grow in Grace and Knowledge. As the Epistle began so it ends, with the affirmation that in the full knowledge of God are our peace, power, and progress to be found.

'To Him be glory, both now and for ever. Amen.'

Dean Farrar points out that in this Epistle are many unique and arresting phrases which are to be found nowhere else:

'to acquire faith by lot'; 'giving things which tend to life and piety'; 'greatest and precious'; 'bringing in besides all haste'; 'to furnish an abundant supply of virtue'; 'receiving oblivion'; 'the present truth'; 'they shall bring in besides factions of perdition'; 'the judgment is not idling, the destruction is not drowsily nodding'; 'to walk behind the flesh'; 'eyes full of an adulteress'; 'insatiable of sin'; 'a heart trained in covetousness'; 'the mirk of the darkness'; 'treasure stored with fire'; 'pits of gloom'; 'calcining to ashes'; 'hurling to Tartarus'; 'blaspheming glories'; 'hurtingly'; 'to the day of the age'; 'the world compacted out of water, and by means of water' (i. 1; i. 3; i.4; i. 5; i. 5; i. 9; I. 12; ii. 1; ii. 3; ii. 10; ii. 14; ii. 14; ii. 14; ii. 17; iii. 10, etc.).

Notice Peter's references to Noah and the Flood; to Sodom and Gomorrah; to Lot; to Balaam and the ass; to fallen angels.

The following should be noted (Revised Standard Version).

'The multiplication of grace and peace' (i. 2). 'Things that pertain to life and godliness' (i. 3). 'His own glory and excellence' (i. 3). 'You may escape' (i. 4). 'Make every effort' (i. 5). 'They keep you from being ineffective' (i. 8). 'Blind and shortsighted' (i. 9). 'Be the more zealous' (i. 10). 'The putting off of my body' (i. 14). 'You do well to pay attention to this' (i. 19). 'A lamp shining in a dark place' (i. 19). 'Day-dawn' (i. 19). 'The morning star' (i. 19). 'Destructive heresies' (ii. 1). 'The way of truth' (ii. 2). 'They will exploit you' (ii. 3). 'Their destruction has not been asleep' (ii. 3). 'Pits of nether gloom' (ii. 4). 'Condemned to extinction' (ii. 6). 'Vexed in his righteous soul day after day' (ii. 8). 'The Lord knows how' (ii. 9). 'Bold and wilful' (ii. 10). 'Like irrational animals' (ii. 12). 'Creatures of instinct' (ii. 12). 'Born to be caught and killed' (ii. 12). 'Suffering wrong for their wrong-doing' (ii. 13). 'Blots and blemishes'

(ii. 13). 'Insatiable for sin' (ii. 14). 'Unsteady souls' (ii. 14). 'Hearts trained in greed' (ii. 14). 'Gain for wrong-doing' (ii. 15). 'A dumb ass spoke' (ii. 16). 'The prophet's madness' (ii. 16). 'Waterless springs' (ii. 17). 'Mists driven by a storm' (ii. 17). 'The nether gloom of darkness' (ii. 17). 'Uttering loud boasts of folly' (ii. 18). 'Barely escaped from those who live in error' (ii. 18). 'Slaves or corruption' (ii. 19). 'Whatever overcomes a man, to that he is enslaved' (ii. 19). 'Again entangled' (ii. 20). 'Better never to have known' (ii. 21). 'They deliberately ignore this fact' (iii. 5). 'Stored up for fire' (iii. 7). 'Kept until the day of judgment' (iii. 7). 'Do not ignore this one fact' (iii. 8). 'All these things are to be dissolved' (iii. 11). 'What sort of persons ought you to be?' (iii. 11). 'Lives of holiness and godliness' (iii. 11). 'Hastening the coming of the day of God' (iii. 12). 'Be zealous to be found by Him without spot or blemish, and at peace' (iii. 14). 'In all his letters' (iii. 16). 'Things hard to understand' (iii. 16). 'Knowing this beforehand'. (iii. 17). 'Beware lest you be carried away' (iii. 17). 'Lawless men' (iii. 17). 'Grow in the grace and knowledge of our Lord and Saviour Jesus Christ' (iii. 18).

THE CATHOLIC EPISTLES

JUDE

Before A.D. 70

Notes

The value of this Epistle is out of all proportion to its length. In its 458 words are utterances of great and abiding worth. It is not the shortest of New Testament Writings, but it is the fullest of the short ones—Philemon, 2 John, 3 John.

Jude was a common name, and there are six persons so named in the New Testament, but of these only two have been regarded as the writer of this Epistle—Jude the Apostle (Luke vi. 16), and Jude, a son of Joseph and Mary, and a younger brother of Jesus (Mark vi. 3). Of these two the author, without doubt, was the latter (ver. 1 and Jas. i. 1). It would seem that in verse 17 Jude distinguishes himself from the Apostles.

Jude was married, and apparently his wife went with him on his missionary journeys (1 Cor. ix. 5).

A tradition, quoted by Eusebius, tells that grandchildren of Jude were brought before the Emperor Domitian (A.D. 81-96), so that Jude must have had a child or children.

If this tradition is true 'it is hardly likely that the death of Jude occurred at a later date than the decade A.D. 70-80, when he would be well advanced in years' (A. S. Peake).

There is no reason for supposing that any of the Nazareth family believed in the Messiahship of Jesus before His death and Resurrection (John vii. 5), but we know that later on they did believe (Acts i. 14); and it is most impressive that two of them wrote Holy Scripture.

These two—James and Jude—do not claim to be *brothers* of Jesus Christ, but *bondslaves*. The reason for this is that 'the Ascension had altered all Christ's human relationships, and His brethren would shrink from claiming kinship after the flesh with His glorified body' (Plummer).

The *James* of verse 1 could be none other than the head of the

325

Church at Jerusalem, the writer of the Epistle, and one of Jesus' brothers. To have claimed relationship with anyone less prominent would have been pointless.

The writer has Jewish Christians chiefly—not exclusively—in view, but we do not know to what Church or Churches the Epistle was sent.

Also, the date of it is unknown, but it is safe to assume that it was written before the destruction of Jerusalem in A.D. 70.

To place the date in the second century only creates problems and contradicts what the Epistle claims (ver. 1).

The author's first intention was to write to Christians on what he calls 'our common salvation' (3), by which he means the grace of redemption—a grace open to all—but before he got started a report, or reports, had reached him which changed his purpose, and constrained him to write a letter of warning, and of denunciation of evil persons who privily had crept into the Church (4).

It's a pity that later Jude did not write on the 'common salvation.' Perhaps he intended to and was hindered!

Who the 'certain men' were we are not told, and many have been the guesses; but the description of them (8-16), makes it clear that their errors were chiefly ethical rather than doctrinal (but see vv. 4, 12), that theirs were evils of conduct rather than of creed. They were libertines rather than teachers.

As these evil persons are actually present (ver. 4), one wonders why discipline was not brought into action for their exclusion from the Church (cf. 1 Cor. v).

One wonders if those to whom Jude refers are the persons to whom Peter refers (2 Pet. ii. 1-3). In Peter they are definitely called 'teachers' (ver. 1), besides being immoral (ii. 12-19).

The relation of Jude to 2 Peter (ii) has been, and must continue to be a matter of controversy. Some scholars are absolutely certain that Jude wrote first, and others are absolutely certain that Peter wrote first; but the only thing we can be certain about is that no one knows who wrote first.

This matter is similar to the controversy over the authorship of the Epistle to the Hebrews.

This Epistle has some notable characteristics.

1. Jude uses 15 words which do not occur again in the New

Testament. 'Contend-earnestly' (3). 'Crept-in-privily' (4): to slip in secretly as if by a side door (para, besides; eis, in; duō, to sink or plunge). 'Having-given-themselves-over-to-fornication' (7). The word means that they had done so utterly (ek, out-and-out). 'As an example' (7). To exhibit as something held up to view as a warning. 'Suffering' (7). 'Dreaming' (8). 'Naturally' (10: cf. 2 Peter ii. 12). 'Hidden rocks' (12, R.V.). 'Autumn trees' (12). Pertaining to the late autumn (R.V.). 'Foaming-out' (13). 'Wandering stars' (13). Comets perhaps. 'Murmurers' (16). It is used of the cooing doves. 'Complainers' (16). Blamers of their lot. 'Make-separations' (19, apodiorizō, from apo, away, dia, through, and horizō, fix a boundary line). 'Stumbling' (24, R.V.).

2. The writer's fondness for triplets is a characteristic. 'Jude-servant-brother' (1). 'Called-beloved-kept' (1). 'Mercy-peace-love' (2). 'Ungodly-turning-denying' (4). 'Israelites-angels-cities of the plain' (5-7). 'Defile-set at nought-rail' (8). 'Cain, Balaam, Korah' (11). 'These are-these are-these are' (12, 16, 19). 'Separations-sensual-not having the Spirit' (19). 'Building up yourselves-praying-keep' (20, 21). 'Some-some-some' (22, 23). 'Before all time-now-for evermore' (25).

3. Another characteristic is Jude's use of Apocryphal literature: the *Assumption of Moses* (9), and the *Book of Enoch* (14, 15).

On account of these references the genuineness of the Epistle has been questioned by some.

But Jude is not the only New Testament writer who makes reference to foreign material. In Acts xvii. 28 Paul refers to Aratus, a poet of the 3rd century B.C. and in 1 Cor. xv. 33, to Menander, a Greek poet of the 4th century B.C., and in Titus i. 12, he refers to Callimachus, a poet who died about B.C. 70. In 2 Tim. iii. 8 he is quoting a non-Biblical tradition.

The Assumption of Moses is an apocryphal book, written in all probability, between A.D. 6-44.

The Book of Enoch, also apocryphal, was composed, it is supposed, by a Jewish writer before the Christian era.

Though this Epistle is so short there is discernible in it a definite plan. In verse 3 the writer urges a *duty*, and in verse 4 he points out a *danger*.

The *danger* is developed in verses 5-16; and the *duty*, in verses 17-23. The following Chart will make this clear.

CHART 183

THE EPISTLE OF JUDE			
1-4	5-16	17-23	24, 25
Introduction	**An Exposition of the Danger**	**An Exhortation to the Duty**	**Conclusion**
THE ADDRESS 1, 2	APOSTATES DOOMED, 5-7	THE BIBLICAL DUTY 17-19	THE GOD ADDRESSED 24, 25a
THE KEYNOTES 3-4	DENOUNCED, 8-11	THE PERSONAL DUTY 20, 21	THE PRAISE ASCRIBED 25b
A Duty, .. 3 A Danger, .. 4	DESCRIBED, 12-16	THE RELATIVE DUTY 22, 23	

'*Beloved*' occurs 4 times (1, 3, 17, 20). '*These*' (*houtoi*) occur 5 times (8, 10, 12, 16, 19). '*Keep*' occurs 5 times (1, 6, 6, 13, 21). In verse 1 we are *kept*, and in verse 21 we are to 'keep ourselves.' The Divine and the human actions must be co-operative.

Jude's epithets and metaphors are most impressive. 'Hidden rocks.' 'Clouds without water.' 'Autumn trees without fruit.' 'Twice dead.' 'Plucked up by the roots.' 'Wild waves of the sea.' 'Wandering stars.'

With these should be compared James iii. 1-12.

Perhaps the triplets in verse 1 should be related: *called* by *mercy*; *kept* in *peace*; and *beloved* in *love*.

In no other Greeting is *love* joined with *mercy* and *peace*. The *mercy* is from God to man; the *peace* is between God and man; and the *love* is of all towards all.

There is such a thing as priority of needs, and if we are alive to this we may have to postpone or abandon some of our good intentions (3).

Conflict in the Christian life is frequently referred to in the Epistles. Sometimes it is with elements within us (1 Cor. ix. 27), and sometimes with enemies without us, as here (3, 4). If we would have the best things we must *contend* for them.

The faith is the substance of evangelical truth.

'The faith which was *once* delivered unto the saints' (3 A.V.) is wrong. The R.V. is right—'*once for all* delivered.' No other faith will be given (Bengel).

That which has been 'once for all delivered' is complete and final (Gal. i. 6-9). Distinguish between *revelation* and *apprehension*. In the Scriptures is the *revelation*, and there can be no supplement, but through all time there can and should be a growing *apprehension*.

Romanism adds to *revelation* many dogmas, such as the Immaculate Conception, the Assumption of Mary, the Confessional, Infallibility, Purgatory, and others; but these are entirely without authority, and are pernicious.

The Canon of Scripture is closed.

In Jude the evil persons are shown to be utterly *immoral* (11-13, 16), but their immorality is due to their *irreligion*; they deny the Father and the Son (4).

All Christians need to be reminded of what they already know. 'I wish to remind you because ye have once for all (3) known all things' (5).

From what follows it would seem that the reference is to their knowledge of the Old Testament.

Of three things the readers are reminded:

(*a*) of the fact that though the Israelites had been delivered from Egypt, many of them afterwards perished in the wilderness because of unbelief (5 cf. Hebrews iii).

(*b*) of the fall of angels who, not *keeping* their exalted position, but leaving their proper home, God is now *keeping* for judgment (6).

(*c*) of the fate of Sodom and Gomorrha (7).

These are typical examples of the Divine retribution, and such judgment awaits the wicked men of whom Jude is writing (8).

What is stated in verse 9 is not derived from Scripture, but from the apocryphal *Assumption of Moses* (see p. 327).

The word '*rail*' which occurs three times (8, 9, 10) is 'blasphemy' (cf. 1 Tim. vi. 4).

In verse 11—Cain represents *rationalism*; Balaam represents *mammonism*; and Korah represents *anarchism*.

In the quotation from the Book of Enoch (14, 15), notice the words 'ungodly,' 'ungodliness,' 'ungodly,' 'ungodly.' It is a terrible thing to be without God (cf. Eph. ii. 12).

Compare verse 16 with James ii. 1-9; 1 Peter i. 17.

The Christian's only security is in up-building, praying, and keeping himself in God's love (20).

How to deal with different classes of persons (22, 23):

Class 1. 'Some indeed convict (15) when they are in doubt'; or 'when they contend with you' (9); or 'when they separate from you' (19). As long as a person is in doubt there is a chance of reclamation.

Class 2. 'Some save, snatching them out of the fire.' These are not unstable and disputatious, but obdurate and presumptuous, and must be dealt with severely.

Class 3. 'On some have mercy with fear; hating even the garment spotted by the flesh.'

There are occasions when those whom we would help are a menace to us. This is the worst class of all. In the endeavour to help the defiled we must beware lest we become defiled.

The first class is in incipient danger; the second is in extreme danger; and the third is a source of danger.

In the sublime doxology of verses 24, 25 observe:

(i) *Preservation*:
'Unto Him who is able to guard you from stumbling.'

(ii) *Presentation*:
'To set you before the presence of His glory without blemish in exceeding joy.'

(iii) *Praise*:
'To the only God our Saviour, through Jesus Christ our Lord, be glory, majesty, dominion and power, before all time, and now, and for evermore. Amen.'

THE CATHOLIC EPISTLES

THE WRITINGS OF THE APOSTLE JOHN

A.D. 90-100

These Writings are the last utterances of Apostolic inspiration, and the tone and outlook of them are in striking contrast to the Writings of Paul. By the last decade of the first century, the questions which dominated in Paul's time had disappeared. Matters relating to the Mosaic Law and the Gentiles, clean and unclean meats, the gift of tongues, the position of women in the Church, Jewish tradition and the Christian revelation, and kindred subjects were no longer matters of interest and of controversy. Other and more important subjects—subjects relating to the Person of Christ, and to the Divine Life in the believer now dominated, as John's Gospel, Epistles, and Apocalypse show (Gospel i. 1-18; 1 Epis. i. 1-4; Apoc. i. 12-16).

In a survey such as this some things must be assumed which there is not room or time to argue, though these assumptions could be argued.

One of these assumptions is that the *Fourth Gospel*, the *Three Epistles*, and the *Revelation* were all written by the Apostle John. The standard Commentaries and Bible Dictionaries present the case for and against this conclusion.

The Gospel shows that the Man of Galilee was God.

The Epistles show that it was God Who became Man.

The Apocalypse shows that ultimate victory over all evil will be by and for the God-Man.

The Gospel may be regarded as a summary of Christian Theology.

The First Epistle, as a summary of Christian Ethics.

The Apocalypse, as a summary of Christian Politics.

In the Gospel, Christ is in the world; in the Epistle, He is in the heart; and in the Revelation, He is in the Church.

That the Fourth Gospel and the First Epistle are intimately connected is not open to question.

The Gospel is objective; the Epistle is subjective.
The Gospel is historical; the Epistle is moral.
The Gospel treats of Christ; the Epistle, of the Christian.
The Gospel enunciates principles; the Epistle enjoins practice.
The Gospel reveals truths; the Epistle applies them.

331

The Gospel was written that men may believe (xx. 31); the Epistle was written to those who had believed (v. 13).

The Gospel was written to shew the way to eternal life (iii. 16); the Epistle was written to assure those who believe that they have eternal life (v. 11, 12).

The verbal parallels between the Gospel and the Epistle are most impressive. Compare:

Gospel xvi. 24 and Epistle i. 4; viii. 37 and i. 10; xiii. 34 and ii. 7, 8; xii. 35 and ii. 11; ii. 25, xvi. 30 and ii. 27; i. 29 and iii. 5; viii. 34 and iii. 8; xv. 18 and iii. 13; x. 10-15 and iii. 16; xv. 19, xvii. 14 and iv. 5; iii. 16 and iv. 9; i. 18 and iv. 12.

Other parallels, though not so close, are: Gospel i. 1 and Epistle i. 1, ii. 13; i. 14 and i. 1; xx. 27 and i. 1; iii. 11 and i. 2; xix. 35 and i. 2; i. 1 and i. 2; xvii. 21 and i. 3; i. 19 and i. 5; i. 5 and i. 5; viii. 12 and i. 6; iii. 21 and i. 6; xiv. 16 and ii. 1; xiv. 15 and ii. 3; xiv. 21 and ii. 5; xv. 5 and ii. 6; i. 9 and ii. 8; xi. 9 and ii. 10; xii. 35 and ii. 11; xii. 40 and ii. 11; xiii. 33 and ii. 1, 12, 28 (*teknia*); v. 38 and ii. 14; xxi. 5 and ii. 18 (*paidia*); xvi. 13 and ii. 20; xv. 23 and ii. 23; xiv. 23 and ii. 24; xvii. 2 and ii. 25; xvi. 13 and ii. 27.

Space does not allow of our quoting these texts, but those who are sufficiently interested will look them up.

The Gospel and the Epistle move in the same circle of ideas; their leading views and representations are alike; the same expressions and images are used.

There are many phrases common to both the Epistle and the Gospel.

i. 6 (John iii. 21). Doing, or not doing the truth.
iii. 8, 10 (John viii. 44). Of the devil.
i. 8; ii. 4 (John viii. 44). Lacking the truth.
iv. 5 (John viii. 23). Of the world.
ii. 6; iv. 13 (John xv. 4ff). Abiding in God.
i. 6; ii. 11 (John viii. 12; xii. 35). Walking in the darkness.
ii. 3, 4, 13, 14; iv. 6-8; v. 20 (John xvi. 3; xvii. 3, 25). Knowing God.
i. 8 (John ix. 41; xv. 22, 24). Having sin.
iii. 15; v. 12 (John iii. 15, 36; v. 24, 39, 40). Having eternal life.
iii. 14 (John v. 24). Passing from death into life.
v. 4 (John xvi. 33). Overcoming the world.
ii. 1 (John xiv. 16, 26; xvi. 7). The Paraclete.

From these and other references it will be apparent that certain words dominate John's Epistles and the Gospel as they do not any other N.T. Writings. *Witness (martureō* and *marturia*): Epistles 18 times; Gospel 47 times. *Truth, true (alētheia, alēthēs, alēthinos, alethōs)*: Epistles 28 times; Gospel 56 times. *The Devil (Ho Diabolos)*: Epistles 4 times; Gospel twice. *World (kosmos)*: Epistles 24 times; Gospel 79 times. *Abide, continue, remain, tarry (menō)*: Epistles 26 times; Gospel 41 times. *Darkness (skotia, skotos)*: 1 Epistle 7 times; Gospel 9 times. *Light (phōtizō, phōs)*: Epistles 6 times; Gospel 24 times. *Sin (hamartanō, hamartia)*: Epistles 27 times; Gospel 21 times. *Life (zōē, psuchē)*: Epistles 16 times; Gospel 46 times. *Know, see (eideō, ginōskō)*: Epistles 45 times; Gospel 179 times. *Love (agapē, agapaō)*: Epistles 52 times; Gospel 45 times. *Phileō* (the weaker word for love) occurs in the Gospel, but not in the Epistles of John. *Commandment (entolē)*: Epistle 18 times; Gospel 10 times. *Manifest (phaneroō)*: Epistles 9 times; Gospel 9 times. *Hear (akouō)*: Epistles 16 times; Gospel 58 times.

In the Epistle the facts of the Gospel are presented only indirectly, but they are so presented.

The Incarnation: iv. 2; cf. Gospel i. 14.
The Baptism: v. 6; cf. Gospel i. 33.
The Sinless Life: ii. 6; cf. Gospel viii. 46.
The World's hatred: iii. 1; cf. Gospel xv. 18, 19.
The Divine promise: ii. 25; cf. Gospel vi. 27; x. 28.
The Crucifixion: iii. 16; cf. Gospel x. 11, 15.
The Resurrection and Ascension: ii. 1; cf. Gospel xx. 17.
The Second Advent: ii. 28; cf. Gospel xiv. 3.

The indirectness of these references but adds to their significance.

John's First Epistle

We may safely conclude that the First Epistle was written in Ephesus in the last decade of the first century, about twenty-five years after the Destruction of Jerusalem.

But for the Writings of the Apostle John, the last thirty years of the first century would be almost a blank.

It is written to the Christians of the Asiatic Churches, who were chiefly Gentiles. There is no reference to Jewish Christianity. There are no quotations from the Old Testament. The readers are warned against idolatry (v. 21), of which the Jews had not been guilty since their return from Babylonian captivity.

Though this Writing has no salutation at the beginning, and no benediction at the end, it is, nevertheless, an Epistle, as the frequent intimate address shows: 'I write to you,' 'I am writing to you' (i. 4; ii. 1, 7, 8, 12, 13, 14, 21, 26; v. 13).

The object of the Epistle is clearly stated: 'that you may have fellowship with us'; 'that our joy may be full'; 'that you may not sin'; 'because your sins are forgiven for His sake'; 'because you know Him Who is from the beginning'; 'because you have overcome the evil one'; 'because you know the Father'; 'because you know the truth'; 'that you may know that you have eternal life' (i. 3, 4; ii. 1, 12-14, 21; v. 13).

The object, then, is to *warn* (ii. 26. *peri*); to *encourage* ('because,' *hoti*); because of forgiveness (ii. 12), of knowledge (ii. 13, 14, 21), of victory (ii. 13, 14); and to *inspire* ('in order that,' *hina*); with a view to Christian fellowship (i. 3), fulness of joy (i. 4), freedom from sinning (ii. 1), and spiritual assurance (v. 13).

The Epistle 'is a solemn warning against the seductive assumptions and deductions of various forms of Gnostic error; an emphatic protest against anything like a compromise where Christian truth is in question' (Plummer).

Like Galatians, James, and 1-2 Peter, this Epistle is a circular letter, and, no doubt, it was read by the seven Churches of Western Asia Minor, and by others (cf. Rev. ii-iii).

In so comparatively short an Epistle one would not look for words exclusive to it, but the following should be studied.

Message (*aggelia*; i. 5; iii. 11). The verb occurs only at John xx. 18.

Propitiation (*hilasmos*; ii. 2; iv. 10). Appeasement. One of the few great words in this Epistle which are not found in the Gospel. Christ wins life for us by being a propitiation for our sins.

'*The last hour*' (ii. 18). The period preceding a crisis in the advance of Christ's kingdom; a changeful and troublous period, marked by the appearance of 'many antichrists' (Marvin Vincent).

'We are left in doubt about this "last hour", whether it covers a period, a series, or the final climax of all just at hand' (A. T. Robertson).

Antichrist (ii. 18, 22; iv. 3; 2 John 7). Peculiar to John in the New Testament. One who stands *against*, or *instead* of Christ; one who opposes Christ in the guise of Christ.

The Church of the first three or four centuries almost universally regarded Antichrist as an individual. Compare 2 Thess. ii.

But Antichrist has been held to be a principle, a tendency, a power, a political system, a dynasty, a succession of rulers, the Roman Catholic Church.

Anointing (ii. 20, 27) *Chrisma*; cf. *Christos*. The anointing is from the Anointed. The Antichrist with his antichrists is contrasted with the Christ and His anointed ones.

Slew (iii. 12; Rev. v. 6, 9, 12; vi. 4, 9; xiii. 3, 8; xviii. 24; nowhere else). Its original meaning was 'to cut the throat', especially of a victim for sacrifice. 'Backward they turned the necks of the fat beeves, and cut their throats, and flayed the carcasses.' *Homer, Iliad*, i. 459.

John's reference is to a very early event in history.

Murderer (iii. 15). *Anthrōpoktonos* means 'to kill a man'; a 'man-slayer'. Compare John viii. 44, of the devil.

John's First Epistle is unlike anything else in the New Testament; it is in a category by itself, and is specially attractive to the thoughtful reader.

Its characteristics are distinctive, among which are the following:

1. PROFOUNDEST THOUGHT IS PRESENTED IN SIMPLEST LANGUAGE.

The words are such as any intelligent child can understand, yet they are charged with truths which have their roots in the Infinite and Eternal.

2. THE EPISTLE IS CHARACTERIZED BY WHAT MAY BE CALLED *Moral Antagonisms*, or *Antitheses*. Moral qualities are personified, and are presented in sharp contrasts: Light and Darkness; Truth and Falsehood; Love and Hate; Life and Death; Love of the World and Love of the Father; Children of God and Children of the Devil; Doing Righteousness and Doing Sin; Sin unto Death and Sin not unto Death.

Truth presented in this way sticks in the mind and memory, and gives an insight into the ultimate realities.

3. ANOTHER FEATURE OF THIS WRITING IS ITS *Rhythmical Structures*

> If we say we have no sin,
> We deceive ourselves,
> And the truth is not in us.
>
> If we confess our sins,
> He is faithful and righteous to forgive us our sins,
> And to cleanse us from all unrighteousness.
>
> If we say that we have not sinned,
> We make Him a liar,
> And His word is not in us.
>
> He that saith he is in the light
> And hateth his brother
> Is in the darkness even until now.
>
> He that loveth his brother
> Abideth in the light,
> And there is none occasion of stumbling in him.

It is impossible to miss the cadence of these sentences, or to forget their lyrical lilt.

4. IMPRESSIVE, ALSO, IS THE *Calm Serenity* OF THIS EPISTLE

It is tranquil, quiet, restful, contemplative. Here is not a stormy sea, but a land-locked harbour. The language is that of an old man who has survived the storms, storms which have made him a saint. Occasionally we hear the rumble of antagonism to specific evils, but it is peace that rules. The fiery nature of former days is not destroyed, but it is purified.

5. ANOTHER CHARACTERISTIC OF THE EPISTLE IS ITS *Tone of Authority*

The writer is one who has 'seen and heard' and therefore knows, and who, in consequence, proclaims. He does not argue, but affirms; he states the truth and leaves it at that. He does not submit, or suggest, but declares. One feels that here he is on sure ground.

Knowledge is everywhere emphatic: *ginōskō* 25 times; and *oida* 15 times. The latter means knowledge generally, and the former, experimental knowledge.

6. THROUGHOUT THE EPISTLE THERE IS A SENSE OF *Finality*

Truth is never stated in a speculative form. The writer is not concerned with propositions, but with principles.

The Writing is not a manual of Christian doctrine, yet it 'completes and harmonises the earlier forms of apostolic teaching' (Westcott). When John says that God is Light, God is Righteous, God is Love, he has said something ultimate and final. The truth he declares is not a stopping-place on the way—it is the goal.

Of the many themes which are dealt with in this Epistle are: the Character of God; the Person of Christ; the Work of Christ; the World; Hatred; Error; Antichrist; Eternal Life; Righteousness; Love; Truth; Belief; Assurance; Spiritual Growth; and Eschatology.

The many and varied outlines which have been given of the Epistle indicate how difficult it is to analyse.

Bishop Westcott says: 'No single arrangement is able to take account of the complex development of thought which it offers, and of the many connections which exist between its different parts'.

The following is suggested:

    I. *The Christian's Advance in the Light Divine* (i. 5-ii. 27).
    II. *The Christian's Attitude towards the Love Divine*
        (ii. 28-iv. 21).
    III. *The Christian's Affinity with the Life Divine* (v. i-20).

CHART 184

JOHN'S FIRST EPISTLE	
PART I—CHS. i. 1-ii. 27	
Introduction: i. 1-4	
I. The Christian's Advance in the Light Divine	
I. CONDITIONS OF WALKING IN THE LIGHT: i. 5-ii. 11	2. HINDRANCES TO WALKING IN THE LIGHT: ii. 12-27
(i) Practical Holiness Selfward i. 5-ii. 2	(i) The Ground of Appeal ii. 12-14
(ii) Complete Obedience Godward ii. 3-6	(ii) The Evils that Threaten ii. 15-23
(iii) Brotherly Love Manward ii. 7-11	(iii) The Secret of Safety ii. 24-27

CHART 185

JOHN'S FIRST EPISTLE	
PART 2—Chs. ii. 28–iv. 21	
II. The Christian's Attitude towards the Love Divine	
1. THE EVILS WHICH NEGATIVE LOVE ii. 28–iv. 6	2. THE LOVE WHICH NEGATIVES EVIL iv. 7–21
(i) Sin Opposing Righteousness ii. 28–iii. 10a	(i) The Revelation of Love iv. 7–10
(ii) Hate Opposing Love iii. 10b–24	(ii) The Inspiration of Love iv. 11–16a
(iii) Error Opposing Truth iv. 1–6	(iii) The Consummation of Love iv. 16b–21

CHART 186

JOHN'S FIRST EPISTLE	
PART 3—Ch. v. 1–20	
III. The Christian's Affinity with the Life Divine	
1. THE POSSESSION OF ETERNAL LIFE v. 1–12	2. THE CONFIDENCE OF ETERNAL LIFE: v. 13–20
(i) The Bond of Possession Faith v. 1–5	(i) In the Boldness of our Spiritual Action v. 13–17
(ii) The Proof of Possession Witness v. 6-12	(ii) In the Certainty of our Spiritual Knowledge v. 18–20
Conclusion: v. 21	

The Introduction to the Epistle (i. 1-4) is the key to it.

1. *Revelation*:

    'That which was from the beginning . . . the Word of Life . . . the Eternal Life which was with the Father' (1, 2).

2. *Manifestation*:

    'The Life was manifested' (2, 3).

3. *Apprehension*:

    'We have heard, we have seen with our eyes, we have gazed upon, and our hands have handled' (1, 2, 3).

4. *Declaration*:
   'We bear witness, and report to you the Life Eternal' (2, 3).
5. *Participation*:
   'That ye may have fellowship with us, and indeed our fellowship is with the Father and with His Son, Jesus Christ' (3).
6. *Jubilation*:
   'That your joy may be full' (4).
7. *Transmission*:
   'These things we write unto you' (4).

In i. 6-ii. 2 note the three pairs:

'If we say' (6)
'But if' (7)
'If we say' (8)
'If' (9)
'If we say' (10)
'And if' (ii. 1, 2)

There is *cleansing* for us, upon a change of course (7); *forgiveness*, upon confession of sins (9); and *advocacy* upon a recognition that sin is not inevitable (ii. 1, 2).

Three holiness theories are:

1. *Extraction*:
   This is against Scripture and experience
2. *Suppression*:
   This is the prevailing idea, but it is ineffectual.
3. *Counteraction*:
   This is true and experimental.

By 'love' (ii. 9-11) is meant, not the love of natural affection (*phileō*), but of moral judgment (*agapaō*); not of emotion, but of principle.

Study John xxi. 15-17 in the Greek, where both words are used.

'I write ... I write ... I write ...' (ii. 12, 13).

'I have written' ... I have written ... I have written' (ii. 13, 14).

Chapter ii. 12-14. 'Little children' (*teknia*); 'fathers'; 'young men'. 'Little children' (*paidia*); 'fathers'; 'young men'. Most probably, 'little children' refers to all believers (ii. 1), among whom are 'fathers' and 'young men'.

'Little children'. *Teknia* (12) conveys the idea of kinship; but *Paidia* (14), the idea of discipline. *Teknon* is a child (and *teknion*, a little child) by birth; *Paidion*, a little child, one still young.

One becomes a *teknon* by forgiveness of sins (12), and a *paidion* by education, by knowing the Father (13, 14) (cf. Eph. vi. 14; 2 Tim. iii. 16; Heb. xii. 5, 7, 8, 11).

The characteristic of the 'fathers' is wisdom, and of the 'young men', strength.

Worldliness Analysed (ii. 15-17).

It is characterized by three dominating desires: the desire of *having*, 'the lust of the flesh'; the desire of *seeing*, 'the lust of the eyes'; and the desire of *being*, 'the vain glory of life'.

They are all in the Temptation in the Garden (Gen. iii), and in the Temptation in the Wilderness (Matt. iv. 1-11). In the one case Paradise was Lost, and in the other, it was Regained.

There are three reasons for not loving the world:

(*a*) because he who does so does not love the Father:
(*b*) because the world in its entirety is passing away: and
(*c*) because he who does the will of God abides for ever (ii. 15-17).

No one can be a Christian who denies the Person and Work of Christ as revealed (ii. 22-24).

The Christian life is here described as 'walking' (cf. Isa. xl. 29-31). It is easier to fly and to run than to walk.

'*Love*'. The word which represents natural and emotional love (*phileō*) does not occur in this Epistle, but the word which tells of the love of choice and principle (*agapaō*), in its various grammatical forms, occurs over 50 times. No wonder it says: 'See what love the Father has given us' (iii. 1).

'*Children of God*' (iii. 1, 2), not 'Sons' as in A.V. 'Son' in this Epistle refers to Christ, not to the Christian.

Paul speaks of '*sons* of God', but John, of '*children* of God'. In both there is *relation* to God, but Paul's 'sons' tell of *adoption*, while John's 'children' tell of *generation*.

This distinction is important.

What we are, and what we shall be (iii. 2). The former we know, but the latter we know not (*nun* and *oupō*). 'We shall be like Him'. The sight of God will glorify us (2 Cor. iii. 18; Rev. xxii. 4).

'This hope in him' (iii. 3). The preposition is not *en*, but *epi*, which means, not that the hope is *in* the believer, but that it is *upon* Christ. The Christian is not the subject of the hope, but Christ is the object of it.

The subject of iii. 4-10 is *Sin* and *Sinning*.

Here is the briefest and most comprehensive definition of sin—'*Sin is lawlessness*'. We are all constituted under a threefold law—to God, to ourselves, and to others. The law *Godward* is *obedience*; the law *selfward* is *holiness*; and the law *manward* is *love*. To break any part of this law is to sin.

The statements in iii. 6, 9; v. 18 must not be explained away, but they must be explained.

> 'Whosoever abideth in Him sinneth not.'
> 'He cannot sin because he is begotten of God.'
> 'Whosoever is begotten of God doeth no sin.'

John has already said: 'If any man sin' (ii. 1), but these statements are not contradictory.

In ii. 1 the reference is to *single acts of sin*, and in the other three passages it is to *continuing in a course of sin, sin as a habit*. Those whose lives are characterized by sin are not children of God, but Christians who fall into sin, and repent, have an Advocate (ii. 1; i. 8-10).

The subject of iii. 11-24 is *Love* and *Hate*, and John says that: (*a*) love is the heart of the Christian message (11); (*b*) love is the evidence of spiritual life (14); (*c*) love is the norm of Christian duty (16); and (*d*) love is the secret of heart-assurance (19-24).

Opposed to this is *hate* which is murder (12, 15), spiritual death (15), and originates in Satan (12).

The subject of iv. 1-6 is *Truth and Error*.

Rival spirits must be tested, and the test is their attitude to Christ (1-3).

'Jesus Christ is the storm-centre; the battle sways this way and that about the person of the King. Every kind of antipathy that Christianity excites, in the modern as in the ancient world, impinges on our Lord's name and person; its shafts strike on the great shield of the Captain of Salvation, from whatever quarter they are aimed.'

(Findlay).

Every heresy in the world is an attack, in some way, upon the Person and Work of Christ.

In a profound passage John speaks of the Love which negatives all evil (iv. 7-21): (a) the revelation of it (iv. 7-10); (b) the inspiration of it (iv. 11-16); and (c) the consummation of it (iv. 16-21).

The Apostle has spoken of Divine Light, and Divine Love, and in chapter v he speaks of Divine Life—the Possession (1-12) and .he Confidence of it (13-20).

Speaking of the *Possession of Eternal Life* (v. 1-12) the Apostle affirms that *the Bond of it is Faith* (v. 1-5), and *the Proof of it is Witness* (v. 6-12).

As to the *Confidence of Eternal Life* (v. 13-20), this is seen to be in *the Boldness of our Spiritual Action* (v. 13-17), and in *the Certainty of our Spiritual Knowledge* (v. 18-20). Mark the thrice-repeated 'we know'.

'He came by water and blood, Jesus Christ' (v. 6). This refers, not to the water and blood which flowed from Jesus on the Cross, but to His *Baptism* at the beginning of His ministry, and His *Death* at the end of it.

Beyond dispute chap. v. 7 must be omitted, and verse 8 must read: 'There are three who bear witness, the Spirit, and the water, and the blood; and the three agree in one'. Dr. Döllinger observes that nothing in textual criticism is more certain than that the disputed words are spurious.

It would seem that by 'there is sin unto death' (v. 16) is meant, not an act of sin, but a state or habit of sin wilfully chosen and persisted in (ver. 18). This has already been said in iii. 6-10.

The 'begotten of God' in v. 18 is not the Christian (according to the A.V.) but Christ. The Christian does not and cannot keep himself (but see ver. 21. cf. John xvii. 12, 15).

The evil one will assault the believer, but he will not get hold of him (cf. John x. 28. R.V.).

THE SECOND AND THIRD EPISTLES OF JOHN

A.D. 90-95

Notes

Several matters of interest are common to these two Epistles, and need not be considered separately.

We can safely conclude, from all the evidence available, that 2-3 John were written by the same person; and evidence leads to the conclusion also that the Fourth Gospel and the First Epistle were written by the same person; and that that person was the Apostle John.

It can also be assumed that both Epistles were written by John in his old age, and most probably in Ephesus.

In both Epistles the writer speaks of himself as 'The Elder' (*ho presbuteros*), a designation which indicates age as well as office. The word *presbutēs* means an old man (Luke i. 18), and aged (Phile. 9; Tit. ii. 2).

The Epistles have been ascribed to John the Presbyter, a resident at Ephesus, and other than the Apostle John; but there is no historical evidence that such a person ever existed. It can be assumed that the Apostle and the Presbyter are the same person.

It would appear that both Epistles are written to an individual, but this will be referred to again under the Second Epistle.

The Second Epistle condemns the spirit of *heresy*, and the Third, the spirit of *schism*.

In both Epistles occur—*love* (1, 5, and 1); *truth* (1, 1, 2, 3, 4, and 1, 3, 3, 4, 8, 12); *peace* (3, and 14); *rejoice greatly* (4 and 3); *walk* (6, 6, and 3, 4); *joy* (12, and 4); *ink* (12, and 13); *face to face* (12, and 14); *I hope* (12, and 14).

The two are classed with the General or Catholic Epistles though neither of them is such. Probably they are to be regarded as appendices to the First Epistle.

Both Epistles have a marked resemblance to the Fourth Gospel in tone and style.

SECOND EPISTLE OF JOHN

Notes

The Address: 'Unto the elect lady and her children.'

'*Eklektē kuria*' may mean 'to the elect lady'; or 'to an elect lady'; or 'to the elect kyria'; or 'to the lady Electa'; or 'to Electa Kyria.'

The question which these words raise is whether this short Epistle (245 words) is addressed to a *Church*, or to an *individual*. Each view is held by able students of the Epistle, and the matter cannot be said to be settled.

Westcott's verdict is:

'On the whole it is best to recognize that the problem of the address is insoluble with our present knowledge. It is not unlikely that it contains some allusion, intelligible under the original circumstances, to which we have lost the key. But the general tenor of the letter favours the opinion that it was sent to a community and not to one believer.'

On the other hand, Dr. Plummer says:

'The common sense canon, that where the literal meaning makes good sense the literal meaning is right, seems applicable here.

'No one doubts that the twin Epistle is addressed to an individual. In letters so similar it is scarcely probable that in the one case the person addressed is to be taken literally, while in the other the person addressed is to be taken as the allegorical representative of a Church. It seems more reasonable to suppose that in both Epistles, as in the Epistle to Philemon, we have precious specimens of the private correspondence of an Apostle.'

Each reader must form his own opinion on the subject; but whichever view is held we are left in ignorance of the identity of the Church, or individual.

The Outline of this Note is simple.

INTRODUCTION (1-3):
1. The Address, 1*a*.
2. The Keynotes, 1*b*-3.
    (i) Love.
    (ii) Truth.

I. THE PATH OF THE BELIEVER (4-6):
1. Walk in Truth, 4.
2. Walk in Love, 5, 6.

II. The Peril of the Believer (7-11):

    1. The Nature of it, 7.

    2. His Relation to it, 8-11.

Conclusion (12, 13).

I. The Path of the Believer
(4-6)

Short as the Epistle is, it speaks to believers of every age most important and timely messages. Not to dwell upon the ennobled estimate of womanhood which Christianity was introducing (and which is reflected in this Letter) and the power of a mother's life and influence in the training of her children, we should give most prayerful attention to the great lesson of this Letter, that God has joined together Truth and Love, and no man must put them asunder.

This keynote is struck in the opening verses, and then we are exhorted to walk in Truth and in Love—certainly in Truth, but not in Truth only, for that would be hard; certainly in Love, but not in Love only, for that would be soft, but in these united.

The supreme illustration of this combination we find in Jesus, as He is presented in the Gospels; and John himself has learnt that, and every other lesson, directly from his Master.

II. The Peril of the Believer
(7-11)

This being the believer's *path*, it is now pointed out that there is a *peril* in the path, the peril of departure from the Truth, and that in respect of the Person of Christ, Who is the crucial test of all doctrine.

Our relation to all such false teachers is plainly stated; we are not to take them into our life or love if they are against the Truth, for Truth and Love are wed. This is a severe doctrine, about which let two things be said: (1) We must be very careful not to assume this exclusive relation towards men who may differ from ourselves in other and perhaps less important matters of doctrine. There is almost certainly a place in the Church for large charity, at any rate in regard to non-essentials; but (2) We must be altogether uncompromising with respect to the matter before us, the full Deity and true Manhood of Jesus Christ, for between those who hold this true God-Manhood, and those who do not, there is, and ever must be, 'a great gulf fixed.'

We cannot give verses 7-11 too careful attention in a day when doctrine, even relative to the Person of Christ, is considered not essential to comprehensive Christian fellowship. By the time that every doctrine is eliminated on which all professing Christians do not agree, what is left that is worth holding?

The foundation of Christian fellowship is laid in the Divine-Human Person of Christ, and His Atoning Sacrifice. If this is denied there is nothing on which to build.

John exhorts his readers not to allow heretics to undo the work which Apostles and Evangelists had done. He who does not follow this advice loses reward both in this life, and in that which is to come (8).

We hear much nowadays about advanced thinkers, but such, so-called, are by no means modern. John speaks of them as 'taking the lead and going on beyond the Gospel' (9).

It has been well said that 'there is an advance which involves desertion of first principles; and such an advance is not progress but apostasy.'

What is to be the attitude of Christians to those in their midst who would deny the New Testament doctrine of Christ? This question is answered in verse 10, and a reason is given in verse 11. Of course this will raise the cry of narrowness and uncharitableness but charity has its limits.

If one tolerates and entertains those who deny Christ he becomes a 'partaker in his evil works' (11).

Love of good cannot exist where there is not hatred of evil.

There is a tradition that John rushed out of a public bath at the sight of Cerinthus, crying, 'Let us fly, lest even the bath fall on us, because Cerinthus, the enemy of the truth is within.'

Cerinthus denied the miraculous conception, and held that Jesus was a mere man; that the Holy Spirit descended upon Him at His baptism, and withdrew from Him at His crucifixion. It is the teaching of this man that John so vigorously opposes in his Writings, in Gospel and Epistles alike.

'Paper and ink'

The word '*paper*' (*chartēs*) occurs nowhere else. It was probably Egyptian papyrus, and was costly and scarce, which may account for John's brevity.

Probably the perishable nature of papyrus accounts for the easy loss of the Apostolic autographs.

'Ink' seems to have been made of soot and water (3 John 13; 2 Cor. iii. 3).